PRAISE FOR *SALES TRAINING SOLUTIONS*:

"This is a wonderful resource guide for any salesperson interested in sales training. Even veteran trainers could benefit from using this book!"

—Maria Edelson
Director, Sales Capability Development, North America, Procter & Gamble

"The content is comprehensive and provides many real-life examples from experienced sources, not just one person's view."

—Matt Gross
President, Sales, RR Donnelley

"An excellent and comprehensive guide to sales training. Both sales executives and trainers will find this book provides the information necessary to design and improve their company's sales training program."

—Kevin P. Hart
Executive Vice President, Sales and Marketing, WNA, Inc.

"Most sales executives believe that developing training should be easy; find a trendy sales program, secure some budget, roll it out, and watch the revenues increase. Unfortunately, efforts like these underwhelm the sales force and are forgotten in a week. *Sales Training Solutions* describes how successful companies define training needs, gain sponsorship, and measure results of dynamic programs that are remembered for years."

—James A. Rocha
Manager, WW Sales Force Development, Cisco Systems

"*Sales Training Solutions* offers a compendium of tips and techniques for sales training practitioners and consultants alike. There's something for everyone involved in designing, developing, and implementing sales training solutions in today's fast-paced world. I've never seen this array of information available on these topics in one place before! I highly recommend it to anyone in the sales training profession."

—Stephen J. Bistritz, Ed.D.
President, Professional Society for Sales and Marketing Training

"I found that *Sales Training Solutions* had all the essential components to enable a corporation to provide appropriate sales training to their target populations in a timely manner. If the guidelines prescribed are followed, you will be able to provide the right (sales) training to the right (sales)people at the right time."

—William G. Skea
Manager, Learning Strategy & Solutions for Sales Skills Development,
Xerox Corporation

"Retaining key customer-facing employees and equipping them with the tools to succeed in today's complex, global business environment is paramount to being both competitive and profitable. Through a diverse collection of mini-cases, *Sales Training Solutions* provides a practical roadmap for firms that take seriously the challenge of developing human capital."

—Lisa Napolitano
President & CEO, Strategic Account Management Association

"In *Sales Training Solutions*, Renie McClay offers us a comprehensive look at how to make sales training work in any organization. Lots of books tell you what to do. This one tells you how to do it! If you want to succeed as a sales trainer, this book can be your guide for years to come."

—Jerry Acuff
CEO Delta Point, Inc.

"Renie McClay has collaborated with a truly outstanding cadre of experienced sales training professionals who discuss, in practical terms and processes, how to create real business value with your sales training initiatives. Don't miss having *Sales Training Solutions* readily available at all times."

—Dennis McGurer
President, McGurer & Associates, Inc.

"This book should be used as a reference for anyone interested in sales training. Each chapter reads like a consultation around sales training and is loaded with ideas, tips, tools, and sound thinking."

—Howard Prager
Director, Lake Forest Corporate Education
Lake Forest Graduate School of Management

Sales Training

SOLUTIONS

Edited by Renie McClay

KAPLAN PUBLISHING

This publication is designed to provide accurate and authoritative information in regard to the subject matter covered. It is sold with the understanding
that the publisher is not engaged in rendering legal, accounting, or other
professional service. If legal advice or other expert assistance is required, the
services of a competent professional should be sought.

President, Kaplan Publishing: Roy Lipner
Vice President and Publisher: Maureen McMahon
Acquisitions Editor: Karen Murphy
Development Editor: Trey Thoelcke
Production Editor: Mike Hankes
Typesetter: Todd Bowman
Cover Designer: Gail Chandler

Printed in the United States of America

06 07 08 10 9 8 7 6 5 4 3 2 1

Library of Congress Cataloging-in-Publication Data

Sales training solutions / edited by Renie McClay.
    p. cm.
    Includes bibliographical references and index.
    ISBN-13: 978-1-4195-8544-9
    ISBN-10: 1-4195-8544-4
 1. Sales personnel—Training of. 2. Selling. I. McClay, Renie.
    HF5439.8.S354 2006
    658.3'1245—dc22

                                    2006016583

DEDICATION

With Gratitude for Many Blessings:

To the authors of this book, I truly couldn't have done it without you.

To my professional and personal supporters (you know who you are), I give many thanks.

For friends and family, my life is richer because of you.

Contents

Preface

Sales trainers are different from other trainers; at least we want to think so. We often are hired from within the sales organization because we have the credibility with the sales force and have demonstrated competency in the roles. What better way to bring knowledge of the products, customers, and competition to training than to hire someone who has done the job – a subject matter expert. However, that means subject matter experts have to learn how to do the job of training. The question is whether to teach a professional trainer the industry and products or teach the subject matter expert how to develop and deliver training. There is another scenario of companies who do not have a dedicated trainer for sales. Here, the sales leader, sales management, or human resource professional is charged with developing the sales force. Any of these scenarios can be successful when done well, and this book is designed to support them all.

The idea for this book came as a result of the limited amount of training and education resources specifically for sales training. There are workshops and conferences galore for the general training or organizational development professional. I vividly remember being in awe at the first Professional Society for Sales and Marketing Training (SMT) conference. Wow! These people were talking about the exact issues I faced in my job – designing complex product training, generating profitable sales as well as volume, customer relationships, managing selling teams, selling to the right levels in a customer organization, sales and marketing collaborating (or not), differentiating products from the competition. Eureka! Consider this book as an extension of a sales training conference – with no travel expenses!

My objective was to provide practical information for the new trainer and the experienced trainer alike without writing a textbook. There is no need to read these chapters consecutively like a book! Go first to the chapters that appeal to you. Read it like you would go grocery shopping. Just pick up the things you need. As with any organization or business, there is no single "fix" that works for all. Organizations are different, cultures are different, budgets and margins are different, organizations in a growing industry are different than organizations in a declining industry. My hope is that you will use this as a dynamic tool with actionable content and find value in seeing what others are doing. This is not the type of book to be stored with dusty binders on a shelf!

The plan here is that you will find some education, some theory, things that will make you think, plus very real-world ideas you can put to use right away. You will be the judge of how well we accomplished that plan.

Training is often a balancing act, and I have strived for balance here. A balance between:

- training leadership and training practitioners
- corporate professionals and solution providers
- strategic, tactical and operational topics
- sales trainers and training generalists who have trained for many audiences

This means I sought balance of people who develop and facilitate with strategic people that direct training. It means a balance of people who have in-depth knowledge of a few companies and others with a broad knowledge of many companies. Where else could you access so many experts who together have either worked for or with 100 Fortune 500 companies!

The authors bring a combined 150 years of training experience to this project. They are subject matter experts, very talented in training and have a great understanding and credibility for the topic about which they are writing. Many I have known for years, through an association with the Professional Society for Sales and Marketing Training (*www.smt.org*). My association with them has been a huge blessing and I have enjoyed this journey to creating what I hope will be a great resource for sales training professionals and others working with a sales audience.

I have tried to maintain the contributor's voice throughout this book. It wasn't about one author sitting down and writing everything they know. Because the topics are interrelated, you will occasionally find some overlap in information, reinforcement of key concepts and different views on the same topic. We hope you will think this blend of information enriches the book and helps make it the valuable resource we intend it to be.

My hope is that you enjoy using this resource as much as we enjoyed creating it.

CHAPTER 1

What Do Salespeople Want?

BECKY STEWART-GROSS, PhD, Building Bridges

WHAT DO SALESPEOPLE THINK OF TRAINING?

Have you listened to the voice of the sales staff lately? Have you questioned them about their expectations, their preferred learning style, or what constitutes a successful learning session for them? How do you know if you are getting a fair return on your training investment? Do you know what sales professionals really think about the training they receive? Very few companies go beyond the "smiley face evaluation form" at the conclusion of a session to conduct an in-depth survey of what the salesperson is actually thinking and learning. According to Steve Cohen, vice president of Learning Solutions for Carlson Marketing Group, a Minneapolis-based relationship marketing company, "What employees feel about their training, identifying how and what they like to learn as well as their learning preferences and then using these to design the training—very few companies engage in that kind of study." (*Training,* July 2004)

As a sales trainer have you given your sales force the opportunity to evaluate their training recently? Given an opportunity, sales professionals will generally evaluate their training sessions based on how the training was conducted: Was it fun, active, "hands on," all lecture, or boring? Were they treated as professionals and adults or like adolescents back in high school? They will assess their training in terms of the instructor's professionalism, personality, skills, knowledge, and experience. They will evaluate the training based on whether or not the content was practical and relevant to their work. Did it provide needed information, skills, and techniques that they can use immediately? They will also gauge the training on how well the goals of the session aligned with their expected outcomes. Did the training meet their personal and professional expectations?

Your sales team is full of opinions about the training they receive and the training that they would like to receive. Have you given them an opportunity to voice their opinions lately? This chapter will examine what instructional methods salespeople prefer, what topics they consider valuable for them, and what personal and professional goals they would like addressed in their training programs. You will also hear salespeople describe some "worst case" sales training programs they've attended. Most important, this chapter will call you to action. A sample training assessment survey is included to encourage you to reassess your sales force in order to determine their training preferences, opinions, and expectations. Similarly, a sample training evaluation form is included to help you revise your current form to include questions about the instructional delivery methods, the training topics, and the participants' goals and expectations. Lastly, the final "call to action" component is to assign follow-up activities. Sample active and passive follow-up activities are presented to assist you in accommodating the various learning styles represented in your sales force. This chapter is about helping you stay in tune with what your sales force thinks about sales training programs.

INSTRUCTIONAL METHODS

Perhaps the most predominant component of any training program is the instructional delivery method. Unfortunately, there is not one best method that can be used for all participants and all training topics. Sales trainers need to match the delivery methods with the participants' learning styles as well as the topics to be discussed and the skills to be acquired in order to be successful. You can learn more about adult learning styles and product training in Chapter 9, "Creating Effective Product Training."

Do you know what *instructional methods* your sales team prefers? Do they prefer to role-play, enter discussion groups, and present the team's work to the entire group? Do they prefer to listen to an expert share his or her knowledge and experience or read about it in a white paper? Do they prefer to use CD-ROM or DVD training materials or participate in a Webinar? Would they prefer listening to a podcast about training on their MP3 players? For an expanded list of questions to ask regarding technology, see Chapter 11, "Developing Strategies for Sales Training Technology Selection."

In a recent survey conducted by Building Bridges,[1] sales professionals expressed their preferred learning styles. Interactive, upbeat, fast-paced, instructor-led, hands-on training programs were favored over lengthy lectures, canned presentations, and highly structured textbook approaches. Some of their specific comments reflect their preference for interactive instructional methods.

- "I prefer case studies in which I develop an action plan based on a scenario that I am currently involved in."
- "I prefer the sharing of 'best practices.'"
- "Discussion, case studies, videotapes, and role playing really drive home the points and allow me to practice my new skills."

- "I prefer training sessions that are upbeat and keep my attention."
- "I prefer a combination of 'live trainer' and e-learning."
- "An entire day of lecture is . . . boring!!"

A recent survey by AchieveGlobal,[2] a performance improvement consulting and training service provider, asked 1,155 full-time U.S. and U.K. workers what instructional methods they preferred. Their top choice was a combination of instructor-led and electronic delivery. Achieve Global reported that 49 percent of workers preferred a combination of instructor-led and electronic delivery methods. Its report indicated that 41 percent of employees preferred instructor-led delivery of training, 10 percent preferred electronic delivery of training, and 49 percent preferred a combination of the two training methods.

Each member of your sales force has his or her own preferred learning style. Do you know the two most predominate learning styles among your team members? If not, a convenient way to find out their preferences is to conduct an informal survey, which would include a component dealing with their preferred learning style. Based on their preferences you can then design your training sessions to include a combination of instructional methods to accommodate the various preferred styles and maximize the effectiveness of the learning environment.

Successful trainers know that people learn in different ways. Various learning methods can be employed to accommodate the diverse learning styles. Some people are visual learners and learn best by reading or observing. Others are auditory learners and prefer to listen or speak about the information or skills to be learned. A third category of individuals learns best as a result of doing.

Learning by doing and learning by speaking are considered active methods of learning, while learning by reading, observation, and listening are more passive methods. Generally, the most successful learning environment includes the active methods of doing and speaking.

Sales professionals generally tend to be extroverts and as a general rule would prefer to be engaged in speaking and doing. Thus, trainers should include a variety of learning activities, such as:

- Hands-on, experiential activities
- Working with a mentor
- Analysis of "best practices"
- Role playing and participant presentations
- Interaction with instructor and participants (large and small group discussion)
- Discussion of relevant, custom-designed case studies
- Question-and-answer time with the facilitator

Because successful learning environments engage participants in a combination of learning methods, sales trainers should attempt to combine or blend various instructional methods—both active and passive—for maximum effectiveness. Training programs need to find the right mix of instructor-led training and Web-based training. Heather Johnson[3] reported that Lucent Technologies increased its sales training participation by 400 percent in just 18 months by using "partnerships and the right mix of training." After a year of experimenting with virtually all Web-based training, Lucent retargeted toward a program that combined 65 percent instructor-based training and 35 percent Web-based training and believes this will be the right mix for its sales force. According to Mary Slaughter, director of global sales training for Lucent, "The problem is that if you just use the cost-only mentality as opposed to a learning effectiveness mentality, it doesn't matter how cheap or expensive it is if people do not engage or use the tools." Heather Johnson reported that in 2001 Lucent was providing 90 percent instructor-led training and 10 percent Web-based training. In 2002, the company opted for the cost-effective Web-based method of training almost exclusively. By 2003, it moved closer to the right mix of training for its staff and has seen "incredible gains in sales training as well as performance."

| | Lucent Technologies | |
	Instructor-Led Training	Web-Based Training
2001	90%	10%
2002	8%	92%
2003	70%	30%
2004	65%	35%

To help enable you to design training programs with the right blend of learning methods for your team, your survey should include questions dealing with the preferred learning styles of your sales staff.

TRAINING TOPICS

Do you know what *information* and *skills* your sales team needs and wants? The members of your sales team have definite opinions about what training topics could help them improve their sales effectiveness and productivity. Generally speaking, sales professionals look for skills and information that can be applied in their sales environment. They look for three to five skills or points of knowledge that they can take away, remember, and apply. Building Bridges' survey of what would help salespeople improve their effectiveness and productivity yielded these familiar training topics:

- Focus on the closing
- Precall and postcall work
- The art of persuasion
- The art of building trust

- Understanding customer motivation
- Negotiation skills
- Presentation skills
- Overcoming objections
- Product training

Reynolds & Reynolds[4], an information services company, recently surveyed its 270 sales employees about the training they needed and wanted. Susan Moll, Reynolds University senior director, explained, "Shortly after I arrived I decided to ask the employees about their training needs rather than just continuing with what had always been done in the past." Moll asked a variety of questions in order to determine what additional training could be provided to improve sales effectiveness and productivity, what was their preferred delivery method, and what types of courses could improve their personal productivity. The survey received a 68 percent return— the highest return rate the company has ever achieved for a survey. Moll said the employees were eager to share their opinions.[5] Based on those opinions she was able to set new exciting training goals. In terms of which skills were needed, a 60 percent majority said they needed more training on how to create and present credible ROI (return on investment) for each solution for their customers. In terms of delivery methods, 62 percent said they preferred classroom training. And, finally, with regard to their personal development, 50 percent said they needed more time-management training.

Has your sales staff recently had the opportunity to provide input into their training topics? Do you know what topics and/or skills they would, collectively, rate as the top two in terms of what they want and need?

A second focus of your survey should address the appropriate topics for your sales staff and their business environment. Your sales force can assist you in understanding what skills and information are needed for the selling environment in which they are working. Once you have determined the content for the session then work to deliver it using several different learning styles.

GOALS AND EXPECTATIONS

A third component in your survey should address the goals and expectations of your sales force. Do you know what *goals* and *expectations* your sales team might have in mind for their training? All training participants view their training sessions in terms of their own personal and professional goals. They value training in terms of what they can expect to get out of it. Because they invest their time, money, and energy in participating in a training session, they evaluate it in terms of what they can expect to gain by participating.

Some sales professionals expect their training program to allow ample time to renew old acquaintances and to build camaraderie among their peers. Others anticipate time to build new friendships with their sales colleagues. For others, their personal goal is to learn to achieve a healthier balance of their work and personal lives. Some merely want to improve their home office productivity. Some have set as their goal to improve their negotiating skills. Here is how a few sales professionals expressed what they had in mind for an upcoming sales training session.

- "I'm anticipating the opportunity to meet and socialize with my colleagues."
- "I am looking forward to the opportunity to step back and renew my energy and my focus."
- "I am looking for some new techniques to help build better relationships with my customers."
- "I am expecting to be inspired and to be welcomed as part of the team."

- "I am expecting to receive information and skills relating to the act of persuasion."

One of your challenges as a sales trainer is to meet or to exceed the expectations of each participant in a training session. How do you go about satisfying such a wide range of expectations? How do you meet your sales team's goals, provide certain information and skills, and do so using their preferred learning style? The place to begin is to hear the voice of the salesperson.

A third component of your survey of your sales force should focus on their professional and personal goals and expectations. What could your sales training program offer that would help your sales force be successful in their careers and their personal lives?

You may find out that what is needed is a tutorial on how to better utilize today's technology, some tips on time and stress management, training on how to work more productively from their home office, or just some time to build some cohesiveness with the geographically disparate team members. You won't know what their goals and expectations are and you won't know what you can do to help them unless you ask.

Once you have a "fix" on the goals and expectations of your sales force, take some time to reflect on whether or not these issues are, indeed, "training issues." They may be, in reality, concerns that are more related to management, customer service, quality control, or perhaps personnel. Even the best sales training programs can't solve or resolve all of these other types of issues. If it is not a situation that can be dealt with through sales training, then perhaps you are wasting your time and that of your sales force. By making certain that the goals and expectations identified by your sales force are, in fact, training issues, you will have a genuine opportunity to help your team create behavioral change.

As a sales trainer, you not only need to "hear the voice" of your sales force, but you must also hear the voices of the sales manager and the company. You need to assess whether or not the goals and expectations of your sales force align with the company's goals and those of the sales manager. Making certain that there is proper alignment will enable you to "sell" the training program to the company's leadership. Moreover, linking your training goals to your company's goals will better position you to demonstrate the business impact and return on investment of your programs. Chapter 3, "Sales Managers as Key Stakeholders," will outline approaches that will convert sales managers into your program's torchbearers.

WORST-CASE SCENARIOS

In our survey of sales professionals, we asked the participants to describe a "disastrous" sales training program that they attended. The worst-case scenarios had similar themes, such as:

- Too theoretical with no practical application
- A large audience and lecture-style format
- A presenter who did not understand "our business"

One "disillusioned" national sales director described his worst training session this way: "Recently, we convened all salespeople, about 100 business managers, team leaders, and senior sales managers for a national training seminar with the founder of the program serving as our key sales trainer and facilitator. At that time, the program was regarded as one of the preeminent sales training programs in the United States. The program was very glitzy. The trainers were highly polished, persuasive, and articulate. Over the course of a three-day training seminar, we were provided with training notebooks, viewed videos, and were promised that if we used the 'XYZ Approach,' we were guaranteed to make the sale of any product to any customer. In other words, we were promised that we could 'sell the proverbial refrigerator to an Eskimo.' We all left the seminar convinced that we could do exactly what we were promised, only to find out it wasn't that easy. What we learned was that

- a canned, foolproof set of sales gimmicks generally never works;
- all customers have a set of real problems that require real solutions;
- selling is an art, and not a science; and
- slick, glitzy programs always look better in the passion of the presentation with a trainer than in real-life business application."

A "misled" account representative says he won't go back and recalls his "bad day" this way: "I attended a seminar that was billed as a product learning session. I found out that it was a sales training seminar designed to go after a specific market niche. Not only did they insist on using their sales 'formula' but they put attendees on the spot by making them role-play their 'formula' and then 'constructively criticizing' them if they didn't follow it correctly. I will never attend another seminar of theirs."

A "frustrated" sales manager highlights an instructional approach that put her to sleep: "This training program started out bad and went downhill from there. It was

- a highly structured textbook approach, lecture style;
- given by someone who has never sold a thing except the training session;
- not interactive or allowing for participation and discussion;

- without practice or application of concepts presented;
- a competitive environment where learning took a back seat to winning; and
- too long and too academic."

SALES TRAINER'S ACTION PLAN

EVALUATE YOUR ASSESSMENT SURVEY

Perhaps this would be an opportune time to review (and redesign if necessary) your sales training program assessment tools; specifically, your assessment surveys, evaluation forms, and follow-up questionnaires. Do your surveys include questions relating to the training delivery methods and preferred learning styles of your sales force? Do your surveys include the desired training topics of your sales staff and the sales manager as well as their goals and expectations? If you are not currently listening to the voice of your sales force perhaps it is time to survey them in order to determine their training preferences, opinions, and expectations. Figure 1.1 provides some sample survey questions that are designed to assess the training delivery methods, the training topics, and the goals of your sales staff.

REVISIT YOUR TRAINING EVALUATION FORM

Review your evaluation form and revise it, if necessary, to incorporate questions about the instructional delivery methods, the training topics, and the participants' goals and expectations. Figure 1.2 provides some sample training evaluation questions.

FIGURE 1.1 Sample Training Assessment Survey Questions

1. Training Delivery Methods

A. What general training delivery method do you prefer?
   i)   Working with a mentor
   ii) Instructor-led
   iii) Web-based, e-learning
   iv) Videoconference
   v)   Individual reading
   vi) Podcast
   vii) Other _____

B. What learning activities do you prefer? (Circle two)
   i)   Hands-on, experiential activities
   ii) Custom-designed case studies applied to real-life situations
   iii) Role-playing new skills
   iv) Large and small group discussion
   v)   Lecture/expert presentation
   vi) Analysis of "best practices"
   vii) Other _____

C. What learning material format do you prefer?
   i)   Audiocassette
   ii) Videotape
   iii) Book
   iv) Workbook/learning packet
   v)   CD-ROM/DVD
   vi) MP3
   vii) Other _____

2. Training Topics

A. What skills, techniques, and information could be provided to enhance your sales effectiveness and productivity? (Circle two)
   i)   How to ask strategic questions
   ii) How to negotiate effectively
   iii) How to close successfully
   iv) How to manage communication technology
   v)   How to build client trust
   vi) How to listen effectively
   vii) Other _____

FIGURE 1.1 Sample Training Assessment Survey Questions *(continued)*

B. What skills, techniques, and information could be provided to enhance the sales process? (Circle two)
   i)   How to develop better sales proposals
   ii) How to manage my territory more productively
   iii) How to develop high-impact direct mail letters
   iv) How to market special events
   v)   How to generate more qualified leads
   vi) How to enhance "precall and postcall" work
   vii) Other _____

3. Goals of Participants

A. What are your top two personal development goals?
   _____
   _____
   _____
   _____

B. What are your top two professional development goals?
   _____
   _____
   _____
   _____

FOLLOW-UP LEARNING ACTIVITIES

Assign follow-up activities to further accommodate the various learning styles represented on your sales force. Here are some examples of active and passive learning methods that can be used for follow-up learning.

Active learning methods:

- Workbooks/manuals
- Webinars, Web conferences
- Discussion groups online
- Teleconference
- Videoconference

FIGURE 1.2 Sample Training Evaluation Form Questions

Delivery Methods

1. Did the facilitator provide learning methods that met your learning style?

1	2	3	4	5
No		Somewhat		Yes

2. Did the facilitator provide helpful learning activities?

1	2	3	4	5
No		Somewhat		Yes

Training Topics

3. Rate the relevance of the material to you professionally.

1	2	3	4	5
Not relevant		Somewhat relevant		Very relevant

4. Rate the effectiveness of the skills acquired in this session.

1	2	3	4	5
Not effective		Somewhat effective		Very effective

Goals

5. Did the training session address any of your professional goals?

1	2	3	4	5
No		Somewhat		Yes

6. Did the training session address any of your personal goals?

1	2	3	4	5
No		Somewhat		Yes

- Working with a mentor
- Case studies applied to real-life situations

Passive learning methods:

- Reading best practices, case studies
- Audiocassette material
- CD-ROM/DVD presentations
- Videotape material
- MP3 podcasts

FIGURE 1.3 Sample Implementation Survey Questions

---

1. Have you found the newly acquired skills or information to be effective?

1	2	3	4	5
No		Somewhat		Yes

2. Have you utilized the skills or information taught in the program?

1	2	3	4	5
No		Somewhat		Yes

3. Have you encountered any obstacles in implementing the skills or information?

1	2	3	4	5
No		Somewhat		Yes

4. How often do you use the skills or information?

1	2	3	4	5
Never		Frequently		Always

FOLLOW-UP QUESTIONNAIRE

Utilize a follow-up questionnaire to help assess how the skills and information were applied and implemented. Figure 1.3 provides some sample questions.

SUMMARY

Training sessions should be customized to meet the expectations, needs, and learning styles of the participants. By employing a variety of learning methods, the sales trainer can address the predominant, preferred learning styles of his or her sales force, thus enhancing the learning situation. By delivering information and skills that are relevant to the sales force and the selling environment in which they work, the sales trainer can create a more productive and meaningful training session. By addressing the professional and personal goals of the sales staff, the sales trainer can create more ownership and participation in the training program.

Remember the four habits of highly successful sales trainers:

1. *Assess.* Use assessment tools to hear the voice of your sales force.
2. *Train.* Provide interactive, relevant, practical, and meaningful training programs based on listening to the voice of your sales force.
3. *Evaluate.* Evaluate your training programs in order to determine how well you heard their voices and delivered programs that met their needs.
4. *Follow up.* Design and implement follow-up activities to accommodate the various learning styles represented on your sales staff.

CHAPTER 2

Getting Leadership Support

JIM GRAHAM, RR Donnelley

There is no magic pill for persuading senior leadership to support your training initiatives! It's a tough, uphill battle, where you are competing for time, tight budget dollars, potential outsourcing, reductions, restructuring, cost controls, and many more worthy projects. Other constituents are just as enthusiastic and eager as you are to get the same support. So here are a few best practices and some success stories for gaining that support for your projects.

But let's be clear, there is no panacea, no one right way, no way that works every time, and no formula that I know of for always getting what you want. We will explore some options and give you ideas, along with a few actual cases, that could work in your organization.

CREDIBILITY

Let's start with *credibility*. As the old saying goes, sometimes you've got it, and sometimes you don't. In getting support from senior management, you must have it! This is not negotiable; you cannot get support for your project without having credibility.

How do you get it? First, you earn it through years of service to the company. You rise through the ranks, become successful in sales or sales management, earn a reputation for effectiveness, take on challenging initiatives, and succeed. Basically, *your reputation precedes you*. It's great if you've got it, but it is tough if you don't.

In today's world, with mergers, acquisitions, downsizing, and rightsizing, many of us don't have years of experience to support our position. Perhaps the VP of sales, who supported you, has now left the company and your champion is gone. (I have a story about a project like this later in the chapter.) As a result, credibility can be hard to come by.

What is credibility? Credibility is doing what you say you will do when you say you will do it. It is your track record of performance. How quickly and professionally have you responded to each request? How successful have your projects been? How visible? Who knows about your past performance successes? Can you or someone who has credibility summarize your successes to impress a decision maker?

One way to gain this credibility is to obtain the support of others who have it. You can't gain it alone; you must get help and support. You gain credibility for your project by the associations you have with those who are seen as credible. The people who coach and support you must be credible, even if you are still earning your stripes. They can actively support you via e-mail recommendations or in hallway conversations (yes, those conversations with the right people do influence decisions), or by attending a presentation and supporting you with their presence. They also may coach you behind the scenes (the invisible coach). What they do and how you use their credibility is very important. The higher this person is in your organization, the better! The general has more clout than either the lieutenant or the captain.

Here is an example from my company:

One of my first experiences selling—yes, selling—a major project to senior management was a large, interactive computer-based learning simulation project. I started by building a very elaborate presentation with well over 100 slides in more detail than a congressional report. Then, I requested two hours with our president. His approval would lead me to the CEO. I started with someone with whom I already had credibility, who had credibility with the ultimate decision maker, and who I thought could influence the decision. I told him I had prepared the presentation for the CEO and wanted him to critique it. After the first ten slides or so, he stopped me and asked what I was doing. He described the attention span of the CEO, and suggested an executive summary of a few slides, without the agonizing detail I had prepared.

I learned a valuable lesson about being *brief* and *precise*. I took the advice, built the executive summary with plenty of detail to back it up, and a few weeks later presented to the CEO. The CEO asked, "Who else have you talked to?" I told him the president (hoping that would seal the deal). He asked more questions. Because the project was for sales, he wanted to know if I had the approval of senior sales leaders across the business units? No. I had not talked with all of them, but I certainly would. I went off to meet with each, get their sign-off and support, and returned to both the president and CEO with support signatures and obtained the finances I needed.

CONSIDER THE AUDIENCE

Sometimes all the support you need from the most senior level, the CEO or president, is a signature on an appropriation releasing the funds. At other times, their *support* is in the form of a message to the organization. It's amazing how much support you get when the CEO or president is behind your initiative. Unfortunately, politically minded people often check the organization chart before making a decision. We all know that there are followers and leaders in every organization. Your job is to gain support high enough to bring the followers along. Here is an example of how this might work:

A well-known midwestern furniture manufacturer wanted to create a "learning organization," an environment of ongoing learning, growth, and development for all employees. With this in mind, a well-seasoned training leader with remarkable credibility set out to create a state-of-the-art facility to provide such an environment. But in order for this project to be successful, it had to have senior leadership support *and*, in fact, board funding approval. This person's credibility made support from the highest levels possible, and the project proceeded, becoming a best-in-class facility not only in the industry and state, but unquestionably, one of the top five in the nation. Most facilitators for the center were internal and well credentialed in their own right. The CEO who supported the project with the board also was an instructor. Can you guess how many other members of the senior management team also were involved in leading sessions in the new facility? Yes, you are correct—all members of the senior team became involved in one way or another in developing talent at the new learning center.

As you can see, sometimes you need a signature and funds, and sometimes you need the direct support and presence of senior managers. As you plan your strategy, think about how to maintain support at this level for much more than just approving the funding.

DEFINING THE RETURN

When faced with a lack of your own earned credibility, as well as a lack of high-level support, you must consider another tactic. One tactic is showing the potential impact this initiative will have on the company's bottom line. Can you prove that changing the behaviors of certain individuals with training will have a return on investment (ROI) for the company? If you have compelling evidence of such an outcome, then you are home free!

Not so fast; we need to think this one through a bit. Why? Because people refute irrefutable evidence all the time!

Most of us at one time or another have completed an exhaustive needs analysis to understand gaps in performance, and have developed plans to close those gaps. It's a good starting point, but the message is sometimes lost in the training minutiae. Have we considered *business outcomes?* Do we know the key business drivers of the organization? Is an earnings per share (EPS) target such a driver? How about growing revenue? Reducing costs? Competing in new markets? Launching new products? Retaining talent?

These questions, and their answers, are as important as your credibility in selling your initiative. Using business terms instead of training terms shows that you are thinking of the business—and the management's definitions of success. If you make the management look good by helping to achieve their goals, you will become a business partner.

Let's dig a little deeper. A few years ago, Rob Brinkerhoff introduced a high-impact learning process called *success case methodology,*[1] which is tied to measurement and evaluation of training outcomes. He should be credited with changing the way that many training people, and businesspeople alike, think about training outcomes. His process can help you gain that elusive credibility we all seek. And if you already have the credibility, it can cement your ability to gain support from senior management. Quite simply, it involves understanding the business-related questions above. Which business outcomes must be produced for the enterprise this year? Every company gets a quarterly scorecard (at least the public ones do) and they are evaluated against their industry peers, forecasts, previous quarters, and more. We, as training professionals, must understand those outcomes if we are to win.

Here is a story that shows this point:

Training at a large medical products company was historically classroom-based for new sales representatives joining the company. Often reps were from outside the industry, so they had to learn about the industry as well as products. Experts were committed. A solid training process was in place. The sales training leader, working with an external consultant, determined it was time to move to an e-learning platform for product training and to institute a "masters" program for senior reps, as well as define a curriculum for overall sales development.

The price tag would be more than $1 million for three years, and included: analysis, selecting an e-learning vendor, design, development, 360 feedback instruments, and, of course, heavy use of the external facilitator. How would you sell this expensive idea to a conservative senior management staff? First, by understanding the company sales culture—what sales needed, sales usually got. Second, by using some ideas from Rob Brinkerhoff about measurement and proving the outcomes of training. Finally, with a well-orchestrated plan expertly presented to upper levels, showing speed of learning and 24/7 access to e-learning modules (many of which were also used by experienced reps for their own quick reference).

The outcome? Complete support from senior management! The metrics offered proof of success, and encouraged continued funding.

In the business climate today, we must be business professionals as well as training leaders. Rob Brinkerhoff provides ample direction for how we get there. Understand the key business drivers of your organization first, and design your training to meet those outcomes. Deceptively simple, and not impossible to execute!

While having discussions with key senior leaders and trying to gain their support for your initiatives, you should be asking what the success drivers are for this year and/or this quarter. When you meet with business unit leaders, you should ask the same questions about those business units. Without sounding too much like a *training geek*, you can ask for the behavioral outcomes they need to see from your sales teams, sales managers, and senior sales leaders. The answers will tell you what your special initiative or your training needs to accomplish.

When you understand the business drivers both for the company and the business unit in particular, you can create "line of sight" training to accomplish those business objectives. (And you will have some very interesting business discussions with those you engage.) Your project, your initiative, and your training plan must be linked to business outcomes if you are to have a chance of winning support, with or without credibility.

Here are some additional ideas and success cases on selling to senior management and getting their support for important projects.

In a large imaging products company, the training manager worked with the vice president and senior directors to conduct the annual needs assessment. They each were asked: What are the three to five top priorities in your business and how can training support them? What do sales representatives need to be able to know or do to ensure your business success? Communications continued (see the questions below) until the VP and each of the directors had identified enough detail to formulate the training plan for the first half-year. Specific training outcomes were identified and agreed on, with dates for completion. This plan was used for quarterly reviews with the directors and VP to make sure they were satisfied with the training focus and the programs offered.

Managers want to have excellent training with the least investment of money and time, so what you offer needs to meet all of those expectations—starting with small projects and increasing to larger projects. Begin with no-cost and low-cost projects that management only has to support by word and deed, then move on to those projects that might be more costly but have more payback. Delivering on each and every commitment and agreement and checking back on a continuous basis with each director resulted in ongoing support and communication from management.

The vice president and senior directors were asked:

- What are your top three to five business priorities for the next six months?
- What do the sales representatives need to be able to know or do to achieve your goals?
- How will you know they have achieved them (examples of evidence)?
- When do they need to be able to do this (month, quarter)?
- Who can we work with to ensure that we are helping you to meet your goals?

Priority	Objectives	Results	Timing	Partners
1. Increase sales	Learn how to sell Product A	Sell 50% more of Product A	Q1	Marketing, product expert
2. Decrease costs	Learn how to use System B	Reduce travel costs by 20%	Q2	Systems group, purchasing

You really must *understand your audience.* We spend a lot of time training class participants to sell to senior executives with programs like "Selling to Senior Executives," "Selling to Vito," and "Selling to the C Level." The message always is if you are going to sell to senior management, you must understand how they buy! It seems simple, and in some ways it is, but not always.

I mentioned earlier that your priorities compete against other priorities. Executives have more on their plate than just your project. Someone (the president of our company in my story earlier in this chapter) must help you identify the "hot buttons" for his or her buying decisions.

You need to *understand the budget.* Are there budget dollars available? Who is going to pay for your program? Will it be billed back to business units? Will the training budget house the costs? There are always budget dollars available for the right idea. You may have to search to find them, but the dollars are there—somewhere. You also have to work with accounting to determine whether your project can be included in the "capital" budget. If a project includes hardware, building improvements, upgrades, or furniture, you may be able to capitalize the costs instead of expensing them. The expense budget is usually much more sensitive than the capital one. Maybe you can amortize the costs over several years, and this will help to reduce the single-year impact.

You must *shape the content of the message* as well. Executive summaries are an excellent place to start. Become familiar with the detail that supports your summary, and find a way to make it short, sweet, and to the point. Realize too that the people you are presenting to are quick studies. They would not be where they are if they weren't. Don't oversell your proposal; get the signature and get out! The content is important, but so is the delivery. Many a great message, proposal, or project with an important payoff for the company has been denied because the delivery was flawed. Just like a good facilitator can make an average training program come alive and a poor facilitator can destroy a good program, so too with a proposal.

Here is an example:

In a large manufacturing company, a proposed system would cost thousands of dollars and expert time from the systems group. It was clear to those in the training department that this system would be beneficial to all managers worldwide, but the challenge was to convince the budget approvers in purchasing and finance that this was a good deal and a critical need for the company that could save millions in training dollars. Gaining agreement for a meeting to discuss the project was a challenge, accomplished primarily through friends of influence. At this meeting, the decision makers were coached on using the system and provided with impressive marketing materials to engage their interest. They really enjoyed using the system and found the materials to be impressive. So they responded well to the internal sales pitch/public relations approach and approved the project. This took a long time (18 months), so patience and persistence were important to the success of this effort.

Your executive summary is like the executive summary often built into a sales proposal, or a request for proposal (RFP) response. Think about your customer—the senior executive—

and build the summary around "what's in it for them." What are the business drivers, will the project deliver results, and why do they need to do it now? Why should they spend the company's dollars on this instead of any one of several important initiatives?

Timing is critical! *Timing is everything!* If your proposal falls in Q1 and the budget was finalized three months before, you will have little chance of getting approval. Unless, and this is a big one, someone very high up wants to support the project. There are always budget dollars available for the right idea.

If your company is completing a good year, timing may be right for your proposal. If, on the other hand, it's been a tough year, quarter, or the next year looks dismal, all bets are off on getting acceptance. And here is another point on timing that you cannot control: a change in personnel. Leadership changes occur without your knowledge (at least not before it happens), and you may find you've been working with the wrong people. Sales training company Miller Heiman, in its program *Strategic Selling,*[2] would call this a red flag—a loss of executive sponsorship.

Here's something that happened in my company:

My team and I had worked for several months convincing a group president and an executive VP of sales how important it was to conduct a fundamental leadership program for the sales leadership team. Our proposal was strong, needs were identified, and curriculum was developed and tied to business outcomes. We had done everything. Our last meeting included four hours with the executive VP of sales defining launch strategies, attendees, and location—detail after detail. Three days later, an organization announcement was made: the company had reorganized business units and these two individuals were not retained. The outcome for my team: no sponsors and new decision makers—we had to start over.

DEFINING OUTCOMES

Your next question is, or should be, how are you going to *measure the success or outcomes* of your project? Put yourself in the chair of the senior executive. Would you ask, what will be the outcome of my investment in your project? Have you measured the ROI? Will the investment make a difference? How will I know? Who else is supporting this (another way of asking, whose neck, other than yours, is on the line)? Companies always measure the ROI of a capital project (new equipment, a plant, system upgrade, or an acquisition), and you can measure the ROI on your project if it's a capital expenditure.

In a large equipment products company, a system was purchased to provide data on the success of sales promotions. The senior management decided that it was worth the investment to purchase and implement this system. It was considered critical to the success of the organization and important to achieve organizational goals. The training group compared the costs of having the external company who designed the system conduct the training to the cost of having internal resources conduct the training. Management was sold on supporting the internal training effort.

While the training was a success, the system was not, so management considered the training unsuccessful as well. The lesson we learned was to spend your training efforts on projects that are more likely to succeed rather than on risky ones, because management cannot often separate the failure of a project from the successful training that was conducted. It was a hard lesson and not one you can always avoid. With limited resources, it is important to prioritize the projects that you can be most successful in supporting, and show positive results for the organization.

Often the results of training are intangible, much like buying insurance: I know I need it, I'm just not sure how much, which type, and for how long. Most would agree it's better to have a trained workforce than an untrained one. Some might argue that if we train them, they might leave. Others might argue that if we don't train them, and they stay, what do we have? Few senior leaders would disagree, but why then are training dollars the first cut from the budget? Many of us have experienced this over the years. We know the organization needs XYZ, and many times so do the executives, but decisions must be made. If you don't have a direct link to business outcomes, you won't get the funding! Sometimes even when you do, the funding is just not there:

> We were conducting a leadership development program through a large midwestern university for 30-plus attendees. The program had budget approval and had been conducted before. In fact, the relationship we had with the university went back several years and several sessions. We had complete approval and support from the business units the participants worked in, and we were four weeks from launch. The university faculty had developed their sessions, correspondence had been distributed to all, and university accommodations were booked. Then I got the dreaded phone call from the CEO's office, and was asked to immediately cancel the program. No discussion, no negotiations—just cancel it. I, of course, being of stout heart, scheduled a meeting with the CEO to explain why this was not a good idea for our company reputation and for the message it would send to participants, and that it was just too darn late to do such a thing.

> I received a quick lesson in economics, which I have never forgotten—what it means when a public company is close to missing quarterly results. The CEO not only wanted to save the cost of the program, travel, and missed

work opportunities (there were a lot of sales leaders in the program), but he wanted to send a very clear message to the organization: *your #1 job is to make the numbers to which we committed.* (I was not in sales, but was leading a major expenditure during a quarter.)

We postponed instead of canceling, and rescheduled six months later. The university, to their credit and our relationship, did not charge the normal cancellation fee, although it would have been impossible to schedule another company in the slot. I made sure the CEO knew what a good partner the university had been. We ran this program and several others there.

BUDGET PROCESS AND TIMING

Timing, as we've seen, can be so critical. The project was right—the purpose, process, funding, support, and agreements at all levels—and it was critical for leadership development.

Sometimes the chief financial officer (CFO), not the CEO, is "to blame" for a project rejection. "Obviously it's the accountants who don't understand the importance of our project and who reject it only because they have veto power! They don't understand the complete merits of our very important endeavor!"

In my CEO example, that CEO was an attorney by background, although he did understand the numbers quite well (as any CEO must!). There are times though when *the CFO or the accounting team can be your ally*, rather than your adversary. Here's another example from my experience:

We were in the midst of an internal consulting project with our large account managers. We were trying to measure the outcome of our very extensive efforts by using additional volume and/or profits from their accounts. The account managers were held to rigorous details and analysis of their accounts. They dug deeper than they ever had into understanding their customers' business. We looked at everything from marketing to operations to sales and distribution. Update meetings were held every three weeks, and each participant presented what he or she had learned and accomplished since our last meeting. There were three follow-up meetings after an initial training program. A lot of time, effort, and sweat went into the program.

We were collecting solid growth numbers, but needed more support to continue our efforts. To gain that support, we developed a presentation, which we delivered to our CFO. We were conservative in the results we were claiming; we didn't want to get caught up in numbers we couldn't support. He looked at our analysis, asked several good questions, as you would expect, and in the end told us our numbers were better than we thought they were! We were surprised, even though we had been conservative. He further pointed out results we could take credit for that we had not considered.

The point is that the accounting team, especially the CFO, can be helpful in selling your projects to senior management. If you have the numbers that the CFO supports, you can't get a better recommendation! Before you present to the CFO, make sure you have worked with someone in accounting to help you understand which metrics make the biggest impression on those who approve the numbers. Is it return on assets (ROA), internal rate of return (IRR), or another measure? How are other projects judged? Do you need to prove a return on investment in three years or five? The better you understand the internal accounting mechanism, the better you will be able to present your story.

SELL IT

How do you really develop that winning presentation and what does it contain? As I mentioned earlier in the chapter, there is no one right way, but there are some elements that must be considered. The list below may help if you have not done this before. Even if you have, it might be worth a quick review of the fundamentals:

- *Know your audience* and how they like to receive information. (If you don't know, ask one of their assistants or *get coaching* as I did from the president.)
- Provide an *executive summary*, which should include answers to:
  - Why are we doing this now?
  - What impact will this have on the growth and development of participants?
  - What is the change outcome that will make a difference?
  - What are the costs? Don't try to hide this at the end as most people do with proposals, present it up front, but then explain why.
  - What time will this save? Almost any project worth its salt will speed the learning process by reducing learner time.
  - How much cost will the project reduce? For example, switching from classroom to e-learning will reduce travel, classroom expense, trainer hours, lost time from the field, and more.
  - Who, other than yourself, is sponsoring?
  - How long is the development time? Give yourself some flexibility here, no matter what your developers or external suppliers are telling you.
  - When will it be implemented?
- Always *underpromise* and *overdeliver*.
- *Keep it short.* Brevity is one of the keys to success.

- *Bring the back-up data.* Don't get surprised with a question you can't answer. (Just as you would prepare for a sales call, anticipate what your audience will want to know and questions they may ask.)
- *Practice, practice, practice.* Don't get fooled by what might seem to be an informal meeting. Even if you are not presenting via PowerPoint, be thoroughly prepared. In many cases, you have only one time to make a good impression. Even if you know your audience, don't be too casual.
- PowerPoint slides can be a great way to present, if done right. Make the presentation *clear* and *concise.* Avoid putting 80 percent of what you say on the slide! Put 20 percent of the information on the slide in bullet points, and talk to the rest.
- *Schedule enough time* for the meeting, and avoid circumstances where they are preparing for board meetings or budgets, and/or or during the busy times in your organization. (Again, an executive assistant can give you insight here.)
- *Be enthusiastic but rational.* They probably will be less excited about your project than you are, but your job is to get them excited.
- Remember your objective is to *get the commitment—once you do, leave.* Don't get caught up in trying to explain more just because you think they should know. Once you get the signature, grab it and run.

PROGRESS UPDATES

As part of your project proposal, you should plan to provide feedback on progress and demonstrate, within a reasonable period of time, that the dollars invested were invested wisely. The story earlier from the medical products company included very detailed end-of-the-quarter and annual ROI analyses. It was a three-year project, so interim accounting of costs and results was critical in gaining additional funding.

In order to get funding from senior management for your next project, you must provide progress reports. These should be at least annually or, even better, quarterly to apprise the leadership team of your success and accomplishments. Again, consider your audience. They don't need length or depth; they need a brief synopsis of accomplishments and measures.

For example:

- *X* people have completed the *Y* program.
- The results we are seeing are as follows . . .
- Our costs savings have been . . .
- Our improvements in process are as follows . . .

They will tell you if they want more information, so you should be prepared.

GAINING SUPPORT

What if you don't have senior-level support? Start with a manager who has a budget and might be interested in your project. You may know of a group that is obviously struggling with a problem that training can fix. Put together a proposal for that manager's review. You would only ask for input on the development of a possible program and, if the manager feels it is appropriate, a pilot session with some of the sales representatives. Based on feedback and success, you can use the results to gain support for implementation in another part of the organization.

You can also engage key influencers who may not be at the senior level. Look for those people that others listen to and engage them in conversations about your proposed project.

Listen to their advice and counsel on how to get more management support. Sometimes they know just the right way to present things and sometimes they can save you a lot of frustration, because they know the project will not get the support that you need to be successful.

Rob Brinkerhoff, who was mentioned earlier, talks about measurement and evaluation in a very practical, logical way that does not require a staff of statisticians to prove results. It can be executed by mere mortals who are willing to follow his process and are diligent about understanding business outcomes and real-world business results. The process of establishing intentionality and preparing participants for a learning experience, linking the learning event to understood outcomes, and providing manager support and reinforcement after the program is deceptively simple. It does not require a staff of statisticians.

You can show performance improvement by providing pre- and post-training test scores, number of participants trained, cost savings using internal experts instead of external, virtual instead of classroom cost and time savings, training participant satisfaction scores, and other measures of success, in addition to increased sales, decreased cost and time to perform, and so on.

Rob also writes at length about what makes training initiatives fail. These reasons should be explored to ensure the project you worked so hard to sell doesn't fail because of poor execution.

Neil Rackham wrote in his classic book, *SPIN Selling*,[3] that 87 percent of skills learning in a training program will be lost within 30 days if not *reinforced by a manager or mentor*, who in fact can coach to the skills taught in the program.

It is important to engage leadership in the implementation and post-training follow-up/reinforcement.

We were designing a leadership development program in a large northeastern city and knew that the CEO of the company was a model leader, so we engaged him in a conversation regarding leadership and what examples he could share of excellent leadership. He told us that leaders need to "walk the talk." We asked how they might do that. He explained that if we wanted supervisors to take the training that their managers should participate as well. We asked if he would be willing to lead by example and he agreed to come into the training pilot session to talk with participants about leadership.

Participants were so impressed and excited to talk with the CEO that they recommended this for every session. So the CEO required all of the company executives to spend 1½ hours at the end of each session discussing leadership. If any executive did not show up for the session because of other "pressing business," the CEO came to substitute and had a difficult discussion with the executive who did not model leadership by showing up to represent management. This really sent a strong message throughout the company about the importance of leadership training!

The CEO also requested feedback after each class regarding the senior management discussions about leadership and the training. He invited e-mails from the participants and responded to each one personally, to reinforce their learning experience. We also instituted an annual 360-degree leadership assessment to track improvements in performance. Results were reviewed by the CEO.

TIPS FOR SUCCESS:

- Start with company or organization priorities and goals.
- Identify what training is required to achieve those goals.

- List all stakeholders (see example below) in the success of the training.
- Create a plan to engage each stakeholder (person who stands to benefit from successful training implementation) and explain how the training will support his or her success.
- Ask what his or her definition of success would be
- Design the training to achieve this definition of success and the learning objectives that would ensure that organization results can be achieved.
- Don't waste time and money on projects that you want instead of what the key managers are requiring.
- Start a year ahead to obtain budget funds for key projects.
- Work with the managers who have the money to pay for the training they want.
- Put together a solid business case for the training.
- Don't be disappointed when they say no. They are often choosing between sales feet on the street and training. (They make money on sales; training is an expense in their eyes, instead of an investment.)
- Keep informed of the state of the business, choose your timing (when they have money to spend), and word requests very carefully.
- If there is no money—be creative. Think of ways to provide the information and skill practice without spending a lot of money (i.e., learning tools, internal coaches, subject matter expert panels, etc.). Don't give up!
- Always keep open communications regarding status of projects, needs of management, and success celebrations with management and stakeholders.

The results of getting leadership support for initiatives might include the following:

- Priorities are always agreed by the end of the year for the next year.
- There is a large budget and support for training.
- Suppliers are engaged as partners for success.
- Purchasing helps with RFP and approval process.
- Finance always says yes.
- Senior management introduces programs and checks for application of new skills.
- Credit for results and high productivity often goes to training.
- Sales representatives and sales managers ask for more training on a continuous basis and tell you they will fund the training if the dollars are not available.
- Training expenditures are approved quickly.
- Training often is highlighted in the company newsletter.
- Senior managers often attend and stop in on training sessions.
- Many managers conduct training sessions, as requested.
- Subject matter experts make it a priority to be available for design, review, and delivery of training programs.
- Managers and the best salespeople make themselves available to coach those who request their support.
- Training results are reviewed on a monthly or quarterly basis.
- Awards and recognition are given to training staff and sales representatives for outstanding performance.

Here is an example.

We were developing a low-cost (Webcasting) approach to training sales representatives on new products and engaged the VP of sales in the design and implementation to save money on travel and training costs and time. The VP agreed to invite participants with our prewritten memo and his signature. He then followed up the memo with a phone message to all sales representatives telling them that he expected their full participation and would be checking to see who attended and who did not. Then he asked for attendance rosters and gave them to his directors to follow up to see why someone had not attended the session. He congratulated those who completed the training and encouraged them to use the techniques they learned in the next few months so he could track the increase in sales on the product. This really motivated everyone to attend and apply the new learning because they knew the expectations and follow-up would be conducted by their managers. They would be responsible for applying the new learning and showing results from the training. Sales on the product on which they were trained were closely tracked to ensure the reps were using the knowledge and skills that had been learned.

In short, what you want to do is:

- Develop a plan to obtain leadership support.
- Find out what the "hot buttons" are for key leaders.
- Use their terms and examples to prepare to discuss what they would like training to do for them.
- Deliver excellence on a continuous basis.
- Make them the leaders of the training effort, but do all the work for them.

Here is an example:

We were asked by the president of the division to create a university where senior executives would learn to use and teach their employees about new products. Our dialogue helped us learn what he was looking for and we agreed to provide drafts for his approval. We quickly worked as a team to design a proposal and some examples for his review. We made him the "dean" of the university, created a curriculum, and brought him sample tools and certificates for the completion of the training. After some revisions based on his input, the program was introduced at the annual executives meeting by the president who expressed his expectation of completion by every executive. He would get monthly reports regarding who had completed the training and who had conducted the training for their sales representatives and he would personally sign and present the certificate of completion to each executive. Ongoing communications from the president (which we created and he signed) were sent to all executives throughout the year. Lists of whom had completed each phase of the university sessions were sent out to all executives on a monthly basis so those who had completed were recognized and those who had not completed were motivated to finish quickly.

YOUR PLAN FOR LEADERSHIP SUPPORT

Answer the following questions in order to get leadership support for a specific initiative. If you find that categories cannot be completed, it is time to do more homework to determine the answers to these critical success factors. This list is just a beginning; you should add other factors that will be important to the success of the project.

1. What critical needs have to be identified?
2. What training is required to achieve organization goals and targets?
3. Who are the key stakeholders?

4. What are the costs?
5. What results need to be achieved?
6. What are the objectives?
7. What is the timing?
8. What is the training plan?
9. What is the schedule for engaging stakeholders?
10. What are the roles and responsibilities?
11. What are the measures of success?
12. What is the communication plan?
13. Is there a design document?
14. What is the implementation plan?
15. What are the results of the evaluation and feedback?

Persuasion is an art and a science, and it is important in gaining other people's support. "Change management" to engage support of leadership often depends on relationships that have been built over time (*trust*) and the numbers to prove success. Senior managers are people too. Find out what they like and especially what they *don't* like. Secretaries and administrative assistants are your *best* friends (or they can be your worst enemies; i.e., gatekeepers). Always make the senior leaders and your manager look good. Find ways to talk to managers on a more casual basis, such as after presentations or at charity, community, or network events that you attend to show your support of their interests. Always tie the training to the goals they are committed to achieving. Show that you value their time by making their involvement brief and preparing everything for them to ensure that things proceed smoothly.

You will likely need to make connections with people you do not naturally connect with at high levels of the organization. Jerry Acuff, author of *The Relationship Edge in Business*,[4] recommends a three-step process for improving these relationships. They include your mindset (are your intentions good and not manipulative), your information gathering (asking questions about their business and them as a person to find common ground), and your actions (consistent, persistent actions over time). This process used consistently will help to find common ground and will improve relationships over time.

SUMMARY

There are a lot of right ways to gain acceptance on the projects you bring to senior management seeking their support, and there are a few things you can do to shoot yourself in the foot, so to speak.

LuAnn Irwin (a contributor to this book) tells me from her Kodak, Xerox, and HSBC experiences, that a Utopia does exist in some organizations and is really worth the work put in to achieve it. Your support can change very quickly. So you often need a plan B. It is a wonderful experience to have the corporate CFO request training for his team, fund it, participate fully in the training exercises and tests, and introduce all of the training sessions himself.

Hopefully this chapter has spurred your thinking about your approach to gaining support. But let me capture what I think is most salient: Selling to senior executives is not completely different from selling to senior levels of a customer or prospect. You must

- have credibility (If you don't have it, you need to find a way to get it!);
- consider the audience and the message content, length, depth, time, structure, level and position of buyers, and more;
- make sure your project provides a return on investment for the corporation because you are competing against other projects that will;
- define project outcomes very clearly, with ROI, time savings, improved efficiencies, and more;

- understand the budget process timing;
- be prepared to answer questions;
- practice, practice, practice;
- get the order and get out;
- plan progress reports and get senior management agreement on when they want to see them; and
- remember that selling internally is not that different from selling externally.

So, let's get going! There are lots of people to persuade!

RECOMMENDED RESOURCES

- Neil Rackham, *SPIN Selling* (and several other outstanding books by the same author)
- Rob Brinkerhoff, *Success Case Evaluation Methods, High Impact Learning Process*
- Robert B. Miller and Stephen E. Heiman, *Strategic Selling*
- Jerry Acuff and Wally Wood, *The Relationship Edge*

CHAPTER 3

Sales Managers as Key Stakeholders

DON STERKEL, formerly of Time Warner

Find a successful sales trainer and you'll likely find someone very adept at "inside" sales. Why? For any training effort to succeed, the support of key stakeholders in the company, such as sales managers and senior managers, or departments, such as human resources, is absolutely essential. Without that support and buy-in, even the best-designed program is very likely to fail. The development and implementation of an effective sales strategy aimed at garnering the full support of your internal stakeholders is essential to the success of your training program. If you can convert those stakeholders into your training program's informal sales team, all the better.

On countless occasions throughout my 30-year career in sales, sales management, and training, I've witnessed the slow death of top-notch training programs that were never implemented or that never made it fully through the approval process primarily due to one reason—the trainer's failure to seek the buy-in and support from sales managers and other key stakeholders as early as possible in the training process. This is a crucial component to making any training program a success.

In this chapter we explore how you as a sales trainer, sales training manager, or training professional can get the needed buy-in and support necessary for your training programs to become a success. You will learn to

- *identify* key stakeholders who need to buy in to and support your efforts,
- *establish* effective relationships with stakeholders based on what motivates them, and
- *utilize* and *galvanize* the sales manager and other key stakeholders as your own internal sales force to champion the value of your services and training services.

In addition, you will also have the opportunity to examine how these techniques are applied in some case studies.

WHY WORRY ABOUT STAKEHOLDERS?

Stakeholders are internal organizational people ranging from top decision makers, such as senior management and key frontline sales managers, to others such as your boss or human resources. A stakeholder's impact on your training program generally falls under one of three categories:

1. You need them to "bless" your training efforts.
2. They actively support you in the design and delivery process.
3. They can "raise an issue" if they don't buy in to the training efforts.

For your training to succeed, it is vital that you identify who the key stakeholders are, in relation to your training program, and then cultivate their support. This is usually accomplished through a four-step process:

1. *Identify* who the key stakeholders are for your project.

2. *Determine* how each relates to your project in terms of his or her power and influence to make it either succeed or fail.

3. *Strategize* how to cultivate the needed support from each key stakeholder based on what motivates him or her.

4. *Utilize* those you have support from as your sales force to convert others.

IDENTIFYING KEY STAKEHOLDERS

To identify key stakeholders evaluate the following:

- Who requested my help?
- Who do they report to who will also need to support this training project?
- Who makes the final decision on whether to proceed with the project?
- Who is paying the bill?
- What approvals and buy-in are required from senior management?
- What other individuals or groups can "raise an issue" with what is being taught in the course or program?

Identifying key stakeholders requires that you not only look at the sales department's organization chart, but the organization charts for other departments such as human resources, organizational development, research and development, marketing, promotion, and finance. Analyze both the formal and informal organization hierarchy within all departments to identify the highly influential organization stakeholders you need buy-in and support from, remembering that the *informal leaders* within the organization are of equal importance to you and the success of your training program. Chapter 2 provided some insights on gaining support from the organization leaders.

UNDERSTANDING STAKEHOLDER INFLUENCE

Once you have identified key stakeholders, you need to understand how they relate to your project in terms of the power and influence role each one exercises. This careful analysis is an essential component in developing a successful strategy of how to get the needed buy-in and/or approval.

One successful method that has been used by salespeople to effectively cultivate the needed relationships with key stakeholders was developed by Neil Rackham, author of *SPIN Selling*.[1] Rackham's model suggests you classify these key stakeholders into *three influence or power relationships:*

1. Focus of receptivity (FOR)
2. Focus of dissatisfaction (FOD)
3. Focus of power (FOP)

FOCUS OF RECEPTIVITY

These are receptive people who are prepared to listen sympathetically; they are individuals in functional areas most likely to:

- Listen receptively
- Provide you with information

Examples of FOR (Focus of receptivity) stakeholders might include:

- New sales managers looking for assistance
- Struggling sales managers looking for assistance
- Experienced sales managers with personnel issues
- Other sales personnel expressing a need for training
- Senior sales management that have observed a need for training based on their interaction with field sales staff

These stakeholders, as individuals in need of your assistance, will be naturally sympathetic to the need for training.

FOCUS OF DISSATISFACTION

This category represents people who are unhappy with the present. This could stem from dissatisfaction with the current way the sales force is interacting with customers, or frustration with the current type of sales training programs or offerings. FODs can be individuals, functions, and locations most likely to perceive problems and dissatisfaction in an area where you can provide help.

Examples of FOD stakeholders are:

- Individuals who have had a bad experience with training
- Individuals responsible for budget who have concerns with cost management
- Managers who, through life experience, have little or no belief in adult learning
- Managers who feel that the benefits of training don't equate to the loss of sales revenues experienced when sales staff are pulled from their selling environment and put into training environments

FOD stakeholders are natural targets for you to cultivate. And, critically, they may also have influence with the stakeholders who are the focus of power.

FOCUS OF POWER

Often it is difficult to identify all of the FOP stakeholders within an organization, as this group not only includes the people authorized to make the key decisions, but also informal leaders and power-centered function areas. The individuals and functional areas in this group possess and wield power in one of more ways by

- approving action,
- preventing action, and
- influencing action.

Examples of FOP stakeholders include:

- Vice-president level management and above
- Division level management
- Individuals who are less than VP or division level but, whom through experience and networking, have influence with senior management and are used by them as sounding boards. These individuals are informal leaders. Their influence is often very persuasive and permeates throughout all levels of the organizational chart.

It is crucial that you get the buy-in of FOP stakeholders to your training services and offerings, because without their stamp of approval there is very little likelihood that you will be successful.

GETTING THE SUPPORT OF KEY STAKEHOLDERS

Once you've identified your key stakeholder targets—and their FOR, FOD, or FOP status—you need to form a strategy on how to build and utilize these relationships to obtain the needed buy-in. Critical questions to consider during this process include:

- How can I get the stakeholders who are already sympathetic to my cause to introduce me to others who will be sympathetic, as well as to those with the power to either approve or block this training?

- What motivates each of these stakeholders and will recruit them to my cause?
- What benefits can these individuals and/or their departments derive from my training program that will be most beneficial to their success?
- How can I communicate the value of my services in meeting each of these person's needs?

To understand this idea, let's look at how a sales training professional needs to interact with one of the most important stakeholders, the sales manager.

THE ROLE OF SALES MANAGERS

Sales managers are vital stakeholders in any sales training effort. They have a tremendous amount of influence over whether your training will succeed. They are not only your internal customer, but often your most important critic. It's most likely their voice that is most listened to by the training program's participants, because the sales manager is probably their boss, or at the very least, has some form of guiding influence on them.

It is impossible to overstate the importance of sales managers relative to their impact on sales personnel. For a salesperson, the sales manager is the person he or she is going to look to for direction on what he or she needs to do to be successful. According to Charles A. Coonradt, author of *The Game of Work*, "A manager, boss, or supervisor is probably the number two or number three most important person in the life of a salesperson, or certainly in the top five ... and depending upon how things are going at home, may rank much higher.[2] Consequently, getting the buy-in from this influential stakeholder is crucial if your training effort is going to succeed.

In terms of his or her focus of power or influence, a sales manager can occupy any of Rackham's *three influence/power relationships*, specifically:

- Those who understand the connection between people development and business results and are *receptive* to the training services you provide
- Those who are dissatisfied with either past or current training and thus have a *focus of dissatisfaction*
- Those who may be in a position to either block the effectiveness of your effort if they don't buy in to it, or to actively champion it if they do, by using their *focus of power*

In fact, in some organizations and situations, certain sales managers will actively play all three roles depending on their influence.

CULTIVATING THE STAKEHOLDER RELATIONSHIP AND GAINING SUPPORT

Given the need to cultivate an effective relationship with the sales manager and other key stakeholders, how do you do it? Chuck Coonradt offers the four best tips I've ever come across for developing and understanding interpersonal relationships.[3] Most people are familiar with the first way of thinking, but the other three mind-sets explore further viewpoints that must be recognized and effectively dealt with in your quest to enlist the support of key stakeholders.

WHAT'S IN IT FOR ME (WIIFM)?

We all know the power of this statement, but how often do we really think about it and express it in terms that are important to your key stakeholders. Put yourself in the shoes of the stakeholders whose support you are seeking. What really is in it for them if they support your training initiatives? Will the training increase sales? Do increased sales equal increased compensation? Can your program help move a manager toward a much desired promotion? Might it help them keep their job? Might it get one of their direct reports promoted? Might it lessen their administrative or paperwork burden? Might it help the sales manager become more efficient, allowing for more family or personal time? What else might WIIFM do for the manager? Determine what the WIIFM benefits are for the sales managers and other key stakeholders you work with, and how the services you provide address *their needs*.

Plan and explore the many options for each person you need to influence or develop a relationship with. Don't forget to list your own WIIFM benefits as well, as this allows you to identify and address potential incompatibility between your goals and those of the sales managers and other key stakeholders.

MAKE ME FEEL IMPORTANT (MMFI)

We as sales trainers at times make a critical error in believing that we, as the developer, teacher, instructor, professor, or whatever program role we chose, are the most important element in the successful implementation of training. Wrong! Our job as trainers includes successfully instilling a sense of central importance and program ownership within the sales manager so, if necessary, the sales manager will carry the torch of our successful sales training. Once convinced and made to feel like the the linchpins or conduits to the program's process and success, sales managers will do the internal selling and promotion efforts needed to gain influence among their peers and superiors.

As discussed earlier, it is important to also work on identifying the real "players" who are often those *informal leaders* within an organization who carry tremendous influence with their peers and with the hierarchy. By recognizing and approaching these individuals, you have already made your first step along the MMFI path leading to their buy-in and support. You can't carry the torch all the way by yourself. Eventually you'll get burned or burned out . . . that's why they pass it off on the way to the Olympics. Think about and list what MMFI tactics you need to successfully employ with your sales managers.

WHY SHOULD I (WSI)?

Are you aware of key sales strategies and plans? How about noteworthy events, such as industry meetings, regional meetings, and other activities that occur outside of routine business? If you are not aware, your credibility with the sales managers will suffer. Reflect on your sales process and the understanding of needs and how, in reality, your role is that of a "solution provider" addressing the needs of the sales managers to help them become more effective at bringing in and/or increasing sales, revenues, and profits. Time is money to a sales manager. If a sales manager sees no value in your programs or training solutions, your credibility is at risk and there is little chance to get on the calendar or get the required time needed for your program. Whether you are offering open courses or working on individualized, customized programs, *a compelling business reason must be the key component in your presentation to the sales manager.*

Speaking of money, remember too that most sales managers are also responsible for their team's budget and travel expenses. Training participants may need to travel quite a distance to attend your programs. The travel expense involved with attending your training program will certainly be a key factor in the decision process of the sales manager, as will the fact that you are taking sales personnel out of the field and out of action. These factors translate to a lot of revenue loss in a sales manager's mind. Remember that a return on investment is always an essential component in the buy-in process, so gear your presentations to include convincing examples of positive returns. Also, if your sales training initiatives do not address specific development, skill, and knowledge areas that meet business demands and resolve business performance issues, sales managers will be reluctant to spend money on travel, preferring instead to send sales personnel on customer calls. Ask yourself, "Am I delivering sufficient value for the time and money expenditure attendees are making?" Include the answer in your sales manager presentations. Think about and list the WSI issues you need to know to influence sales managers within your organization.

DIFFERENT STROKES FOR DIFFERENT FOLKS (DSDF)

The title of this viewpoint category brings me back to the '60s and Sly and the Family Stone's hit *Everyday People*. It reflects that each of our unique personal and professional experiences have shaped our opinions. If the sales trainer's job is to gain influence with the sales manager to support training, it is also the trainer's job to understand not only the top- and bottom-line objectives and goals, but to also understand the inner workings of your sales manager(s) and what turns him or her on or off. Find out how they perceive their involvement throughout the project's development and implementation stages.

For example, some sales managers may wish to play an active facilitation role in your training programs, but others may prefer a passive or "hands-off" position. For some, an arm's-length coaching approach with facilitation by their staff represents a unique style. Other managers may liken training to college or even high school classroom training and believe the lecture approach works. You'll only know if you ask the questions and get the answers. *Each manager is unique and each has been shaped by individual experiences.* Ask probing questions and determine what these experiences are.

Also, understanding how sales managers approach humor, creativity, off-site activities, and the myriad of other details can make or break a training program, your credibility, and an essential trust. Occasionally during the buy-in process you'll encounter a stumbling block involving a sales manager's preferences that may present a conflict or an inconsistency with adult learning theory or our knowledge of "best practice" training. You, as the trained professional, understand the potential negative impact the conflict will create on the training process and outcomes, but what do you do? Prepare yourself with a second buy-in and support presentation fully prepared to cite facts, figures, and desired outcomes versus the reality that will occur. Remember three key points:

1. You understand who your customer is. Employ that understanding during the presentation.
2. Always state your case professionally, but unemotionally.
3. Emphasize the benefits and highlights of a successful program, stressing the tie with its proper design and implementation.

If the sales manager (your internal customer) and you still have differing opinions, or if the sales manager is adamant or forceful about desires, work to meet those needs while not compromising your core values or the relationship.

The best way to learn DSDF is to ask questions and to pay attention to the little things including the quirks and the idiosyncrasies that are unique to each manager—inattention to those can make or break your training programs and can often place a lot of unnecessary roadblocks in your career.

Identify the DSDF characteristics that are really distinctive and/or contrasting between you and the sales manager with whom you're working. Think about age, education, experience, attitudes, interests, and lifestyles as starters.

WIIFM, MMFI, WSI, and DSDF are the four essential steps to discovering how to build the necessary relationships, trust, and commitment needed to enlist sales managers and other key stakeholders as your training program allies and informal sales force.

A necessary component in any training professional's job is to interact with all members of the organization in such a way that you are perceived as their key support manager, someone whose primary focus is to develop relationships with your customers—the *internal customers*, such as the sales managers.

ENLISTING STAKEHOLDERS AS YOUR INTERNAL SALES—THIRD-PARTY SELLING

In the late 1960s, I enrolled in a sales training class that was conducted primarily by distance learning and featured one evening course a week in Milwaukee, led by a Marquette University business professor. From this course emerged one key sales technique that continues to resonate with me today and is still considered the most successful skill to acquire in order to gain influence and close sales—*third-party selling*. What exactly is third-party selling? It is providing some type of value or service that is so extraordinary that the customer (internal or external) is compelled to pass it on to others.

Third-party selling has always reminded me of Tom Sawyer, Mark Twain's great character who always seemed to get someone else to do a lot of his work. That's the power of third-party selling, as seen in testimonials, references, influences, and "best of class" awards. It's the key to successful life insurance, real estate, auto, and equity sales. Even commissioned salespeople at high-end stores such as Nordstrom make well over $80,000 per year using this technique. It takes an unswerving commitment to providing consistent, good service to collect third-party references. But once the good referrals begin coming in, they work like an annuity that continues to flow.

The third-party stories discussed among sales managers about your training programs will have a profound impact on your success as a sales training professional and the support you receive for your training programs. Think of the stories and experiences you've heard about other third parties over coffee, meals, or drinks. In fact, this is where the real evaluations, expectations, and perceptions about products and people take place.

When you work to cultivate relationships with sales managers and other key stakeholders, and then provide honesty and great service, the testimonials from customers (external and internal) will provide most of the promotion needed. Third-party selling is, was, and always will be the most effective way to gain sales, influence, and trust. The sales training professional who delivers quality product, value at fair price, and is the "best in class" will consistently win the respect of the internal customer and key stakeholders.

DESIGNING SALES TRAINING SOLUTIONS THAT MEET STAKEHOLDERS' NEEDS

Besides cultivating their support, it's critical that you actually provide training offerings that meet your stakeholders' needs. Here are some suggestions on how to make sure that the training solutions you design meet the needs of sales managers and other key stakeholders.

- Spend less time on developing perfect content (pleasing to the training staff) and more time communicating with line managers so you are aware of what is happening "out there" on the line and in the field.
- Toss the belief that any training developed is worth the sales reps time to attend; ensure that training has relevance to the job, current business issues, revenue, profits, or other metrics.
- Develop a dynamic and ongoing dialogue with sales managers.
- Utilize highly knowledgeable and trusted subject matter experts and facilitators to deliver training; if none is available, look for an outside practitioner who can deliver a quality program.
- Work to get along with the manager, even if there are personal frictions or reasons you "just don't get along." You're not inviting each other out for dinner; you are business professionals with common needs and goals. Position yourself as a resource, support, and asset for the sales managers.
- Become a recognized expert in the field of training through certifications and training association memberships.

STRATEGIC PROCESSES THAT ENSURE TRAINING PROGRAM SUSTAINABILITY

Another way for the training professional to help ensure the ongoing success of training programs and the effective transfer of information to staff is by involving management, specifically sales management, in the pre- and post-training process. To varying degrees, management has some level of responsibility for preparing its staff for training, ensuring staff can attend training, and giving attention to ongoing follow-up after training sessions. Because managers are not training professionals, giving them advance input, support, and guidance is up to the training manager, and, if properly executed, will certainly help you attain successful training program results.

Let's use the sales manager as an example to demonstrate the ways in which the training manager can facilitate pre- and post-training activities that will have considerable impact on the sustainable success of the training program. After the training manager has secured the buy-in and support of the sales manager, the next step is to obtain that manager's assistance and commitment to performing critical "make or break" pre- and post-training program processes. As a torchbearer for your training program, the sales manager should respond to that form of appeal. Once the commitment has been agreed upon, the training manager is responsible for preparing materials, providing support, and coordinating actions in a timely manner.

THE SALES MANAGER'S PRESESSION ROLE

A few weeks prior to the start of training the training manager should communicate the training session details. These details would include such information as training start time, what time training will wrap up, the name of the training site, directions to the training site, a map to the site, phone numbers for the site office, your phone number/cell number, and the "rules" for attending training. The participant's rules for attending training should include:

- Arriving early to ensure no parking hassles, to give time to find the training room, and to get comfortably settled
- Advising all "need to know" external or internal customers that he or she is not available while in session and ensuring voice mail and messages will be

responded to during the specified break and lunch periods; also, providing customers with a number to call in regard to urgent situations

- Turning off the cell phone for the entire session and saving callbacks and message checking for break and lunch periods
- Completing and bringing all presession work
- Thinking of some real-world challenges, problems, and scenarios that he or she can contribute to the training sessions' discussion and problem-solving segments
- Being prepared with appropriate questions
- Coming prepared with an open mind
- Not letting late-night activities interfere with the purpose of being at the training session

Review the information with the sales manager, and ask the manager to share expectations of the training session with the salesperson. Let the salesperson know why the session is important to his or her job.

The flyer and the meeting overview are meant to produce five direct preprogram benefits:

1. To build training momentum and job relevance
2. To build pretraining enthusiasm among participants
3. To provide a forum or means for participants to ask questions prior to training
4. To help relieve participants' pretraining "nerves"
5. To directly demonstrate a dedicated commitment to the training by the sales manager through tangible pretraining participation

The training manager is responsible for setting the sales manager's post-training process into motion by preparing materials, giving instructions, and reviewing the materials, actions, and techniques with the sales manager while also acting as the ongoing support system and coach. The sales manager's role is to implement a critical fourfold post-training process:

1. The sales manager should demonstrate a full and ongoing commitment to training by regularly observing the salespeople who have been trained and by providing honest feedback through use of corrective and reinforcement coaching techniques.
2. The sales manager must put training on the agenda. One method of doing this is to assign a training topic to be presented for group review and discussion as a highlight of regular team meetings. Each trained sales rep gets a chance to present and is always given at least two weeks' notice to prepare his or her training session.
3. The sales manager should hold the salespeople accountable for applying what they've learned and for producing desired results with successes and failures directly linked to the training program and its objectives.
4. The sales manager must "walk the talk." Nothing is more unmotivating to staff than a manager who does not practice what is preached, trained, and expected!

The training manager can gain a high level of credibility for future training programs by creatively supporting the sales manager's training follow-up efforts. Key support actions would include:

- Providing corrective and reinforcement coaching technique training
- Ensuring understanding of the various techniques that can be used in face-to-face encounters, over the phone, and through e-mail and other written forms
- Attending the sales meeting when the reviews are being held

- Providing reinforcement workshops to the sales manager that can be conducted at district meetings
- Providing further training development for the sales manager
- Providing resources and materials about coaching and training techniques
- Inviting the sales manager to cofacilitate training sessions to help the manager stay current with content

CASE STUDIES

The following two sales training case studies are based on shared experiences and provide a fair representation of typical sales training management and sales management personnel training initiative interaction, along with the nuances involved in different training situations. In Case Study #1, the sales trainer actively sought the necessary stakeholder buy-in from the start, and achieved a highly successful result. Case Study #2 was a different story. As you read the two cases, evaluate to what degree, if at all, the mechanisms and strategies for success discussed within this chapter were used. A questionnaire, which can be used as a diagnostic recap tool, is provided at the end of the chapter.

CASE STUDY #1

Background. During the early 1990s, senior management recognized that the business and customer contact environment was changing. There was a need for a more intense customer relationship focus, and a need to differentiate product offerings from those of competitors while ensuring that products weren't being treated as commodities. The sales culture of "asking for the order," or what consultant Rick Gibney refers to as the "show up and throw up," was to be replaced with *consultative-type selling*, which features buyer interaction.

The initiative. A new initiative was developed, with the goal of retraining the entire sales force at two regional meetings. The learning objective was to retrain staff, taking them from the heavily product-focused, traditional product sales process, which always focused on features, advantages, and benefits, to a *new sales process*, which placed the focus on the customer.

The initiative was assigned directly by the division president to a training manager who was empowered to interview, attend vendor sessions, and make final vendor recommendations to the president and VP of sales. The training manager has long had the ear and trust of senior management through development of other successful programs and so had no difficulty selling recommendations internally.

The training process. In order to develop an understanding for the level of customization needed to make the new training relevant to the sales force, the training manager attended the full vendor train-the-trainer course. One key decision was whether the program was to be facilitated by the vendor or conducted by in-house staff. That decision was quickly made when it was discovered that there were no funds available to pay for outside facilitation. This oversight occurred because the costs of meetings had run over the budget allotment.

The training manager began the buy-in process to gain support, trust, and influence at the top with the field vice president. Their discussions included asking the VP for recommendations as to which sales managers had the intelligence, skills, competencies, and desire to become group leaders. As a result of the internal customer selling and influencing of the VP by the training manager during this process, the required time and financial commitment needed for the selected field managers to attend a two-day, in-house facilitated train-the-trainer program was secured.

Eight of 18 potential participants were sent materials and leader guides in advance of the basic program. The materials consisted of lecture, video role-plays, vignettes, and group exercises.

The two-day session began with key general issues listed and posted on a flip chart by the training manager. The training manager provided input on overall program objectives, course material, and adult learning theory and then withdrew from the leadership role to assume a passive observer/coaching role, turning the session over to the group, much to their surprise.

Group transformation and change dynamics began within a few minutes, as leadership and other roles began to emerge based on skills and competencies. Areas such as content understanding, creativity, planning, and logistics emerged. As the observer, not the facilitator, the training manager was in a position to view the entire "field of play" and evaluate which players were going to be successful in what positions.

The group's challenge was to demonstrate an understanding of the basic material and develop course facilitation to change selling behavior from a product focus to a customer focus. With the group members working on what they now understood to be "their program," the buy-in occurred and they began to understand the consequences of developing a high-quality program—realizing it would be a program judged by senior management, but more important, by their sales peers.

For the classroom sessions, group members paired up in teams consisting of one sales manager with solid subject matter knowledge and one sales manager with more creative flair and facilitator skills. The team dynamic fleshed out the course in detail and enabled them to engage in substantive dialogue about course design, facilitation, and customization.

Gambling was the theme selected by the team, which actually meshed well with the overall theme of the meetings, and which centered upon competitive risks and market opportunities. In retrospect, the opening cocktail party had served as a portent for this training theme, by using oversize playing cards for the icebreaker, a questioning "meet and greet" game. Participants could develop poker hands, which, in turn, won prizes. The creative types developed methods to make the program fun and entertaining, while the content experts at times had to temper that enthusiasm and reinforce the goal of the program, which centered on how to achieve higher quality sales calls to increase revenue and market share. Teams were committed to learning the material cold, yet couldn't resist being theatrical and humorous (when appropriate) in the classroom.

Once in session this gambling theme continued with each classroom taking on the name of a casino. Facilitators used cards to reward successful answers and correct problem solving, resulting in poker hands winning awards. A theme song also evolved, using *The Gambler* by Kenny Rogers, to which the words were changed to reflect the keywords and jargon of the sales process for further reinforcement.

Results—feedback, follow-up, and sustainability. As sales trainers, we are always striving for the elusive ROI that says the program was a success. So how did this program rank on the Kirkpatrick scale? (See Chapter 6 for more information about Donald Kirkpatrick's model.)

- **Level 1**—*Reaction of participants to training:* High marks on the course evaluation forms (i.e., "smiley sheets").
- **Level 2**—*Measure of what participants learned:* Upon leaving the course all attendees had shown increased skill and knowledge in understanding the sales process as measured by activities and quizzes within the program and other testing methods developed by the group.

- **Level 3**—*Incorporation of learning into day-to-day work:* How did the Level 3 measurement work? It began by asking questions of the VPs and sales managers and in observing what behavior change they observed each month for the 120 days following the program. The training manager sent out a monthly survey that highlighted the key learning expectations and goals of the course, and what observable behaviors were considered the result of changes in the selling process. Rather than developing complex quantitative charts of the results, the focus was on anecdotal evidence and the success stories addressing increased skills, focus on the customer, product knowledge, negotiation, gaining commitment, and—yes—increased sales.

  At about the 90-day post-training point, a customer feedback survey was conducted. The survey reflected noticeable call improvement marks in the area of customer/salesperson interaction in key areas, such as understanding the customer's business, the customer's customer (the consumer), and general industry trends. Also tracked were the use of sales aids and other new sales tools.

- **Level 4**—*Results reporting:* The training manager tracked and compiled results, and presented them through oral presentations with a one-page support handout at monthly management staff meetings.

The critical buy-in support of the vice president allowed for the training and use of sales managers as program facilitators who were continuously utilized to train new employees in the sales process. In return for their extra efforts, sales managers were compensated with a small stipend for their time out of territory.

The ongoing support and continued vigilance to the process was crucial to its success and completed the training cycle needed to obtain complete buy-in from all stakeholders. Over time this led to observable results and to tangible sales gains with key customers—all of which were tracked back to the training program.

This program registered as a major success for the organization. The key factor was the early involvement of the sales manager and VP in the planning and execution, combined with the empowerment of sales managers to develop and lead the program. An unexpected program bonus, that continued for years after, was the positioning of sales managers as facilitators who not only provided the additional and ongoing sales force training, but evolved into "experts" and "go-to persons" regarding questions and clarifications. The sales managers enjoyed the additional responsibility as team leaders as it provided them with a form of notable status among peers and in the eyes of senior sales management.

CASE STUDY #2

Background. Let's move forward a decade to the new millennium, which brought with it major changes across all industries as we experienced consolidations, reorganizations, outsourcing, downsizing, big-box stores, Wal-Mart, China, India, measurement metrics, and regression analysis compiled by personal computers able to model multiple scenarios. In this world, products are being commoditized and buyers are shunning meetings with salespeople unless they can bring in new competitive information, have intimate knowledge of the customer's business, or something else of value to which the buyer does not have access. In other words, *salespeople must provide value to the customer.* In an attempt to do so, specialized account teams were formed consisting not only of sales personnel, but marketing and finance persons as well. These specialized teams called on the single customer, or single classes of trade, seeking to create, provide, and deliver the elusive and mystical product known as "customer value."

Although the sales force in this case understood and had responded to some macrochanges introduced through a number of other initiatives over the previous few years, it still remained overinvolved in selling product rather than providing value solutions to the customer.

In addition, the sales force in the area of customer interaction had become enamored by the laptop PC, PowerPoint, Excel, and accessible online data from CRM (customer relationship management) systems. For creative and financially oriented sales professionals, IT became the tool of choice. With the ability to present detailed and highly animated presentations, previously learned customer interaction and dialogue began to disappear.

These customer presentations were laborious, lengthy, and uninformative, yet highly satisfying for salespersons given the time, energy, and labor of love creativity put into them. Conversely, to the buyers and key executives these shallow, empty, and nonvalue-added presentations were time-consuming shows causing them to further shun face-to-face sales calls.

In most cases, presentation content focused on features, advantages, and benefits—information of no interest to buyers and key decision makers engaged in strategic initiatives and whose time was at a premium. From the customer's perspective, this type of content was better served up via e-mail or fax.

The initiative. The genesis of this initiative came from the president who, after making a few calls with field managers, deemed "our people can't sell anymore." This statement served as the only needs analysis.

The executive VP and several new senior-level sales managers had all recently joined the organization from outside companies and industries bringing unique expertise, training experiences, and expectations with them.

The executive VP, at the request of the president, directed the training manager (who reported directly to the executive VP of sales) to activate a vendor search to find the "best practice sales process" to meet the new millennium challenges. After considerable dialogue with the training manager, the executive VP of sales made the final vendor decision.

The strategy, in the view of the executive VP, was to have field VPs become "champions" of the new sales process.

The training process. Pretraining work consisted of reading the best-selling book from which the course was developed. The book provided the context, common language, introduction to selling, financial acumen, and expected behavioral changes in areas of research and diagnosis of customers. It also provided an overview on how to appropriately develop a dialogue with a customer that included asking pertinent and pointed business questions aimed at uncovering future customer value creation opportunities.

The initial train-the-trainer session scheduled for two and a half days with the VP sales group (the"champions") changed into a one-day overview of the program when customer-scheduling conflicts arose. The training was conducted by vendor facilitators who were experienced with the sales process of the program, but only superficially knowledgeable about the industry, organization, and real situations and problems. Written case studies, which had been developed using the vendor and three national and key account managers as subject matter experts who provided real-world context and content, were presented during training sessions.

Training then consisted of three half-day sessions for the entire strategic account managers group, consisting of national and key account managers as well as the field VPs and the executive VP of sales. During the sessions, the VPs and senior management assumed the roles of support and coaching, but did not participate in the actual facilitation of the course.

Initial response was exceptional to the new set of selling and customer interaction paradigms and hypotheses. Senior management as the internal customer was pleased and the course reviews (Level 1) were exceptional. The training manager passed course feedback on to the executive VP, who in turn briefed the president.

Results—feedback, follow-up, rescue, and sustainability. During the next three months the training department engaged in work to track the success of the program in an effort to try to quantify the ROI of the training at Level 3 by gathering success stories on process implementation. *The results were slightly better than dismal.* Reports from the field revealed little evidence of the field VPs or other senior management embracing or modeling the process on sales calls. Except for a few exceptions, prework on customers and the use of the available tools was not happening. Customer questions were generic, not customer-specific as required, nor designed to unearth problems. Participants were saying, "Why should I change my selling behavior, when it's not modeled by my manager or their manager."

As sales training had been charged with the success of the program, gathering data, and advising senior sales management of results, it decided to take on the challenge to resuscitate the program and strive for a positive ROI for the intellectual and monetary investments. The rescue process began with a vendor facilitator and selected field managers meeting. Program development was placed in the hands of the selected field subject matter experts who had been chosen for their knowledge, application, passion, and leadership/coaching skills.

What emerged was a field-level peer-driven mentor program aimed at integrating the sales process into daily sales routines and at reenergizing the sales force. This began with the mentors promoting their success stories with teams of three or four sales peers. (Might this be third-party selling in action?) Every other week a meeting or a conference call reviewed assigned skill development areas taken from post-course materials. With demonstrated success, the VPs again became highly engaged to the point that at regional sales meetings, half-day sales process training—which included additional knowledge, review, and skill training modules—was reintroduced. At the six-month point, a diagnostic video tool containing sales scenarios and questions was introduced. This tool, which was scored and analyzed on-site, provided managers the opportunity to focus individually on specific skill and knowledge areas for future development.

Within 8 to 12 months of commencing the rescue process, the initiatives and efforts began to show evidence that the needed change was happening.

Why did it take so long to take hold? The involvement of field-level personnel who do the job every day was critical to helping their peers in understanding the process as they shared it with them, along with demonstrated customer successes, enthusiasm, and a belief in the system.

Monthly calls between the mentors and the training department provided fodder for success stories published in a monthly newsletter highlighting individuals and teams advancing toward customer goals and highlighting strategic sales initiatives of the sales force, as it moved from transactional salespeople to customer value creators—another example of third-party selling in action!

After senior management was finally comfortable that sufficient training had taken place across the sales organization, and that the process was imbedded, the annual performance appraisal process was modified to evaluate use of the learning and new selling behaviors. This set into motion the linkage of behavior change to consequences within the organization.

Job responsibilities specifically detailed the jargon, common language, goals, and selling behaviors of the program. Responsibilities, knowledge, and skill areas were linked to measurements in a set of 25 selling competencies. These created a quantitative score for each salesperson that represented a proportional percentage of his or her total sales bonus and annual compensation awards.

CASE STUDY DISCUSSION AND ANALYSIS

The following questions are designed for discussion and analysis.

1. Cite examples of WIIFM, WSI, MMFI, and DSDF within each of the two case studies.
2. Which of the strategies introduced within this chapter were successfully executed within each of the two case studies?
3. Which of the strategies introduced within this chapter were unsuccessfully executed within each of the two case studies?
4. What more could have been done by the training manager to ensure training program relevance, buy-ins, and successful program development and delivery in each of the two case studies?
5. Which case study delivered the most value for the organization? Why?
6. Which case study created the most beneficial long-term behavioral change within the sales organization? Why?
7. Did both programs provide the Level 3 and 4 evaluations needed to validate success? If not, what more could have been done to accomplish this?
8. What role did the sales manager play in each case and was it appropriate? Was it effective? What more could have been done by the sales manager?
9. What role did VP-level management play in each case? Did they make an appropriate contribution? Did they make a successful contribution? What more could have been done by the VP-level executives?

ANALYZING YOUR TRAINING ROLE

1. Given the dynamics of your organization, which approach models and initiatives introduced in this chapter would be most useful?

2. What impact can a sales trainer directly implement within the field sales force to obtain their immediate input?

3. Given the current responsibilities and accountability of your position, do you have the access needed to be able to build an internal support network of "relationships"?

4. As a sales trainer, do you report to the sales division? If not, how does your reporting relationship affect your training efforts within the sales division?

5. Within your organization, is sales training a true initiative supported by the entire organization or only by the sales department/division?

6. Do you have to fight for a training budget? Do you control a budget?

7. How do you measure your relationship quotient (RQ) with each sales manager?

8. Within your organization, do you know which sales managers will be supportive of your programs and push their boss for development of their sales teams?

9. Do you utilize sales managers' opinions as well as real-world feedback (garnered through surveys and e-mails) to advise you of what training initiatives may be needed and in what time frame?

10. Within your training department, do you have a Kirkpatrick or other type of measurement scale in place? If not, how have you been measuring training performance/results?

11. Outline how you would utilize the approach, tactics, and mechanisms introduced in this chapter to create a more successful training for your organization in the future.

SUMMARY

In this chapter you, the training professional, have learned some key mechanisms that you can use to successfully sell your training programs. Foremost among these concepts is obtaining training program buy-in and support, as that is paramount to your success. In addition, we've introduced fundamental yet vital strategies that if followed will provide you with a smooth transition from training concept to successful delivery. You've learned:

- How to identify key stakeholders and strategic allies
- Techniques for establishing effective relationships based on developing and introducing benefits that will motivate the key stakeholders
- Approaches for converting sales managers into your program's torchbearers
- Methods to identify and circumvent the four mind-sets that make your stakeholders tick
- How to distinguish the three power relationship types that will make or break your program's acceptance

So what now, you ask? Application of what you have learned! Isn't that what we teach our training participants? Don't put off implementing what you've just learned by waiting for a training need to present itself. Plan and create the success of your future training programs by putting these strategies into action—*now!*

RECOMMENDED RESOURCES

- Neal Rackham, *SPIN Selling*
- Charles A. Coonradt, *The Game of Work*

CHAPTER 4

Building a Business Case for Sales Training

BOB RICKERT, Aarthun Performance Group

During the past ten years the sales training profession has weathered its fair share of economic booms and busts, downsizing, rightsizing, and resizing of the sales organization. We find ourselves at yet another crossroad—how to sell the business case for sales training during an uncertain economy and as the number of competing, high-priority initiatives grow daily. Whether it's deploying a new CRM technology, hiring additional salespeople, investing in marketing campaigns, or introducing a new product line, the fact is that in every organization there are too few budget dollars chasing too many important initiatives. Perhaps more so today than at any other time in recent memory, decisions regarding training and developing the sales organization are squarely focused on how a company's overall profitability will be impacted. This is why sales trainers must learn to position their solutions in terms that executives will understand and act on. Jim Graham gives a framework of how to gain leadership support of training in Chapter 2. He helps you gain financial support for your specific initiatives through strategies that build credibility in the eyes of executive management: being clear about your audience, shaping your message, and selling the right outcomes.

In today's environment, the pressure for earnings is forcing management to scrutinize all expenditures the company makes. By learning to speak the language of business and financial return, sales trainers can begin to position their group's capabilities and services as a profit improvement strategy and not be relegated to the dreaded overhead black hole. Moving sales training decisions from the expense line to the profit line is not easy but it can be done.

The annual budgeting process is not a perfect science for most organizations. Every department starts out with a strong idea of their needs and how current or higher levels of funding will help them do their jobs. More and more, every department is challenged to be accurate in their estimates. For the sales training group, there is usually one question asked that will impact whether the sales training budget will be funded or "temporarily deferred": *Will this training investment help us deliver immediate revenue and profitability?*

If the answer is anything less than a resounding yes, then you can expect the next question to be: *Can we achieve our financial goals without it?*

A strong business case for training linked to financial success will be extremely difficult for senior management to cut from the budget. But you might ask, providing a sales skills program is difficult to measure and even more difficult to tie to profitability. That has been true in the past but it does not have to be true today. There are ways to link specific sales skills and behaviors developed during training to profitability.

For example, one of the biggest concerns expressed by most sales executives I work with is defending price. No single measurement is more important to the financial health of a business. Yet, most salespeople do not fully understand or appreciate the impact that pricing has on profitability. The prevailing view is that a small discount required to win a piece of business is a small price to pay for securing the business. However, senior management knows that every dollar lost to pricing will negatively impact year-end profits. This has been our experience at Aarthun Performance Group in working with nearly 100 companies who have focused on improving their margins through pricing. We have discovered that getting a 1 percent price increase, everything else remaining the same, will increase operating profit by as much as 8 percent to 10 percent. For most companies, that is a huge number and a reason why top management puts so much pressure on the sales organization to defend their pricing. By having the skills and doing a more effective job of selling a company's value and discounting less, salespeople can have a major impact on profitability. In looking at it in terms of price erosion, we also help companies understand that a 1 percent discount will conversely drop operating profit by that same 8 percent to 10 percent. And, if a salesperson provides a 5 percent discount, it might take 15 percent to 20 percent of additional sales volume to make up for the loss in profitability based on their current operating margins. That means it takes a lot more effort to produce the same result. Another way to look at it is, the organization has to invest more just to stay even and, lets face it, making a profit is hard enough already.

Sales training leaders must elevate their game if they want to have a voice in their company's financial decision making. It requires a new mind-set and learning to speak the language of business and profitability. In this chapter, we will explore the economic realities that are impacting your organization and what it takes to build a stronger business case for sales training. We will also review strategies for identifying measurements tied to the company's key business drivers and objectives that you can use to make a persuasive business case for training.

NEW ECONOMIC REALITIES

A lot of things changed in this country on September 11, 2001, and not just in terms of our security. Virtually every industry and business has been affected. Some more than others, such as the airline industry. Within five years of 9/11, three of the top four airline companies were in bankruptcy, attempting to deal with the economic and structural changes to their business. Some industries got a tremendous boost from the huge capital investments being made in the buildup of security following 9/11, as well as from the wars in Iraq and Afghanistan. But even more fundamental changes have occurred. Companies have had to invest heavily in beefed-up security to protect employees and customers—video surveillance, smart card technology, data security, and terror strike contingency plans to name just a few. In fact, a new role has emerged at the executive committee level, the chief security officer (CSO).

Businesses have also had to put a great deal of their attention on business continuity, that is, making certain that their supply chain is protected and that the vital products and services needed to sustain their business are in place should another terror strike hit the United States. So how is this relevant to sales training? In short, these new challenges are putting a strain on profitability, constantly changing the priorities for funding, time, and effort. Basically, the new realities are stealing mindshare from other important initiatives facing the company. There are now more initiatives competing for funding than ever before.

Most of the new funding required for security and business continuity comes out of operating expenses, the same budget dollars for which sales training is vying. These days you might not be surprised to hear some suggest that security is a necessity and training is not. Training will only be viewed as a necessity if it is an integral part of executing the company's business strategies.

The good news is that within five years of 2001, the United States has emerged from the recession and is experiencing economic growth. There are more budget dollars to go around and investments are being made in other areas, including training. Job growth is up in the United States and by definition the means development needs are going to increase. But unlike times in the past when that meant training budgets were automatically increased, there are now more priorities to deal with and it is becoming more difficult to make the case for sales training. The best way to describe our current business climate is one of caution. Senior management is more hesitant to make financial commitments too far out ahead of the business. This has led to a great deal more consensus decision making and greater aversion to risk. Living in this environment has become a way of life, and for sales trainers, it will be important to reposition the role that sales training plays in the overall economic picture of the company to compete for support and funding. Competition for funding will only get more intense and that is why it is necessary to prepare a business case that deals with these new realties.

At a 50,000-foot level, how are some of these new realities impacting your company? What can you look at to assess the challenges you might face when putting together a business plan for training? Here are four examples of environmental factors that might be directly or indirectly impacting your company's financial health and could prevent senior management from making an investment in training:

1. *Cost constraints.* Are you in an industry that is experiencing huge fluctuation in the cost and availability of raw materials such as oil and gas, power, food ingredients, steel, and more? Is this causing your cost of goods or services to go up faster than you can pass through price increases to end users to maintain your margins? When this happens, companies have to eat into their profits to maintain their current levels of business. This puts tremendous pressure on margins and causes a pullback on expenditures.

2. *Consumer spending.* Are you in an industry that is impacted by consumer spending? When consumer spending trends downward, inventories build up, purchasing slows down, and price pressures surface as a key strategy for selling products that may be building up in inventory, further pressuring the company's financial health.

3. *Job growth.* Are you in an industry that relies on strong job growth—white-collar jobs, for example—to expand your business? When hiring slows down, senior management will begin to adjust their plans and scrutinize costs to ensure they do not get expenses out ahead of revenue.

4. *Executive changes.* Have there been key executive changes at the top of your organization due to performance or attrition? This will also impact the environment for training. Typically, when an organization is experiencing leadership change at the top, the entire organization becomes preoccupied with job security. At the very least, there will be a climate of uncertainty during the transition. Until the priorities of the new leadership team are communicated, senior leaders are hesitant to commit to future investments in training.

Top executives are under growing pressure to produce immediate results for their company. It is particularly challenging given the nature of business today—living and dying by quarterly earnings reports. This is causing CEO turnover to reach an all-time high. The pressure CEOs face will always involve the financial performance of their companies. However, compliance to new rules put into place after the Enron and Tyco failures, such as Sarbanes-Oxley, create even greater pressure. It is not unusual to see a CEO forced out due to an ethical lapse, or because actions that were taken in some way hurt the credibility of the company. You will also see the board of directors playing more of an activist role in advocating for the shareholders' best interest, mainly because the members too are being held liable for financial and business ethics failures.

It is important to assess your company's environment and how internal and external changes or challenges are impacting senior management's view on investments, especially as it relates to training. Understanding these pressures will help you prepare a business case that addresses the immediate financial and organizational concerns of senior management.

WHAT YOU NEED TO KNOW

With these new economic realities comes a new level of responsibility not just for the manager of sales training but also for the entire organization. Business and economic cycles in the past were reasonably predictable, generally slow to occur, and easier to manage around. In today's environment having a stronger knowledge of the business will prepare you to respond quickly to new emerging challenges.

KNOW YOUR COMPANY'S FINANCIAL PRIORITIES

I have spent the last five years with Aarthun Performance Group working with Fortune 500 companies on installing financial literacy and value selling skills. Most of the CFOs and sales executives I have interviewed readily admit that employees and managers at virtually every level do not fully understand how their company makes money. It's a huge gap in corporate America and the consequences are great. In fact, the former Federal Reserve Board chairman, Alan Greenspan, wrote about the need for Americans to increase their financial knowledge when he said, "The Federal Reserve has a keen interest in encouraging and measuring the effectiveness of financial literacy programs."[1] So why do you need to understand the company's financials? Every decision an executive team makes can be directly or indirectly linked to the company's financials. Understanding the key trends in your business and understanding the key financial indicators that are driving executive decisions will assist you in positioning your business case for training in a way that addresses executive management's biggest concerns.

UNDERSTANDING YOUR COMPANY'S BUSINESS

Generally speaking, everyone who works for a company understands whether the company is making money or not. The proof is all around in the form of hiring or downsizing, profit sharing or no profit sharing, a pay increase or not, new computer for the department or keep using the old system for a while longer. Pick up the local paper's business section or *The Wall Street Journal* and you will read about your company's latest financial releases. Most people understand it when the company announces that revenues are up, profits are strong, and shareholders are getting a dividend. They also know when the opposite is true. However, I have found though these performance numbers are useful, they don't really tell you the whole story. Most of all, they won't tell you about the challenges the company had to overcome, or will have to overcome to be successful. Only when you can interpret the meaning of the numbers "operationally" does it begin to tell a story.

You may work for a privately held company that by law is not required to report earnings publicly. I have found some private companies are fairly forthcoming about their financial situation. Many are not. But, understanding a few of the top-line numbers that are usually revealed can help to get a picture of the company's key challenges and priorities.

Pick up any annual report and you will see two basic financial statements that report on company's performance: the income statement and the balance sheet. The income statement is an accounting of how much revenue a company brought in and how it spent those dollars to operate its business. Basically, this is a financial view of how well the company operated or performed to generate profit. How well did the company predict revenue and expenditures, and how efficient were they in running the business and returning value to shareholders? Here's a simple income statement used by most companies:

Sales
  Less Cost of Goods Sold or Cost of Service Provided
Equals Gross Profit
  Less Operating Expenses (salaries, benefits, rent, etc.)
Equals Operating Profit
  Less Taxes and Interest
Equals Net Profit

The primary purpose of the income statement is to report a company's earnings over a specific period of time to investors. The income statement is also referred to as the profit and loss (P&L) statement. It is the most widely used financial report on Wall Street. Many times, investors make decisions based on the reported earnings from the income statement without considering the balance sheet or cash flow statements. It is the most visible report that a company publishes regarding the health and viability of the company. You will find an example of a hypothetical income statement, with revenues and expenditures, in Figure 4.1.

The balance sheet is a snapshot at any given time of the worth of the business, that is, assets less liabilities will equal the value of the business. One of the biggest shortcomings in corporate America is the lack of understanding of the balance sheet of a business. Most understand, as reported, whether a company made a profit. But returning value in the form of higher stock price or dividends paid is the ultimate metric on which executive management is compensated (and/or fired).

The balance sheet gives a snapshot of the assets, liabilities, and equity for a given day. Often a balance sheet shows

FIGURE 4.1 Sample Income Statement

**Charlie's Widget Company Income Statements for the
Years Ending 2003, 2004, 2005**

Income Statement	2003	2004	2005
Sales	$920,000	$950,000	$990,000
Less Cost of Goods Sold	(230,500)	(250,000)	(262,500)
Gross Profit on Sales	**689,500**	**700,000**	**727,500**
Less General Operating Expenses	(129,500)	(128,000)	(127,500)
Less Depreciation Expense	(29,000)	(30,000)	(30,000)
Operating Income	**531,000**	**542,000**	**570,000**
Other Income	30,000	50,000	30,000
Earnings Before Interest and Tax	**561,000**	**592,000**	**600,000**
Less Interest Expense	(30,000)	(30,000)	(30,000)
Less Taxes	(54,500)	(50,000)	(54,500)
Net Earnings	**$476,500**	**$512,000**	**$515,500**

information for two successive years, which gives an investor a better view of the company's operations by showing areas of growth. You will find an example of a hypothetical balance sheet in Figure 4.2.

It is not the intent to cover finance in detail here; most training professionals understand the basic components of the income statement and balance sheet. And there are plenty of online resources and tutorials that explain the fundamentals of finance. The important thing for this discussion is learning how to interpret the numbers, ratios, and trends that provide insight to the decision-making priorities at the executive levels of your company.

ANALYZING YOUR COMPANY'S PERFORMANCE

For a person without a financial background, finance can be intimidating. Yet, at the executive levels of every company,

FIGURE 4.2 Sample Balance Sheet

Billy Bean Soup Catering
Balance Sheet Ending December 31

	2004	2005
ASSETS		
Current Assets		
Cash and Cash Equivalents	$10,000	$10,000
Accounts Receivable	35,000	30,000
Inventory	25,000	20,000
Total Current Assets	**70,000**	**60,000**
Fixed Assets		
Plant and Machinery	$20,000	$20,000
Less Depreciation	−12,000	−10,000
Land	8,000	8,000
Intangible Assets	2,000	1,500
TOTAL ASSETS	**88,000**	**79,500**
LIABILITIES AND SHAREHOLDERS' EQUITY		
Liabilities		
Accounts Payable	$20,000	$15,500
Taxes Payable	5,000	4,000
Long-Term Bonds Issued	15,000	10,000
TOTAL LIABILITIES	**40,000**	**29,500**
SHAREHOLDERS' EQUITY		
Common Stock	$40,000	$40,000
Retained Earnings	8,000	10,000
TOTAL SHAREHOLDERS' EQUITY	**48,000**	**50,000**
LIABILITIES & SHAREHOLDERS' EQUITY	**$88,000**	**$79,500**

Total liabilities and shareholders' equity equals total assets.

the language most often spoken is that of financial ratios, trends, and the implications of certain decisions on short- and long-term profitability. Getting up to speed can be a daunting task. However, there are some very basic things you can learn that will provide the insight required to understand the company's current situation and, most of all, key priorities. To sell a sales training initiative today requires a working knowledge of the business and financial levers that address executive management's highest priorities.

There are three simple things you can learn that will dramatically enhance your discussions with sales leadership and your development of an effective sales training business case—sales trends, cost trends, and asset management. How does the training organization fit into the company's financial picture? And why should the sales training department learn how to interpret the company's financial goals and objectives? Because speaking the language of business and profitability is the best way to earn credibility and align your sales training plan to the most important financial issues.

THE NUMBERS

The key numbers to understand are revenue or sales, cost of goods sold (raw materials or services rendered), gross profit (sales less cost of goods), gross profit margin, operating expenses (salaries, benefits, administration, etc.), and operating profit.

Numbers are very transparent. Are sales up over last year and by how much? Are costs (cost of goods or services and operating expenses) going up? Did they go up faster than sales? This is a critical sales executive issue because the weight of that difference will land on the sales department. I suggest that you compare the numbers going back three years. Looking at three years will provide the view that analysts take to evaluate a company's key trends. You should also pick one or two of your competitors and compare the numbers. That too can be very revealing in terms of what the market and shareholders look at in terms of what the future performance expectations might be for the company and whether it is a good investment versus your competitors.

THE TRENDS

Perhaps the most important analysis you can do to learn about your company's financial performance and priorities is to look at the trends. On an annual basis, look at the last three years. Are sales going up each year? Are they growing at a consistent percentage or are there fluctuations? Is the cost of goods going up faster than sales? Are gross profits growing and by what percent? This is the first key measurement that management, shareholders, and Wall Street look at to evaluate whether a company is competitive in the market or if they are being forced to discount to win.

Are operating costs (overhead required to run the company) going up at a faster or slower rate than revenue? Executive management will also assess the trends and ratios because they are leading indicators of future performance. Most of all, a trend in costs like raw materials can alert them to margin pressures down the road. That is why cost cuts in salaries, training, travel budgets, and more are often done quickly because management knows that the pressure to adjust costs to produce promised profits will be surfacing soon.

There are other implications to trends. These trends will also be leading indicators of the need for training. If the company is growing, new hiring and speed to performance will be keys to sustaining the growth. You can anticipate training needs based on the key financial trends of the company. Most of all, demonstrating a working knowledge of these trends will elevate the training group in the eyes of senior management.

WHAT MANAGEMENT IS SAYING

You can learn a lot about your company's current and past performance and future strategies by what they are saying publicly. The numbers tell a story about what is happening in a business. The CEO will interpret those results (positively, regardless of what the numbers say) through the letter to shareholders in the annual report and during earnings calls with Wall Street analysts. You can gain a good understanding of how the members of the executive team are viewing their business success and challenges and how they intend to execute their plans to deliver value to shareholders. Pick up any CEO's shareholder letter and you will read about results and the priorities for the following year. Identify key strategies (and/or challenges) and align your training and the benefits to help address the business needs. Use their language and nomenclature to show a working knowledge of the business. Here is an example of how one public company's CEO described his company's performance in a quarterly earnings press release in October 2005 (actual company name and specific data withheld for confidentiality):

XYZ Company Delivers Solid Third Quarter Results: Revenues Increase 8.7 Percent

Sales grew 8.7 percent in the third quarter to $854.89 million, including 7.1 percent in *organic improvement* that excludes foreign currency impacts. *Of this improvement, price represented 6.3 percent.* Hurricane disruptions somewhat reduced sales growth rates . . . *Net income rose to $18.9 million, or 14 cents per share, from $3 million, or 2 cents per share, in the third quarter of 2004.*

"Pricing contributed $47 million to our third quarter growth, putting us ahead of year-on-year cost increases of $38 million for the first time in 12 months. *Year-to-date, however, almost unprecedented cost increases for freight, raw materials, and other materials of $132 million have risen faster than our price increases of $97 million. We will stay focused on protecting price and restoring margins* through at least the remainder of the year," the CEO said.

The Company *expects lower "real" growth*—excluding the price increases that will be passed on as higher costs—will continue for the rest of the year. "Once we recover the latest round of cost increases in our pricing, our salespeople will quickly refocus on generating new business. With today's high energy costs, energy savings from many of our product and process services provide even greater value to our customers. We will be more aggressively promoting the benefits of our programs introduced last week to existing customers."

WHAT'S NEXT?

Now that you have taken a look at your company's performance, what should you do next? The next step is conducting a business analysis, that is, learning about the key strategies and specific challenges facing the sales VP. Clearly, the performance of the business, the current trends, and future objectives of senior management will be reflected in the company's financial statements and what they are saying about the business.

THINK LIKE A SALES EXECUTIVE

It will be important to put yourself in the shoes of the VP of sales to truly understand his or her challenges. It has been my experience that sales executives tend to view sales trainers as experts in learning and skill development. Most do not view sales trainers as a resource for executing their go-to-market sales strategy, but rather as a resource for enabling the skills. That is certainly not wrong, nor is it a bad thing. But it does become limiting when it comes time to address business needs. Speaking the language of the sales executive—gross margins, ROI, operating margins, discounting, and profitable business—will cause the sales leadership to view you as someone who understands their world and, more importantly, their challenges.

You should think of yourself as a business consultant when dealing with a sales executive. You contribute more than just training solutions; you will translate your solutions into business results. The only way to do that is to link your solutions to the sales goals of the executive.

To prepare a strong business case for sales training, you need to understand what keeps a sales executive up at night. Revenue growth is certainly number one, but it will be more than that. Other questions causing insomnia might include:

- Is the company's position in the market strong and is the sales force winning against your key competitors?
- Are sales growing faster than your largest competitor's? This is one way analysts and shareholders measure the effectiveness of the sales organization and its leadership.
- Are you protecting price and growing, or defending your margins? Knowing the importance that pricing has on overall profitability will be the single biggest metric for most sales executives.
- Are you growing the business faster than your expenses? Some of this is outside the sales executive's control; however, within the sales organization, cost management will be huge. And because the sales department typically pays for training, this trend may be the single most telling in terms of availability of budget dollars for training.
- Are you retaining your high-profit customers? In some industries, losing one customer can have a devastating impact on the business. In fact, read the company's 10-K report, which is an annual SEC required document and you will see references made to the types and sizes of customers, as a way to illuminate risk factors of which investors should be aware. This can be an area that training can directly support.
- Is the sales organization motivated by their compensation plan and are they staying with the company? Turnover can be very costly from the standpoint of short-term revenue declines as well as speed to perfor-

mance for those new salespeople joining the company. Again, this is another key area that sales training can cost justify—the return that accelerating the speed to performance can have on the bottom line.

ASSUME THE ROLE OF BUSINESS CONSULTANT

You are skilled at conducting training and competency assessments and applying development strategies to address development needs. But to elevate your game, you need to leverage your understanding of the business drivers discussed earlier to conduct a business analysis as part of your assessment. As you conduct your training needs assessment, you should include the following business questions of the sales executive to identify where his or her pressure points are and what the business priorities are:

1. **What are your key strategies for growing the business this year?**

   Question rationale (what you want to know): There are only so many ways you can grow the business—hire more feet on the street, raise pricing, acquire new customers; call higher and accelerate the sales cycle to close more deals in a shorter period of time, sell more products to existing customers, sell new products, bundle products into an overall solution, target specific competitors and exploit their weaknesses to win new business. Understanding these strategies and priorities will help you formulate your training strategy, but also begin to identify the targeted outcomes that training can impact and measure.

2. **What challenges do you see in accomplishing your goals this year?**

   Question rationale: One challenge might be an inability to hire new salespeople; competition may play a factor if they are attacking your company's customers with lower price and free offers; another challenge may be not calling high enough in a customer's organization to sell solutions (strategy); the economy might have an impact on demand, requiring the sales force to have to explore new markets or work harder to defend the business they have.

3. **Has the sales organization been able to protect price and defend margins?**

Question rationale: This is the big one! You can look at price as a key growth strategy. As McKinsey found, defending price, not to mention increasing it, can dramatically reduce the pressures on the sales organization to sell more wisely and in a more efficient manner. This will also be a function of who the salespeople are calling on. If they are calling on purchasing, then pricing will remain an issue. The information you uncover with this question will serve you well as a consultant to the sales executive. Sales training can absolutely have a direct impact on margin protection and that is a very measurable outcome that you can factor into your sales training business case.

4. **Can you point to one or two critical success factors?**

Question rationale: How the sales executive views his or her most important success factor will be very revealing. It will help you focus your attention on addressing the training needs associated with the factors that can be controlled or managed, for example, calling at higher levels where price is less of a factor, or calling on other functional areas to influence a decision. If there are uncontrollable external factors—for example, supply chain disruption due to weather—that puts added pressure on the sales team. This will force you to identify linkage to strategies in place to deal with current and future challenges that you can impact through training.

5. **How skilled is your team in executing your go-to-market sales strategy?**

> *Question rationale:* This should purposely be the last question because if the sales executive truly believes the sales organization is sufficiently skilled, you have been confronted with a challenge. Will your needs assessment uncover skill gaps, especially those you find that address the key business strategies uncovered through your questioning? I find sales executives intuitively know the weaknesses of their sales teams and individuals in some cases, but a good business consultant can help articulate the specific need and potential solution. More than that, the business consultant will be able to link the financial consequences or impact to a specific competency gap.

So how do sales executives think? They think in financial terms 24/7. Growing the business in most industries means taking business away from competition. It means winning business without giving away unacceptable levels of margin or gross profit. This usually means salespeople must sell on value versus price, call higher in customer organizations where economic decisions are made, and differentiate not only what they sell but also how they sell it. Salespeople are the first line of defense for margin protection and your business case should always address the skills and performance drivers that help sales executives manage this critical business driver.

MAKING THE BUSINESS CASE FOR TRAINING

Too often I hear about well-prepared sales training plans being initially approved and as soon as the next quarterly financials get announced, the priorities shift and training is shelved or deferred. It is important to think about positioning your training plan as more of a business proposition designed to improve the financial performance of the company, than a budgetary expenditure. Certainly, all of the findings from your skills assessment remain the centerpiece of what you are delivering; however, positioning it as a business improvement strategy could be the difference between getting the funding or not. As discussed above, leading with a working knowledge of the financial and business priorities will lay the foundation for selling training as a profit improvement strategy critical to the success of the company.

COMPONENTS OF AN EFFECTIVE BUSINESS CASE

Based on the key trends driving your business, you must start by anticipating the challenges the sales executive is facing. You need to establish the financial and business need before you can effectively assess the competency gaps sales training can address. Next, you must identify the key measurements that should be used to track success—revenue growth, acquiring new accounts, pricing key products differently, customer retention, and so on. Start with the end in mind: What financial outcomes are needed? From there you need to identify the key sales and sales management strategies that will address the desired outcomes. This might include calling higher or targeting only a certain market segment that can drive results more quickly.

Once you understand the business needs, key measurements, and management sales strategies, then the selling skills needs assessment can provide you the ability to map skills to the key business drivers. Are the right information, tools, and feedback mechanisms in place to help you deploy, coach, and reinforce the skills needed to achieve the outcomes? Only then can you put in place a way to measure the return on training investment. Here are the components of the business planning approach:

Business needs. Identify the business opportunities and link them to the sales executive's key financial objectives:

- Review the numbers
- Review the business trends
- Analyze what management is saying

Key measurements. Strategies for measuring the impact of your training include measuring the effectiveness of sales training and its impact on bottom-line business outcomes. In Chapter 12, Gary Summy provides strategies for measuring the impact of training. He examines operational excellence and business impact as part of articulating effective measurements for training financial return. Developing high-level metrics for evaluating the success of trainees early in the training cycle allows you to identify progress as early as possible. Here are a few more:

1. Separate the impact of training from other performance factors, giving you the opportunity to truly know when performance is due to other issues.
2. Understand the extent to which each of your field managers contributes to, or detracts from, the knowledge, skills, and abilities cultivated in training.
3. Reduce turnover and increase satisfaction and organizational commitment by identifying the characteristics most conducive to success in *your organization.*
4. Develop leading indicators of sales success, giving you the opportunity to identify your potential sales superstars as early on as possible.

Key sales and sales management strategies. Based on the business and financial needs, the VP of sales will typically have a clear idea of what the management team will need to be focused on to achieve their goals. What are the specific areas they feel they need to address; it could be targeting the market differently, retaining the top ten accounts, going after new markets, in the first two quarters, or increasing price to the largest users. These strategies will be an excellent baseline for training to determine what skills are required to be successful.

Required skills and activities. What are the required competencies to achieve the desired business results and what sales training content, implementation, and reinforcement approach will most effectively address the need? Identifying the areas that sales training impacts and quantifying the impact will be the most effective ways to address the sales VP.

Information, tools, and feedback. Many organizations have invested a lot of money in customer relationship management (CRM) software programs and enabled the sales force with the technology to manage customer information more effectively. Others have installed sales libraries with product and market information. Review what is available in your organization. Chances are, even if you have a robust system it is likely not being used, yet has the potential to provide exactly what you need to support the overall business case for training. Most of all, finding additional applications for past investments will score high with executives.

Return on training investment. Measurement and documenting return on training is covered in other chapters in this book. But, the key to any return on investment is having the benchmarks established going into the initiative. The groundwork you have done to understand the business, strategies, and key areas for skill development will provide you the quantifiable measurements needed to complete an ROI.

DO YOUR HOMEWORK

Review the training provided in the past two years. A VP of sales and the CEO love nothing more than to hear that you can repurpose or leverage investments already made. It also helps you put into context that the skills in place may not have been adequately addressed in previous training. It also will highlight the importance of driving management behavior to be successful in the current environment.

Identify areas that have dealt with product, pricing, raw materials, and value propositions around the total value that the company delivers. That will be central to positioning price increases. Recommend that existing programs be repurposed to address the specific skills needed to be successful in driving price increases and retaining the company's most critical customers. That will make the case for a new skills program easier to sell if it is required and additional budget dollars are needed.

HAVING THE CONVERSATION—A REAL-WORLD SCENARIO

So you have listened in on the CEO's analyst call, and you learned that margins will be challenged this year due to the steep rise in resin costs, your core product raw material. Even the CEO acknowledged that passing along all of the costs will be very difficult because of competitive pressures. The one person feeling the greatest pressure will be the VP of sales.

You have a meeting planned to talk about the training plans agreed to in the last budget cycle, and you have heard the rumors that all budgets are under review and that deep cuts are likely. So, how do you approach the discussion knowing that factors outside your control and that of the VP of sales are impacting all of the plans you have? Based on your experience with the sales organization, you should be prepared to offer a recommendation. A sales VP in this position is looking for ideas and quick remedies to address the immediate need to position price increases with key customers and to defend the total value the company delivers. Do your homework. You know now that the conversation will center on budget cuts and deferring the training plans already agreed to. Figure 4.3 provides a business analysis worksheet that can guide your research and discussions.

Once you have identified the high-level business needs, you are ready to build a business case using the information you have gathered. Figure 4.4 provides a business case worksheet you can use to prepare a recommendation.

The conversation might go as follows:

> "Jim, during the CEO analyst call I noted the greatest challenge facing us this year is the escalating cost of resin, our key raw material. The key to hitting our growth and profitability targets will be our ability to sell the industry on the continuous rise in resin costs. Even though we have been dealing with this for the last two quarters, it seems now that it will be a challenge facing our sales organization through the year. We had a plan to support the sales team with advanced skills but because our business focus will need to change, I would like to provide a few ideas on how we could retool existing skills and add a component that directly addresses our need for selling price increases."

PRESENTING YOUR BUSINESS CASE

Sales executives are busy and most don't like to get bogged down in details. They want to know what is being recommended or the business proposition being offered, what will be required of them, what does it cost, and what is the return on investment. They will want to know how confident you are

FIGURE 4.3 Business Analysis Worksheet

1. What was the company's financial performance last year?

Example: Sales are up but margins are flat due to the increase in the price of raw materials. This is impacting costs. Operating expenses are up and that means senior management will be looking to cut expenses. Training is usually one of the most visible expenses to cut.

---

2. What are the trends from last year?

Example: The last two quarters of last year were particularly weak. That means management will be tightening expenses and also deferring decisions until the picture gets clearer. This impacts training either through the budget or just plain indecision.

---

3. What are the CEO's stated strategies for this year?

Example: CEOs always address their biggest business and financial challenges every quarter. They also articulate specific strategies to address the need. Herein lie opportunities to align training to the key business needs.

---

4. What are the key impact areas for the sales team?

Example: The sales team is always the first line of defense when it comes to growing the business. Based on the big issues, there will be connections to how the sales organization needs to focus their attention, and what skills are required to be successful.

---

5. What can training directly impact?

Example: Virtually every strategy the CEO and VP of sales put forth will be connected to sales organization. It is sales training's job to identify the skill gaps and present a solution designed to address the most pressing needs in the shortest period of time.

FIGURE 4.4 Business Case Worksheet

1. Critical success factors
Get specific numbers by rep, territory, customers, product

_____

_____

_____

2. Key measurements to be used to track success
Sales, margin improvement goals, retaining customers, retaining volume

_____

_____

_____

3. Key sales and sales management strategies to achieve outcomes
80/20 targeting, call above purchasing in critical accounts, document or justify price increase, quantify value

_____

_____

_____

4. Required skills and activities to achieve success
Inventory current skills in place, review curriculum, look for skills you can repurpose, introduce targeted application-specific remedies

_____

_____

_____

5. Information, tools, measurement, and feedback
Does the company provide product, market, customer, and/or competitor information to the sales force? What information could assist in implementing the key skills and activities to achieve the stated objectives?

_____

_____

_____

6. Return on training investment
How have the skills and activities acquired through training impacted the key measurements identified by management? Get specific numbers by rep, territory, customers, product, etc.

_____

_____

_____

that the outcomes can be achieved, how you plan to measure the results, and how much time is required on their part and on the part of the sales team to implement the training solution. Here are a few things to remember when approaching the sales VP with your business case:

- *Position the targeted results up front.* To get the sales executive's attention, be prepared to demonstrate the kind of business impact your project will have on the organization. Nothing speaks better than numbers, especially for a busy executive. You should quantify the impact in terms of sales growth, margin improvement, new customers, etc., and be prepared to defend your numbers.

- *Set time frames for return on training investment (ROTI).* Be realistic. It may take six months to begin to see impact, but be specific about the milestones that can be anticipated on the way to results, what steps it will take, what will be observable, and how results will be tracked. A 1 percent improvement in price on a handful of deals, for example, may be enough to fully pay back the investment in training in the first 90 days following training.

- *Link your project to other important initiatives.* Where possible, link your project to other key initiatives to demonstrate that you are aligned with the key strategies on which the sales executive is focused. This could be CRM, new product development, or a new marketing campaign.

- *Present the training plan.* Present your project plan with the end in mind. Link the training content and skills to be developed in terms of how each impacts the financial and business outcomes you are promising. The sales executive will get a stronger picture of how the competencies being developed will directly and dramatically impact his or her sales goals. This will create a sense of urgency and importance for the training.

- *Close for the business.* Demonstrate your selling model and close for the business! Most sales VPs will appreciate that you approached the training need in a professional and bottom-line fashion. Even a trainer without experience "carrying the bag" can use a selling model when presenting (selling!) ideas. The reaction, questions, and objections you hear will be easier to overcome if you know the underlying financial and business factors that are directly impacting your internal customer's business.

SUMMARY

There are a new set of economic rules driving business today and for everyone in the organization, change will continue unabated. For sales trainers, the challenges have never been greater. Business as usual just won't get it done in the coming years. There is a need to understand how your company is performing and what impact external and internal decisions have had, and will have on results. Knowing your company's financial situation and providing solutions that address executive's highest priorities will earn you a seat at the table when the key financial decisions are made. This will require analyzing the business and proposing training solutions that address the behavioral and financial performance of the sales organization. Aligning with the sales executive will earn you the right to sell your services and fund your programs because they are viewed as mission critical. Building a business case for success is the only way in the current economic environment to win your share of a shrinking annual budget.

CHAPTER 5

Creating a Stellar Customer-Centric Sales Force

SUSANNE CONRAD, Dechert-Hampe & Company

Organizations intuitively know that remarkable growth and performance are, at least in part, driven by a remarkable sales force. In today's ever-increasingly competitive, changing, and fast-paced marketplace, the best a good or average sales force can do is to maintain market share. The success of any organization depends on the ability of its sales force not only to maintain current customers and sales but also to grow that customer base and volume. That task of growing the business is increasingly difficult because of growing pressures from competitors who can disrupt even the most long-standing vendor-customer relationships. The most progressive organizations engage their training function in building a sales force with the skills, competencies, and experience to meet these challenges.

The key to creating a stellar customer-centric sales force that can take on the challenges is to ensure that the following four elements are in place:

1. A solid and consistently executed sales process and selling methodology

2. An objective customer relationship management methodology for determining the customer's desired relationship type and aligning the organization against it
3. A development curriculum that ensures the sales force has the skills, competencies, and experience necessary to execute 1 and 2
4. Effective tools that help the sales force execute 1 and 2

The training function plays a unique role in this effort. That role is to partner with both sales management and human resources to understand the methodologies and impact of the sales process, selling methodology, and customer relationship methodologies; to assess the knowledge, skill, competency, or experience gaps; to develop strategies and plans for quickly closing those gaps; and to execute the strategy and plans effectively and efficiently.

Each of the four elements listed above could easily be a chapter, even a book, in and of itself. There are, in fact, many books written and readily available on each of these subjects. Consider that a search on "customer relationship management" on Amazon.com's Web site results in over 1,500 book results. The purpose of this chapter is to show how these elements are related and how training can support their application to move the organization closer to creating a stellar customer-centric sales force. We will examine some of these elements in more detail than others and encourage you to consider how they are augmented by information and discussion in other chapters of this book.

SALES PROCESS AND SELLING METHODOLOGY

There is a common misconception that all an organization must do to develop a great sales force is to identify and teach the ideal sales process. So training is tasked with identifying and recommending a sales training program. More than likely, sales management has a hand in selecting the program to ensure that what is presented matches management's sales approach and philosophy. Then, the program is rolled out to the sales organization, which learns the methodology, approach, various tips, techniques, and tricks and then attempts to execute that methodology. Perhaps the sales force is successful. But, perhaps it is not; it may not be able to meet goals and make its numbers. What's gone wrong? Very often, the organization decides that the answer to that question is that the sales force simply has not learned the sales process very well and needs additional sales training. So again training is tasked with identifying skill gaps and a program that will close those gaps. That may work, but before significant resources and effort are expended by the organization, it would be wise to step back and look at the role of the sales process and selling methodology in a larger context.

To begin, the sales process and a selling methodology are not the same thing. The sales process is simply a relatively defined series of steps through which all sales progress. It is presented or described in several variations, but always includes some grouping of the following seven elements:

1. Prospecting
2. Interviewing
3. Needs analysis
4. Presentation
5. Negotiation
6. Closing
7. Servicing and follow-up

It really matters very little how an organization *describes* the sales process as long as it can do so with a consistent clarity that guides the sales force in its efforts to sell the organization's products or services. Understanding the sales process is basic knowledge that every sales person must acquire quickly.

The selling methodology—how a salesperson actually executes the steps of the sales process—is another matter. Researching the available literature and the offerings of various experts provides a number of methodologies that have evolved over the years from the persuasive selling of the 1950s to the consultative selling approaches of the 1970s, which are augmented by strategic selling developed during the 1990s and into today's businessperson/strategist salesperson concept.[1]

No single methodology, however, can be considered the ideal. Which methodology is adopted by an organization is a situational decision. It depends entirely on the requirements of an organization's customers and the type of sale in question. An organization with a complex sale, such as the aerospace industry, would not choose the same methodology as an organization with a high-churn sale, such as that of the insurance industry.

Once an appropriate selling methodology has been chosen, success depends not only on how well the sales force learns, internalizes, and applies the methodology, but also on the alignment of the organization's key elements to support and facilitate execution of the methodology. These elements include the organization's (1) structure, (2) mechanics, (3) culture, and (4) motivations. (See Dechert-Hampe's Organizational Alignment Model™ in Figure 5.1.)

Briefly, as the figure illustrates, Structure relates to the physical structure of the sales force within the organization—reporting relationships, position hierarchy, number of people in each position, physical location of the positions. Mechanics relates to the work processes, workflow, systems, and technology required to accomplish the day-to-day work of the organization. Culture, of course, encompasses the organizational norms, guiding principles, and other intangibles that determine its ways of working. And, finally, Motiva-

FIGURE 5.1 Dechert-Hampe's Organizational Alignment Model

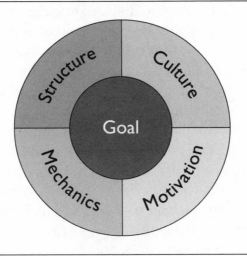

tion relates to the incentives—pay, incentive programs, nonmonetary incentives—as well as disincentives the organization has in place.

It is imperative that the sales process is aligned with these elements. Consider an organization that relies heavily on strong communication and internal cooperation to respond to a request for proposal with a tight timeline defined by its customer. To successfully deliver the proposal requires a structure that allows quick access to key stakeholders and decision makers and sufficient support staff to provide the information and production resources on which the salesperson must draw. It also requires a robust costing and deal evaluation tool as well as a defined process for guiding the salesperson through the steps required for preparing an acceptable proposal to the customer. The stakeholders must work in a culture that values quick response to customer requests, prompting and rewarding a "whatever it takes to meet the deadline" mentality. Finally, incentive and performance review programs might include metrics on response rates to further support the process.

Whenever training is called on to teach a selling skills program or, for that matter, to deliver any program to the sales force, it should consider the alignment or misalignment of these elements with that program. Alignments indicate a strong possibility of success in achieving the behaviors and results desired after the program. Misalignments indicate that some work needs to be done to rectify the misalignment or to open a discussion of the impact the misalignments will have on the desired outcomes of the program. For example, consider being asked to teach the sales force to sell more profitable deals even if that means selling fewer deals. If the organization's incentive program pays bonuses based on number of deals, one can readily predict what will happen—a continuation of mostly volume-oriented rather than profitability-oriented behavior. Of course, the options in such a case are (1) restructure the incentive program to be based on profitable sales; (2) impose disincentives that encourage compliance, such as giving credit toward bonuses for sales volume but a reduction for nonprofitable volume; or (3) adjust the organization's expectations about the amount of behavior change to a realistic level if neither 1 or 2 are implemented.

Thus, what is critically important is not the specific descriptions of the selling process or the selling methodology itself (assuming that the methodology chosen is appropriate for the type of sale and customer requirements), but how well the organization is aligned to support the sales force in executing that methodology. Training has an opportunity to establish its credibility and relevance in the organization by not only delivering excellent training and development programs covering the sales process and selling methodology, but also by partnering with sales management and human resources to assess and discuss gaps in the elements of the Organizational Alignment Model™. Doing so would positively impact the effectiveness of the training and development it delivers.

CUSTOMER RELATIONSHIP MANAGEMENT

A customer-centric sales force is one that understands the type of relationship and what deliverables the customer wants and then delivers exactly that, perfectly, every time. *Deliverables* in this case does not refer to products or services, but instead to how the organization works with the customer. These deliverables are often referred to as the "touchpoints" between organizations. Touchpoints will differ slightly from industry to industry and company to company and must be customized to your business. However, they typically include some variation of the following:

- Strategy and planning
- Product design
- Sales process
- Order process
- Physical delivery
- Billing and collections
- Demand creation
- In-store execution (if applicable)
- Product/technical support
- Damages/returns

A pervasive myth is that an organization should develop a strategic relationship with its largest or most important customers. Dechert-Hampe's research indicates that it is more effective and profitable to develop exactly the type of relationship the customer wants, and then perform better than the competition against that type of relationship.

For example, let's consider the case of a company that produces a line of baby booties, and let's call them the BabeBoots Company (BBC). BBC sells 60 percent of its annual volume to Wal-Mart and 40 percent to other chain retailers and specialty baby products stores. It may be a mistake for BBC to focus its efforts on pushing for a strategic relationship with Wal-Mart simply because that is its largest customer. Wal-Mart typically wants a transactional relationship with most of its suppliers— a "give me as much of your products as I want, when I want them, where I want them, at the lowest possible price, and that's all" philosophy. Some of BBC's specialty baby shop customers, however, may want a more strategic relationship—a "provide me with a new line that no one else carries based on my specific consumer demographic, let's work together on our annual plan, and let's establish a price point that maximizes both our profits and start an EDI initiative to work most efficiently together" approach. It would be a waste of BBC's resources to attempt to establish the strategic relationship with Wal-Mart. Likewise, it may be infinitely more profitable on a per-sale basis to devote the strategic relationship resources to its specialty customers. (Of course, volume, profit margins, and other issues that must be examined in detail will determine the type of resources BBC can ultimately devote to any customer.)

Once an organization has identified the correct relationship type for each customer, the next step is to assess how well the organization is performing against the relationships. A gap assessment based on a relationship type is incredibly powerful because it indicates where training will deliver the greatest ROI and, therefore, where training should focus its efforts. Regardless of relationship type desired by the customer, the sales force's job is to deliver against that relationship better than its competition. Consider which organization will be most successful with a customer: one that has a strategic relationship with the customer but performs poorly or one that has a transactional relationship with the customer but performs perfectly in every transaction? Of course, the latter.

Training often mistakenly believes that because its immediate customers are sales management and trainees, it should focus on delivering the products and services requested by those customers. In reality, to become a true business partner with the organization, training must focus on the same ultimate goal—profitable growth. Its role is to help the organization grow by recommending, creating the business case for (Chapter 4 provides some great insights into developing a business case for sales training), and developing a sales force with the exact skills and competencies required to provide the customer with superior performance. Training's greatest contribution to the sales organization is to focus its resources on what will provide the greatest impact on improving the customer's satisfaction. Understanding and paying close attention to customer relationship requirements across various customer segments will help training accomplish this.

SALES SKILLS, COMPETENCIES, EXPERIENCE

Focusing training's resources and efforts against those sales force characteristics, skills, competencies, and experiences the *customer* believes are most important to *its* business begins with understanding the customer requirements. Often the sales organization believes it knows what the customer wants because it has continual contact with the customer. The only true way to determine customer requirements, however, is to ask the customer.

Dechert-Hampe has done primary research with both manufacturers/vendors and their customers to determine whether there is congruence in their perceptions of what is important. The results of the research indicate that there are gaps in what the customer believes is important and what sales believes is important.[2]

Findings from the studies indicate that manufacturers/ vendors and their customers agree that communication skills and traditional selling skills are important and that manufacturers/vendors, in general, are very good at these. Customers, however, view these basic skills as no more than the manufacturer's/vendor's "foot in the door"—excellent performance is expected from everyone as a baseline. Manufacturers/vendors would like to be more involved in and, therefore, have more influence in the customer's critical processes such as strategy and planning. Customers usually do not want this kind of involvement from their manufacturers/vendors because they believe their staff has not been able to demonstrate a good understanding of their business. What the customer truly wants is for the manufacturer's/vendor's sales force to bring them demand generation ideas based on solid consumer knowledge. In essence, the customer is saying, "Help me sell more to *my* customer rather than sell more to *me*." Of course, manufacturers/vendors tend to focus a great deal of effort against internally focused attributes such as cost reduction efforts and compliance with internal procedures. Despite the fact that customers place little value on such attributes, it must remain a part of the sales force development process to ensure effective and efficient operation of the business.

Traditionally, the vendor-customer relationship was held to be that between the account executive (or the person with the "direct" relationship with the customer regardless of that person's title) and the buyer (or whatever the title of the person actually purchasing the goods or service). Dechert-Hampe's research shows that the dynamic that defines the relationship is much broader (See Figure 5.2.)

This dynamic indicates that the sales force must not only be skilled in dealing with their primary customer contact, they must also be skilled at managing the total relationship between their organization and the customer. These skills must be customer-facing, but they also need internal-facing skills to be able to work effectively and efficiently within their own organization. Such skills include influencing without direct authority, communications, consensus building, negotiation, and conflict resolution to name but a few.

FIGURE 5.2 Vendor Customer Dynamic

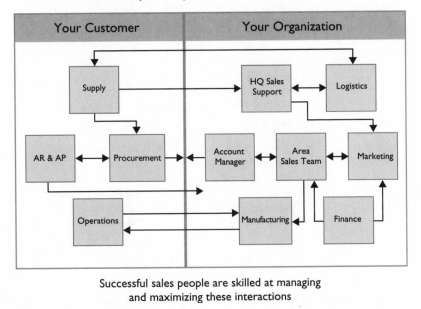

Today there are more touchpoints & Interactions –
both Internally & with your customer – than ever before

Successful sales people are skilled at managing
and maximizing these interactions

Dechert-Hampe's research indicates that every industry and organization has a set of skills that are considered baseline skills—skills every salesperson must have just to meet basic customer requirements. In addition, there are differentiating skills that separate the salesperson from the pack in the customer's mind. These are the differentiating skills that the truly outstanding salespeople in any organization will exhibit. See Figure 5.3 for an example of the baseline and differentiating skills for a typical consumer-packaged-goods organization.

These baseline and differentiating capabilities, once identified for the industry and organization relative to its competitors, can be grouped into a set of core competencies against which the training and development curriculum can be established. (See Figure 5.4.)

FIGURE 5.3 Baseline vs. Skills Example

DHC has conducted multiple studies & research projects (including the Great Selling Organizations Survey) to identify the capabilities necessary for today's sales organization to be effective.

Baseline Capabilities
- Influencing & Negotiations
- Selling Skills
- Communications
- Account Management
- Trade Promotion/B2B Marketing
- Presentation Skills
- Relationship Management
- Interpersonal Skills
- Analytics
- Product Knowledge
- Channel Knowledge
- Project Management

Differentiating Capabilities
- Cross-functional Collaboration
- Consumer/In-store Marketing
- Creativity & Innovation
- Conflict Resolution
- Category Development
- Supply Chain Knowledge
- Team Skills
- Managing & Influencing Without Direct Authority
- Industry Direction & Insights
- Leadership

Training's role is to use its understanding of the sales process and adopted sales methodology combined with the customer relationship evaluations as described above to provide opportunities for salespeople to develop their capabilities and skills in these core competencies and to gain the experiences that allow them to perform excellently against the customer's needs. Focusing on this as its goal rather than on delivering training programs is what allows the training function to become a true business partner to the organization and builds its credibility and relevance.

Executing against this goal is not an easy task. Often training, just like the rest of the organization, does not have the resources to address all of the opportunities before it. A well-planned strategy for addressing the most important, most impactful sales training challenges, however, is what will make the most difference. It is relatively easy to deliver a program because it is what sales management has requested and what

FIGURE 5.4 Sales Core Competencies

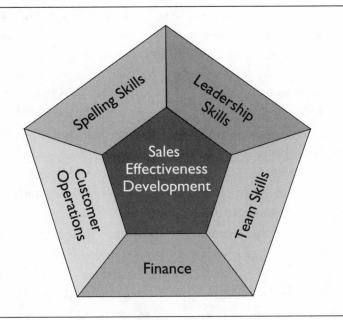

training is used to delivering, rather than analyzing and recommending an alternative approach that requires more strategic work. For example, it would be relatively quick and easy for training to plan a sales training program to address the performance in a sales process touchpoint in an attempt to get excellent rather than good performance. In contrast, addressing the sales force's skills and competencies with the order process would require not only a training program, but perhaps some process reengineering, culture change, and/or systems work. Training often shies away from such undertakings because it believes it has little clout to influence the organization in areas outside of training and development. In fact, if training were to take a collaborative role with other areas of the organization in such situations, it would be much better able to impact true change that improves corporate performance in addition to becoming a more integral part of the organization's operation.

Experiences are as important to building a stellar sales force as developing skills and competencies. Training's role is to work with the organization to create opportunities for the sales force to gain these experiences, either by working with sales and human resources to provide career paths that allow new experiences or by bringing experience into the classroom in the form of application of the principles taught during a training or development program. The first step is for the organization to identify the requisite experiences for each level within the sales organization and where this experience may be obtained. For an example of what an experience matrix such as this might look like, see Figure 5.5.

There are numerous ways for training to collaborate with the organization to provide experiences, including incorporating the day-to-day work of program attendees as activities in training programs, creating hands-on workshops, basing case studies on actual business situations, postprogram coaching and mentoring, etc.; basically anything that allows program attendees to actually apply the learning in a live or as close to a live situation as possible. For example, if asked to develop a program to teach participants account planning, training could design the course so that participants bring the information and data with them to develop an actual account plan for one of their customers during the program. This makes the activity and learning much more real and immediate for program participants.

Finally, training's role also includes determining the appropriate format for true learning and experience generation. Today, there are significantly more options available to the training professional than there were in the past. In addition to the traditional classroom, on-the-job, and independent study formats, there are a number of electronic formats that can be as, if not more, effective in place of or in combination with the traditional formats. Training has an opportunity and a responsibility to create the most effective training and development possible given the content and its resources. (For more information, see

FIGURE 5.5 Sample Experience Matrix

Sample Career Experience Model for Regional Vice President

Experience/Skill	Type	Good	Depth Chart Better	Best
Large scale people management	True Experience	• Warehouse Retail Mgr. • DSD District Mgr. ✓	• Warehouse CBM • DSD RVP +	• Warehouse RVP • DSD AVP +
Fix it/Turnaround	True Experience	• Category turnaround in a customer ✓	• Customer turnaround for business +	• Business unit turnaround—domestic or international N/A
Etc.				
Global Perspective	Exposure	• International Project Team +	• International Special Assignment +	• International Line Experience +
Supply Chain	Exposure	• Customer Service/ Logistics Project Team ✓	• Customer Service/ Logistics Special Assignment +	• Customer Service/ Logistics Line Experience +
Etc.				
Consumer Insights	Knowledge	• Public Seminars • Online Resources ✓	• Corporate University Training Classes +	• University Partner Classes +
P&L Management	Knowledge	• Public Seminars • Online Resources ✓	• Corporate University Training Classes +	• University Partner Classes +
Etc.				

✓ = Requirement   + = Enhancement

Chapter 6 on designing training and Chapter 7 on outsourcing.) Again, this issue of choosing and creating training in the most effective format can fill an entire book on its own.

SALES TOOLS

The final requirement for creating a stellar customer-centric sales force is a set of sales tools that allows sales to effectively and efficiently execute the sales process and methodology against the requirements of the customer relationship. These sales tools include the appropriate processes and procedures as well as IT systems.

Solid, appropriate methodologies/processes, like customer relationship management, are also important sales tools. An example of a methodology that is a critical sales tool would be that of a trade spend methodology based on a trade spend philosophy adopted by the sales organization. To be truly effective with a retailer, a consumer goods manufacturer's sales force must understand and be able to execute the trade spend methodology. This will require IT systems for calculating, tracking, and reporting trade spending, a process for communicating policy and impacts to the retailer, and processes for taking action should performance not match agreed to approaches. Another might be a process for determining an appropriate sales price for the organization's products. One organization that leases corporate fleets to its customers provides price breaks based on the number of vehicles the customer leases. To assist its sales force in determining the correct pricing, each salesperson's laptop is loaded with a link to a program on the organization's extranet that allows the sales rep to simply enter the customer number and number of vehicles for the proposed order. The tool then calculates the appropriate pricing based on the customer's year-to-date order history. The result is a sales rep able to quote accurate pricing within seconds based on history that would ordinarily require lengthy order status checking.

The training function's role in this area of sales tools is to understand their importance and impact and incorporate training on these tools into its development curriculum. It is also tasked with suggesting, recommending, and, perhaps, providing additional sales tools based on its experience in training the sales force. For example, training may find that creating job aids or documenting processes and procedures could support the salesperson in his or her execution of the sales processes. Proactively developing or recommending the development of such sales tools can build training's relevance and credibility as a true partner with the sales organization in building the organization's business.

TRAINING'S CHALLENGE

Everything discussed so far equips training to help the organization develop an outstanding sales force. One thing to consider in this equation is the role the organization will allow training to take on—how involved training will be in strategy, planning, and becoming involved as a full business partner. To take on such a role, training must continually demonstrate its relevance and credibility to the organization and the sales force. Too often, even trainers and training professionals who have held sales positions are seen to be out of touch with the "real world" the sales force faces in the field. Therefore, the training organization must always remain close to the front line. It must see and interact with the sales force in action and with the customer. Let's consider how training can develop the credibility and prove its relevance.

Salespeople are interested in improving performance so they can make quotas and earn a bonus. When training has a direct tie to the sales team and provides the type of information, programs, and support that improve the sales team's performance, training has relevance to the salesperson. Because performance with customers has a great impact on the ability of salespeople to do well, training must demonstrate that it understands the customer and must apply that knowledge to training development. That means that training must either bring timely firsthand experience or work closely with subject matter experts—in this case, salespeople—when developing its programs. In working with clients, the most effective and well-received programs are those developed by a sales subject matter expert in conjunction with an adult education expert (meaning a trainer). In this scenario, we combine current, leading-edge customer knowledge and practices with the teaching disciplines and techniques that truly drive behavior change and learning for programs the sales force finds important and useful.

Training is constantly battling for credibility. It must continually fight the "those that can, do; those that can't, teach" mentality. Veteran and talented salespeople often come into a training session asking, "What can you possibly teach me?" The trainer gains credibility with this group when he/she can discuss actual customer interactions; when the trainer can say, "I was at Wal-Mart last week and . . ." and they aren't talking about shopping! Salespeople are much more receptive to learning and development when it is delivered by someone they know has shared or understands their experiences. And, the experience the trainer should demonstrate must be relatively recent. Organizations often make the mistake of assuming that if someone in training has been a salesperson at some point in their career, salespeople will view them as a peer. Experience working with many organizations shows that a trainer's sales experience must be recent and constantly refreshed to be considered relevant and credible by the salespeople in the trenches. Otherwise, it is assumed that the trainer's knowledge and understanding is dated and out of sync with the real world.

So, how do trainers keep their experience with the front line fresh and up-to-date? Here are some tips:

- Regularly accompany salespeople on customer calls. Work with new reps to see where they are on their learning curve. Work with veterans to see how they integrate the selling process.
- Talk with the sales manager after the day in the field. Give them your observations and ask questions to get their perspective. Let them know you care and are connecting with the business issues, not just skills issues.
- Share your learning and observations with other trainers. Encourage and proactively seek out information from other trainers who have been in the field or attended sales events/functions.
- Stay open to curriculum changes if you see trends emerge from your learning and observations and share these trends with other trainers.
- Sit in on account team meetings, regional or national sales meetings, or any other meetings that salespeople attend. Meet people at all levels in the organization and listen to their issues, problems, challenges, and opportunities. Learn how they interact with the customer to see how to better support the sales force.
- Be involved in corporate meetings and discussions where sales discusses day-to-day operations. Watch for efficiency or effectiveness issues that can be impacted with training, process redesign or tweaking, job aids, or education.
- Offer assistance in planning and conducting sessions or assisting in facilitation at sales meetings, especially national or regional meetings. Facilitate regular feedback meetings to listen to what all levels of salespeople have to say.

What will happen when you integrate these types of actions? You become more integrated into the sales function. Word will spread in the organization that training is grounded in the business. Trainers may even remove themselves from being aligned with "corporate" rather than with sales. Proposed solutions in the classroom will have more credibility if the trainer actually has such hands-on experience because the solutions proposed will be reality-based, pragmatic, and practical solutions specific to the way sales operates in your organization. The trainer presenting the solution will have greater credibility because of his or her experience in the field and exposure to the business. The key is to have as much direct involvement with the sales force as possible. Every person in training should have a performance objective for a certain number of field visits or direct, hands-on contacts with the day-to-day work of sales each year.

Training leaders, designers, and, in fact, the entire training department should stay close to the business. To do this, many training departments rotate their salespeople through training as part of their sales career development. Doing so provides the sales force insights into developing people that will be helpful as they manage a sales team. In addition, the training department gets the most current knowledge and experience as staff rotates in and out of the field and management by providing training the sales subject matter experts to augment their adult education expertise.

In addition to focusing on continually remaining abreast of the training and adult education developments, trainers should make an effort to remain abreast of their industry developments as well. There are a number of ways for a training organization to stay close to the changes in the industry and the customer. For example, training professionals usually attend training association functions (such as the American Society of Traning and Development or the Professional Society for Sales and Marketing Training's annual conference). They should also consider attending industry events, such as the hardware show for tool manufacturers or the Grocery Manufacturers Association conference for the grocery industry. Consider equivalent events in your industry.

Generally speaking, training should make an effort to determine how it can best add value. Creating opportunities to interact with the sales force and customers to better understand the issues and the industry is an excellent way to determine what will add the most value.

SUMMARY

The training function plays a unique and important role in developing the sales force to be ready for the tremendous challenges it faces in today's marketplace. The most effective training organizations are those that go beyond developing and delivering training programs to truly collaborating with the rest of the organization based on a solid understanding of both the business and the marketplace. Training must consider how it can support the organization to realize sales goals not only by providing training, but also by partnering with both sales management and human resources. Training should understand the methodologies and impact of the sales process, selling methodology, and customer relationship methodologies; assess the knowledge, skill, competency, or experience gaps; develop strategies and plans for quickly closing those gaps; and execute the strategy and plans effectively and efficiently. To become a true business partner with the organization, training must focus on developing the credibility and relevance that buys it a seat at that table.

RECOMMENDED RESOURCE

- Jeff Thull, *Mastering the Complex Sale*

Building a Training Program

MICHAEL ROCKELMANN, Driving Results, formerly of United Airlines, Dade Behring, and CDW

So you have decided that your sales force needs a new training program, or that you need to update your current program. That is the first of many important decisions necessary to make this a successful initiative with true business impact. This chapter looks at what needs to be completed in the beginning stages of any training initiative, whether new or a revision.

Many companies skip this step altogether and jump into outsourcing or building a program. To be truly effective you must start with the basics. Even if you decide to outsource your training project, do not skip over this section on building your own program. The model and key concepts are important in the building of any program, whether you are doing it yourself or with an outside firm.

This chapter will also help you identify if you should consider outsourcing; if you can't complete a step in the process you may need outside help. If you do outsource, you should also hold the firm to the same process and standards as if you were building it yourself. (See Chapter 7.)

We'll begin by defining your initiative, including forming a project team and performing an analysis of your needs. Later in this chapter we discuss how to build your very own training program.

We will be using the Course Design Model in Figure 6.1, which is a modified version of the evaluation model most widely used in training and developed by Donald Kirkpatrick in 1959. If we simply flip over the steps in the evaluation model, we have a process to help define and build the program. You may be familiar with Kirkpatrick's model, but here is a quick review.

Kirkpatrick says that there are four main levels of evaluation:

1. Reactions—How did participants react to the training? Did they enjoy the experience?
2. Learning—Did participants learn the intended knowledge or skills?
3. Performance—Can participants apply the skills on the job?
4. Results—What is the business impact of the training?

Some more recent models also include a fifth level— ROI—but it is very difficult to measure and not often used. It can be included or left out of the model as appropriate to your objectives.

DEFINING THE INITIATIVE

CREATING A PROJECT TEAM

The first step in any project is to create a project team. Such a team should be assembled for every project, as it is better to have multiple viewpoints rather than one person making all of the decisions. The purpose of a project team is to make decisions on the needs of the project and on the final product. The tasks of the team will not change with the size of the project, but the size of the team may differ and the number of steps required may change because larger projects are more difficult and time-consuming.

FIGURE 6.1 Course Design Model

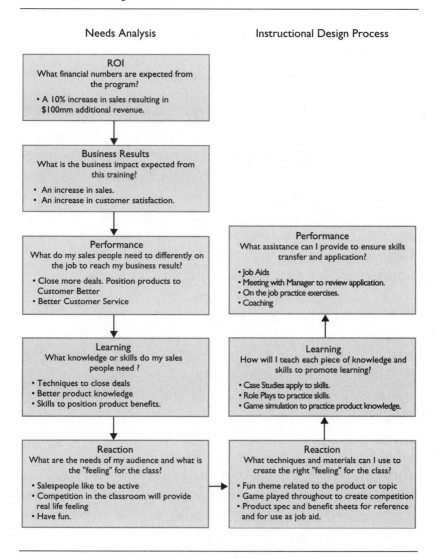

Needs Analysis   Instructional Design Process

ROI
What financial numbers are expected from the program?

• A 10% increase in sales resulting in $100mm additional revenue.

Business Results
What is the business impact expected from this training?

• An increase in sales.
• An increase in customer satisfaction.

Performance
What do my sales people need to differently on the job to reach my business result?

• Close more deals. Position products to Customer Better
• Better Customer Service

Performance
What assistance can I provide to ensure skills transfer and application?

• Job Aids
• Meeting with Manager to review application.
• On the job practice exercises.
• Coaching

Learning
What knowledge or skills do my sales people need ?

• Techniques to close deals
• Better product knowledge
• Skills to position product benefits.

Learning
How will I teach each piece of knowledge and skills to promote learning?

• Case Studies apply to skills.
• Role Plays to practice skills.
• Game simulation to practice product knowledge.

Reaction
What are the needs of my audience and what is the "feeling" for the class?

• Salespeople like to be active
• Competition in the classroom will provide real life feeling
• Have fun.

Reaction
What techniques and materials can I use to create the right "feeling" for the class?

• Fun theme related to the product or topic
• Game played throughout to create competition
• Product spec and benefit sheets for reference and for use as job aid.

The main tasks of any training project team may be defining the outcomes and objectives of the course and then overseeing the design and implementation of the program. The team may also be involved in the decision to outsource, if the expertise is not available in-house.

When deciding how many people to have on the team, your decision should obviously be based on the scope and impact of the project. A major new initial sales program may have a team with representatives from multiple groups and regions. A small job aids or reference materials project may only require two people, one doing most of the work and one giving ideas and content input. A good rule of thumb is to avoid having more than eight to ten team members, no matter how large the project. Having more than eight to ten members often complicates the process. Many experts claim six as a good number, but the important idea is that everyone who has a stake in the project should be represented. Every organization differs in structure, but in the best scenarios for a large project you might have representatives from sales leadership, training or HR, product support, and the sales force. In the small project, it may be yourself and one person from the sales force.

Note that in both situations I recommend the sales force as a key component to the team. The sales force is probably the most important but often overlooked. Sales leadership or training may think they know what is needed, but we've all had experiences with someone who thought he or she understood the problem, but was off target.

For example, I was once approached by a senior sales manager of one of our most profitable regions. He was known within the company as one of the best and always was on top of the needs of his people. He insisted on delivering a one-day team-building and motivation training program for his salespeople. He insisted that their sales numbers were falling because they just were not motivated to sell anymore and needed to be reenergized. He knew they could sell and had great skills, but did not understand why their numbers were falling. After some discussion, I received his permission to hold a focus group with a few of his people. In that meeting, I discovered that motivation was not the issue. They still wanted to remain a top selling unit, but they were having problems understanding some of the new products and features, and how to position them to customers. While they could sell the old products and knew all of the benefits, they felt if they knew more about the new products and specifically how to position their benefits, they could sell more. We ended up delivering a one-day course with specific job aids that helped the salespeople understand the new products and features, and how to correctly position the benefits. Within no time the region was back on top.

This story shows that even a senior manager who typically understood the needs of his people could be mistaken. It is important to include salespeople in the project planning because they are the target audience and it is important to have their input and buy-in. They can provide a realistic view of how the training will be accepted, give advice to avoid pitfalls, and offer real-life scenarios for the program. Having salespeople on the project team can also create "champions" who can deliver your message and build internal commitment to the training program.

As with any team, it is important to follow good team-building practices. It is not the intent of this chapter to offer details on setting up a team (that is the topic of entire books), but once your team is assembled it is important to define team goals, roles, responsibilities, time commitments, and decision-making authority. It should also be clear who the stakeholders are, and set the appropriate communication strategy to ensure the stakeholders are clear on the decisions and progress. The stakeholders should include upper management who requested the project, as well as management in groups that will be impacted by the program.

NEEDS ANALYSIS—DEFINING YOUR OUTCOMES AND OBJECTIVES

Your project team's first task is to conduct a needs analysis. This analysis will define the outcomes and objectives of the

program, as well as evaluating what people are currently doing that is not leading to your intended business result. This
step is necessary whether a new program is being built or an
existing course is being revised, or even if you already know
you want to outsource the project. Everything defined by the
needs analysis will be the basis for the design of the course, or
will be included in the request for proposal (RFP) providing
important information that is crucial to an outside vendor.
Whether replacing or revising an existing program, don't
make the all-too-often-made mistake of inadequately defining
the target outcomes and objectives for the new program before
assessing the existing one. Always define the desired future
state in the beginning and use it as your benchmark for all
future activities. Doing so can also help you in making a buy-
or-build decision, because if you don't have the expertise or
resources to complete the project, then you should look to the
outside. (We look at that in more detail in Chapter 7.)

Your team should at least be able to answer the business
results question in the design model in Figure 6.1, and in many
cases the performance question. If you can't answer the business results question, then you have to ask yourself, why are
you doing this? There has to be a reason and it will be hard to
receive funding if you cannot answer this question.

You will also need to consider the following four issues:

1. *Define your return on investment if necessary.* What monetary return are you expecting from the business
   result? If you are expecting a 10 percent increase in
   sales, what is the increase in revenue? If you are expecting a rise of a point in customer satisfaction ratings,
   what monetary value will this lead to? This step is difficult and not often approached by many organizations. It is difficult to isolate the training as the factor
   for many of these increases. Use this section cautiously
   and only present if it is expected.

2. *Define business results or the outcomes.* Every project should lead to a business result—an increase in sales, a rise in customer satisfaction, and so on. Though improved product knowledge or increased sales skills can lead to business results, they are not themselves business results. Be sure to identify why you are building and delivering this training.

3. *Define the desired change in performance.* Once you have identified your expected business results, you can identify what your salespeople need to do differently to achieve the results. This is where your internal assessment will begin to help you identify what should be done differently. What are salespeople doing or not doing that is causing you to not meet expectations?

   If you know that you want to increase sales, but don't know how, you have to conduct a survey of salespeople to find answers, or look for an outside vendor to help. This is where the internal assessment on what salespeople are currently doing that is not leading to your expected results comes into play. Are they not closing deals, are they not positioning products well, or are they unable to use the systems correctly? Chapter 5 discussed the importance of listening to the customer, which is crucial to defining your desired change in performance.

4. *Define your learning objectives.* The learning question will lead to a tangible list of knowledge or skills that are needed to change performance and impact the business result. Determine what people are doing now, what you want them to be doing in the future, and what they need to accomplish this. This is where you may learn that training is not the real issue; it may be a lack of support or a software issue impeding the desired performance. If the salespeople know how to do the job but still are performing below expectations, then what is stopping them

from achieving the performance? You will need two levels of definition in most cases, your learning objectives and enabling objectives. You can start at a higher level and then break that down further, which will also help you to identify the content needed for the course. The enabling objectives and identification of content will often require the use of a subject matter expert (SME).

COMPARING FUTURE AND CURRENT PERFORMANCE

Information on the desired state of performance can come from many different sources. It may be based on a competency model or it may be derived from your team based on the project request. Even in a project as simple as creating job aids, there should be defined business results and an expected performance. From these you can identify the skills or knowledge needed to achieve the results.

Defining the current performance of the audience and their current skills and knowledge can occur through surveys, interviews, or focus groups; with the use of job observation; or from formal assessments. Once these skills and knowledge have been identified, you can perform a gap analysis to determine what needs to be trained or provided. Figure 6.2 shows a simple format to use and an example.

Next you would identify how to deliver the information identified in the gap analysis. In our example, it is not a skill, but information that is needed. This information could be conveyed with a job aid, without the need for a class.

The situation in Figure 6.3 is a bit more complicated. Both skills and knowledge gaps are present. This would probably require a training solution.

The reaction question will define what you want the training experience to be like for participants. You may determine that, based on the learning step, the knowledge can be transferred by a manager in a sales meeting. You may also determine

FIGURE 6.2 Job Aid Example (simplified)

Expected Business Results: 10% increase in selling XX product category

Desired Performance	Current Performance	Gap
■ Properly discussing product specs and features to customers without use of specialist ■ Immediate response to customer questions	■ Can correctly communicate specs and features to customers only after having to contact a specialist for product details therefore delaying information to client	■ Immediate response of specs and features of current products to customers

Required Skills or Knowledge	Current Skills or Knowledge	Gap
■ Complete understanding of product specs ■ Complete understanding of product features	■ Basic product description and basics	■ Information on product specs and features

a class is needed. Either way, you will also define the atmosphere you want to create in the training or meeting. This will help you with the instructional design process, or aid in finding an appropriate vendor by including it as a requirement in your RFP.

This section of the design model is an audience assessment, which helps define what you want people to feel when they leave training. Many instructional designers skip this step or do not put in the thought and attention needed. The content, material, and experience in the classroom are all critical in designing an effective program. We have all been to training programs in which the content is important and will help us on the job, but the delivery is less than exciting. We sit and listen to the best of our ability, but just cannot seem to be engaged. We may have also been to training programs in which it was an exciting and motivational experience, but in the end we are not sure what we should have taken away and applied on the job.

FIGURE 6.3 Selling Skills Example (simplified)

Expected Business Results: 10% increase in sales

Desired Performance	Current Performance	Gap
■ Close more deals after quotes are extended	■ Deals lost due to lack of follow-up	■ Close more deals after quotes are extended
■ Position products to meet customer needs	■ Deals lost due to lack of positioning and communication on product benefits	■ Position products to meet customer needs

Required Skills or Knowledge	Current Skills or Knowledge	Gap
■ Ability to gather information on the decision-making process	■ Do not follow a process to gather information	■ A process to follow up and gather additional information
■ Ability to follow up in a timely fashion	■ Do not follow up in a timely fashion	■ A guideline for timely follow-up
■ To position products to meet customer needs, sales people need to: – Identify the customer situation – Describe the product features – Describe the product benefits – Use information to position benefits to meet customer needs	■ When they do follow up, ask if a decision has been made but do not continue the selling process	■ Skills and knowledge to gather information in order to properly position products

A basic requirement for all training is that it be interactive and fun. This is essential, but you will also have other items to define. Salespeople, more than typical learners, do not like to sit and listen for extended periods. They like to try what they are learning and apply it immediately. Salespeople are often competitive, so working in some games or activities that include competition can engage learners. See Chapter 8 for more ways to make things fun and interactive, but just remember to give your program thought and to define the experience.

Figure 6.4 is a simplified example of the needs analysis. Many of these areas can be broken down further, but this should give an overview of the process and results from each section.

Our example provides just a snapshot of how the process works. No doubt you will find much more going on in many of the steps. For example, defining the learning and enabling objectives and content will often require the use of subject matter experts. These experts can help define what is important to teach. This is especially true with product information. Experts on the products can provide the information on feature and benefits. Key salespeople or sales trainers can help identify methods and techniques for selling skills.

A FEW WORDS ON WORKING WITH SUBJECT MATTER EXPERTS

You most likely will have to work with SMEs in defining and building your program. This is often one of the toughest tasks in designing training. They are a wealth of information, but they are usually very busy and often their depth of knowledge is beyond what is needed for salespeople. SMEs often want to teach everyone everything that they know when it is not needed. You must remain in control of the content and ensure it is at the appropriate level of detail for your audience. Always refer back to your objectives and do not let SMEs lead you on their agenda.

A few other tips for working with SMEs:

- *Engage them at the right time.* Make certain the needed work is complete and the objectives are defined before engaging the SME. This will help keep them in check and ensure you are collecting what is needed. This is not to say that they will not offer some good ideas and that you should not be open to making adjustments, but do

FIGURE 6.4 Needs Analysis

1. ROI	Increase revenue to $550 million
2. Business results	To reach $550 million in sales we will increase sales revenue by 10%
3. Performance	To increase sales by 10%, salespeople need to: ■ Close more deals after quotes are extended ■ Position products to meet customer needs
4. Learning objectives	To close more deals after quotes are extended, salespeople need to: ■ Gather information on the decision-making process ■ Follow up in a timely fashion To position products to meet customer needs, salespeople need to: ■ Identify the customer situation ■ Describe the product features ■ Describe the product benefits ■ Use information to position benefits to meet customer needs

Enabling objectives (a few examples of the learning objectives broken down further)	By the end of this program, participants will be able to:
	
	■ Gather information on the decision-making process:
	    – Ask appropriate questions to identify the factors preventing a decision:
	        - Determine competitors
	        - Determine if pricing or service is the issue
	        - Use techniques to identify the decision makers
	        - Communicate with decision makers without negatively impacting the relationship with the contact
	        - Use positioning techniques to build a case
	
	■ Identify the customer situation:
	    – Use a set of questions and technique to better understand the needs and requirements of the customer
	
	■ Describe the product features:
	    – Explain the key elements of the product
	    – Describe the features that differentiate the product
	
	■ Describe the product benefits:
	    – Explain how product's key features can benefit customers
	    – Identify other benefits that can be derived from the product features

FIGURE 6.4 Needs Analysis *(continued)*

	■ Use information to position benefits to meet customer needs:
	  – Link information on the customer situation to key product benefits
	  – Explain the key benefits of competitors
	  – Position the benefits of our product against the competition

5. Reaction	During the session participants need to: ■ Be active ■ Work as teams ■ Use researching skills to apply learning, as they would on the job ■ Apply the skills to real life scenarios ■ Compete for prizes by using the skills and knowledge learned in the course ■ Use a theme to create energy

---

not let them dictate what is needed. Be confident that you have identified what you need from the SME.

■ *Remain in control of the content.* Do not just ask for their open opinion on what is needed and have them send you what they would teach. They may prepare more than you intend to teach and it will be harder to cut out details after the time and effort was put into defining what the SME felt was important. Lead the effort and ask the questions. They may want to teach how to build the bathtub when you only want to teach how to fill the bathtub. When looking for feedback, ask, "When filling the bathtub, is this accurate?"

■ *Be prepared when meeting.* Prepare a list of questions and information to gather for the meeting. An expert's time is often limited, so be sure to know what you are looking for. Send the questions ahead of time to allow them time to prepare. Many people do not like to be asked unexpected questions and will provide more complete answers if they have time to think ahead of time. Use follow-up meetings or e-mail to review the answers you have collected.

BUILDING A TRAINING PROGRAM

THE BUILDING PROCESS

If you have resources and time to build the program internally, then follow the process identified by your needs analysis to ensure that you build a course to meet your requirements. Your assessment should have identified what people are currently doing that needs to change in order to reach your desired business results. This information will be important in building your program (or for working with a vendor if you outsource the project, as discussed in Chapter 7).

THE INSTRUCTIONAL DESIGN AND DEVELOPMENT PROCESS

After the course and content is defined, you can begin the instructional design and material development process, which is covered in the right side of the process diagram. If you defined the course well, this part of the process should be easier to complete. While we outline this process here, Chapter 8 covers making sales training and meetings interactive and fun, and provides specific strategies and examples.

Reaction. It is time to identify techniques to create the environment you have defined. In other words, this is the time for brainstorming and creativity, which will set the context for identifying how to teach each learning objective (which we'll get to in a moment).

In our example, we identified that during the training session we wanted the participants to:

FIGURE 6.5 Course Design Model

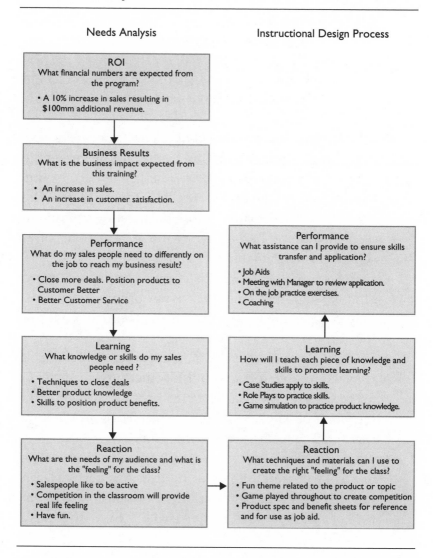

- Be active
- Work as teams
- Use researching skills to apply learning, as they would on the job
- Apply the skills to real-life scenarios

- Compete for prizes by using the skills and knowledge learned in the course
- Use a theme to create energy

Now we can brainstorm ways to achieve these ends. Some examples my colleagues and I have used include:

- *Create a theme based on the location of next year's sales meeting.* Many organizations hold annual sales meetings where the top performers are identified. Because this training is meant to drive sales, link it to the theme. One organization was to hold its annual meeting in Orlando, so their training had a Disney theme. The focus of all activities was on making it to Orlando.
- *Create activities in which teams work together to discover solutions.* People learn best from others, which not only enhances learning, but fosters teamwork back on the job.
- *Conduct real-life research.* If salespeople will have to research competitors and put together proposals to win business, have them conduct research as they would on the job. If possible, provide Internet access and provide less detail so teams can research solutions.
- *Offer real-life scenarios for participants to solve.* If available, use real scenarios both won and lost. An effective learning technique may be to use bids that were lost to a competitor and have the groups explore how they could have done better.
- *Build a competition throughout the program.* Have review "quizzes" or activities with reward points and prizes for the teams that accumulate the most points. Humans are by nature competitive, especially salespeople, so this is an excellent way to engage them. Many trainers avoid competition in the classroom out of fear that some participants will be disengaged, but this is usually not

the case with salespeople and a well-developed program will avoid any pitfalls.

Learning. We have looked at the program overall and what we want to achieve in the instructional design of the course. Once you have identified the theme and techniques that should flow throughout the program, you can begin to identify how to teach each objective. It's time to look at each individual piece of the program, though they should all build on the techniques and themes identified and create a cohesive program; don't use them here and there—work them throughout each objective. Designing a fun, interactive, and social learning experience will make your training more effective and increase the return on your investment (see Chapter 8).

While you consider the design of your training, let's pause to take a look at the history of training. I don't mean in the past 20, 30, or even 100 years. I mean looking back to how cavemen learned. Has anyone heard of a caveman sitting through a lecture? No. Even well into the 19th century, people learned by being active in the educational process. People have always learned by observing others and being part of the process. Our ancestors used storytelling; early artisans had apprentices; Socrates used questioning; each and every one of these used interaction and social learning as a core value. Somewhere along the timeline of history, the typical modern school system was developed and the notion of sitting in a room and listening to an instructor became the best method of learning. The truth is that people still learn best from being involved in the learning process and this process should be fun, interactive, and social. This is the key to unlocking the potential of your sales training. Technology and techniques may have changed over the years, but the main fundamentals of learning have not; people need to be active and engaged.

To be effective in designing a quality learning experience, you need a full understanding of the entire learning process.

This means always keeping the end objective in mind and designing everything in the program to achieve this objective. Most programs are designed as a lecture followed by an activity, but it doesn't have to be that way. You must identify creative ways to teach material to be truly effective. Too many instructional designers and trainers hold on to the notion that varying their techniques to meet all needs will lead to better learning. While they are not incorrect, it is important to broaden your view to look at the entire process.

A basic learning model states that learning a new skill includes three basic steps:

1. Tell
2. Show
3. Do

This often leads people to lecture, demonstrate, and have a hands-on activity, then repeat for the next objective.

Here's another way to look at this three-step learning model that will start to broaden your perspective:

1. Introduction to material
2. Guided practice
3. Individual practice

Notice how changing the terms we use can open our minds to different ways to achieve each step, to meet each objective.

Many instructional designers fall short by grouping all three steps into one and applying it to all learning styles. They believe Bob, who is an auditory learner, will learn during the lecture; Sue, who is a visual learner, will learn during the guided practice; and Dave, who is a kinesthetic learner, will learn during the individual practice. This attempt to shorten the learning process is inadequate. All learners, no matter their style, need to practice and apply new knowledge in order for it to become a skill. This is especially important in sales training. If you are teaching product knowledge, simply offering the knowledge in different ways will not lead to learning for everyone.

It is very important to keep in mind that people prefer to be introduced to new information in different ways, but true learning for everyone needs to include all three steps. Will Bob, the auditory learner, learn a new skill or be able to apply the knowledge after only hearing the information? No. He must also use this knowledge. The same is true for Sue and Dave as well; after being introduced to the material, they must use it for it truly to become a learned or usable skill.

Think back to high school or college. Did you truly absorb the information simply by sitting through a lecture, or did the true learning occur after taking notes and then applying the knowledge to a paper or assignment? The truth is that people learn and retain knowledge by applying it.

So your sales training should use a variety of techniques to introduce learners to the material, and they must apply this knowledge so it is truly learned. Because the objective of your sales training is not just to teach product knowledge, but to teach how to use that product knowledge to sell, you must do more than create a fun way to teach. You must see that the knowledge is then used so that they can take that knowledge and those skills back to the job.

Another result of teaching by lecture is that participants will need breaks from learning during an extended session. Many instructional designers and trainers use exercises and games, but these are often not implemented well and do not reinforce the learning objectives of the course. While it is true that taking participants away from the "traditional" type of class for interaction and fun can benefit learning, the problem is the traditional class. A traditional class is one focused on the instructor and involves long periods during which participants listen but do little else. If a course is designed well, it will include interaction and fun throughout and these activities will reinforce the objectives of the course. The participants will not feel like they are learning, but they really will be.

Here are a few additional tips for designing your course:

- *Link new information to existing information.* Everyone entering a classroom, regardless of age, has some information, preconceived ideas, or related knowledge. The key to a good design that aids retention is to tap into this knowledge and build upon it. It can be as simple as first referring to the current specs of a product, system used to enter orders, or way of selling, and then linking the new to the old. It can also include relating the information to something outside of work that is common among all participants. You can relate information to ordering at a fast-food restaurant or how to drive a car. The content and your audience will define the examples. The key is to know your audience and their knowledge and build.

- *Make sure you explain why this training is important to the learner.* The "what's in it for me" factor cannot be overlooked. People will be more engaged and receptive if they understand what they are learning, why they are learning it, and how it will positively impact them.

- *All learning, as all writing, should include an introduction, body, and review.* The old adage of "Tell them what you will tell them, tell them, and tell them what you told them" is as true now as ever. While this doesn't mean that you have to lecture, do let the learners know what you will cover and why, present the material, and then review to ensure understanding.

In our previous example on positioning products to meet customer needs, the learning objectives were that salespeople would:

- Identify the customer situation
- Describe the product features
- Describe the product benefits
- Use information to position benefits to meet customer needs

Figure 6.6 shows a sample high-level design of a section to teach these objectives which is linked to our course design concepts.

Note that in Figure 6.6 there was no lecture, but the key objectives of having a technique to define the customer situation and identify features and benefits were achieved. We included the elements of the class we identified earlier, including activities, teamwork, real-life scenarios, research, competition, and the Disney theme. We could have lectured on a process to identify the customer situation, the features and benefits of the products, and how to link the two, but instead used social and fun activities that had participants applying the information at every step. Participants will remember the activity and how they created the answers when back on the job.

Performance. The final step in the instructional design process is to ensure that participants can perform the skills and use the knowledge back on the job. This is one of the hardest areas to achieve because once participants leave the classroom you are no longer in control of their actions. Management support can aid in the process, but still you cannot control these interactions. You should focus on what you can control.

Using application and real-life scenarios will help, but one other option is the use of job aids. Look for ways in which you can provide a quick reference to participants. In the example in Figure 6.6 we used a job aid to help define the customer situation that could be used on the job. We also had participants use their existing resources to identify features and create benefits, which again can be replicated on the job.

FIGURE 6.6 High-level Design

Objective	Method
Identify the customer situation	■ Distribute a worksheet to aid in defining a customer situation. This would include key information to collect. ■ Quickly review the main points to ensure understanding. ■ Hand out a scenario of a customer situation. ■ Have groups define the situation using the aid. ■ Review the results and identify missed information. ■ Hold a discussion on what information was gathered and why it was important.
Describe the product features	■ Discuss the difference between features and benefits. ■ Give each group the same or a different product (depending on your product mix). ■ Have the groups use the resources they have on the job to list the product features. ■ Review the answers and correct any mistakes.
Describe the product benefits	■ Have groups go back to their lists and define the customer benefits to each feature. ■ Review the answers; have other groups give input into possible benefits. ■ Further discuss why benefits are more important than features to the customer. Example: Features of a printer include: ■ Prints 20 pages per minute ■ Allows duplexing (two-sided printing) ■ 500-page paper tray ■ A proprietary technology that allows 20% more pages from an toner Benefits: ■ Prints faster to limit time waiting for a job to be complete. ■ You can print on two sides and not have to print and then copy to achieve two-sided materials. ■ The paper tray is the largest on the market and you will not need to fill it as often. ■ You will spend less money on toner refills because you will have more prints.
Use information to position benefits to meet customer needs	■ Have the groups use the customer situation definition from the first exercise and the features and benefits defined in the second exercise to prepare a sales presentation. ■ Have sales managers visit the classroom for the presentations and score on meeting the criteria of solving the customer needs and positioning the products.

FIGURE 6.6 High-level Design *(continued)*

- Award 100 Disney dollars to the highest-scoring group, 50 to the second, 25 to the third, and 10 to all groups (this rewards everyone for their hard work).
- Discuss with the sales managers and class why some were better. Flip-chart the key learning points.

One other method that can be derived from the example is to type up, or have participants type up, the list of features and benefits they developed. They can begin creating documentation that can be used as a reference in the future. This technique can be very effective because participants created their own material, which can be used in management classes to identify best practices in leading and coaching, or many other applications. The sense of ownership frequently leads to future use of such material.

MATERIAL DEVELOPMENT

Creation of materials needs as much attention as the design phase because you do not want to lose the impact of your great ideas in the delivery. One common mistake is thinking that the larger the participant guide and the more information provided, the better the course. This is not at all true. The most effective sales manager class I created had a participant guide that included about 20 pages. It consisted of four models, two cases, four worksheets, and ten blank pages. The participants created their own materials on what they felt were the most important takeaways. In the sample module in the previous section, the only needed materials for a participant guide were the job aid to define the customer situation, the case, and blank pages to take notes and complete activities. The truth is that if you have creative activities, substantially fewer materials will be required. Time will still be required to create job aids and cases, but there will be no need for pages of information. Remember to put effort in the creation of materials and present them in a professional manner.

SUMMARY

This chapter contains a lot of information and the process may appear to be overwhelming. The process will differ from organization to organization and project to project, of course, and the level of detail will obviously be greater in the development of a six-week program than in developing job aids. The important thing to remember is to complete your due diligence in defining your project before building and once you begin building, refer back to your overall objectives and the themes and techniques to ensure everything is working together to a common outcome.

The most important takeaways from this chapter are an understanding of the process, the intent of each step, and what should be produced or completed at the end of the step. To make sure you have a complete understanding of the process of building a training program, and that you can use this process in any situation, I suggest copying the outline below and then reviewing this chapter and adding what you feel are the most important learning points for each bullet. Be sure to include the intent of the step and what should be produced or completed. Record what you feel is important to remember and how you will complete each step in your project. Keep your outline handy and refer to it whenever you begin a new project.

1. Define the initiative
   - Form a project team
   - Conduct a needs assessment
     a) Define your required outcomes and objectives

   b) Complete an analysis of current performance, knowledge, and skills
   c) Complete a gap analysis of required versus current

2. Build a training program
   - Ensure you have adequately completed the needs assessment
   - Define your objectives
   - Work with subject matter experts to gather content
   - Design your course to be educational while being fun and interactive
   a) Follow the basic design process
   b) Apply adult learning concepts

This technique of putting information into your own words is a very effective way to aid the learning process and another example of how you can build activities into your program that will ensure learning. Completing the outline will help solidify your learning and aid your retention. This technique can be used in any training program and is a great exercise at the end of the program.

Remember, people retain information that they create and when it is in their own words. Simply reading this chapter is just consuming information, but creating your own outline and deciding how you can use the information leads to true learning.

ADDITIONAL READING

- Dave Meier, *The Accelerated Learning Handbook*
- Mel Silberman, *101 Ways to Make Training Active*

CHAPTER 7

Making an Outsourcing Decision

MICHAEL ROCKELMANN, Driving Results, formerly of United Airlines, Dade Behring, and CDW

You have decided to offer a new training program. The next decision, to buy it or build it internally, is one of the oldest and toughest in the training profession. This truly strategic decision is based on factors including, but not limited to: time, resources, money, expertise, and audience acceptance. If you decide to buy, more questions must be answered: What do we need to outsource? What supplier do we use? Do we use off-the-shelf or customized training? Do we use internal or external trainers? Even if you decide to build internally, there are still many questions to answer: Who are the content experts? Do I have a selling model? How do I design the course? Who is the best trainer?

The buy-or-build decision is not an easy one to make, but this chapter offers you information and tools to decide and to effectively implement an outsourcing solution. Let's start with defining the initiative and making the buy-or-build decision, before moving on to basic supplier sourcing and management techniques later in this chapter.

DEFINING THE INITIATIVE AND MAKING A BUY-OR-BUILD DECISION

The process for outsourcing starts exactly the same way as the process for building your training program as discussed in Chapter 6. In considering whether to buy training, however, your definition of the initiative must include an internal assessment of resources. As with building a program, you first form your team and conduct a needs assessment (see Chapter 6). If you find that you cannot complete the needs assessment, then you have identified your need for outside help.

CONDUCTING AN INTERNAL RESOURCE ASSESSMENT

After completing your needs analysis, the next step is to conduct an internal assessment of resources to determine whether you should look outside for a vendor, build internally, or use a combination of both. Sometimes you may need help in only one area.

A recent survey of members of the Professional Society for Sales and Marketing Training conducted by Renie McClay asked about outsourcing.

Do you ever buy training products or services from outside vendors?

Yes, products (training programs, customized programs)	87%
Yes, services (assessment, consulting, facilitation)	77%
I never buy products and services from the outside	0%

When do you purchase products and services from the outside versus developing your own?

Tight deadline	42%
Don't have the expertise internally	87%
Want a neutral viewpoint	23%

Insufficient resources   61%
Other (Don't want to reinvent the wheel,
    Useful for benchmarking,
    Specialized technical training,
    External provider has a best practice)

So we see that all companies that responded to the survey outsource at least some tasks, and well over three-quarters of companies outsource at least some services, if not all of the process. These results also provide some insight into the main reasons for outsourcing. The two most critical reasons include not having the internal expertise (or a vendor having better expertise) and not having the resources available.

Your internal assessment will address these and other criteria. The questions in Figure 7.1 will aid you in your internal assessment, and the answers will be a starting point to making your buy-or-build decision.

There is a lot of information to consider in making your final decision. Having clear-set outcomes and objectives will help you make the decision.

MAKING YOUR DECISION

With your internal assessment completed, you should have an understanding of the outcomes and objectives for the program, as well as which tasks can be completed internally and which ones need to be outsourced.

You can now begin the task of making your decision. If the decision is to outsource, this information will flow into the requirements of your request for proposal (RFP). If you will build internally, you have the base information to build your program.

You can outsource any or all of the four basic areas of building a training program—needs analysis, identification of the content, course design, and delivery. The chart in Figure 7.2

FIGURE 7.1 Outsourcing Internal Assessment

Question	Yes/No
Can you complete the entire Needs Assessment?	_____
Are funds available to outsource a section or the entire project?	_____
Is there a tight deadline?	_____
Is the content already available from a vendor, or do you need outside expertise?	_____
Do you have internal resources with the skills and time to build a training program?	_____
Do you have internal trainers with the expertise and skills to deliver the training?	_____
Will your audience accept an outside program? Will it fit the culture?	_____
Will your audience accept an outside trainer?	_____

will help you identify which sections of the project should be outsourced or which ones can be completed internally.

There is no simple answer to what you should outsource; your answers to the questions in Figure 7.2 should paint a picture of what outside resources are required. If the answer to the first question is no, you should consider outsourcing the needs analysis. You can then make decisions on building the program after the analysis is complete. When funds are not available and you cannot build a case for funds or locate internal resources with the expertise, you may have to consider forgoing the project or delivering a different solution. If forgoing the project is not an option, it is important to communicate your concerns to the stakeholders and make clear that the appropriate expertise is not available internally.

The remaining questions in Figure 7.2 will help you clarify which portions of the project should be outsourced. You have many options for what to outsource and what to complete internally.

No matter which decision you make, the completed internal assessment will provide the detailed information to build

FIGURE 7.2 Outsourcing Decision Making

Question	Yes/No	Consider . . .
Can you complete the entire Needs Assessment?	_____	If no, outsource at least the analysis to a consultant or training firm.
Are funds available to outsource a section or the entire project?	_____	If no, build a case for funds or locating additional internal resources with the needed skills.
Is there a tight deadline?	_____	If yes, an outside vendor can complete in less time or may have an off-the-shelf course.
Is the content already available from a vendor, or do you need outside expertise?	_____	If yes, consider outsourcing so you do not spend time and money reinventing material. You may be able to purchase the course and teach internally.
Do you have internal resources with the skills and time to build a training program?	_____	If no, outsource for the expertise and to allow internal resources to focus on the other tasks.
Do you have internal trainers with the expertise and skills to deliver the training?	_____	If no, consider outsourcing the delivery aspect of the training.
Will your audience accept an outside program? Will it fit the culture?	_____	If no, build internally if you have the resources; if not, buy and customize an off-the-shelf program.
Will your audience accept an outside trainer?	_____	If no, outsource the needed parts of the project but hold on the trainer and deliver internally.

whichever case is required and present the finding to the stakeholders.

You will have outsourcing options for each area of your internal assessment.

Needs analysis. This one is simple; you either complete it internally or outsource it.

Content gathering. When the needed content already exists, it can save time and money to purchase an off-the-shelf program. An off-the-shelf program that is designed in a way that will meet all of your objectives and provide an acceptable design can be purchased and used as is. If the content is specific to your organization, then you can outsource the content gathering. If the off-the-shelf content needs to be customized, you can outsource this process and work with the vendor to have an appropriate course.

The survey by Renie McClay mentioned earlier asked why organizations decide to customize an off-the-shelf program instead of building internally from scratch. Here are their responses.

Factor	Most Important Criteria
Time	19%
Budget	13%
Expertise	26%
Quality	19%
Technical issues	3%
Other comments	Political need to make it have the company's brand
	Relevance to our audience needs
	Fit with all of our established programs/culture
	Internal resources (in addition to budget)
	Intellectual property ownership, copyrights, etc.
	Suitability of solution to meet business problem

Course design. The decision to buy or build the course design will be heavily influenced by the choice from the content gathering. A course you purchase that meets your design requirements can be used as is. If you want to change the design to be more appropriate for your audience, you can do this internally or outsource the process. For example, you may decide your audience will want more interactivity or more relevant case studies. You may want more of a mix of activities than the vendor has built into the program, you may want to build a theme into the training, or you may want to include visits from key internal resources during the course. (Some of these ideas are discussed in Chapter 8.)

Course delivery. This is one of the more overlooked aspects of the training process. Salespeople are often a tough audience and it is important for the trainer to have a full understanding of their job and the nuances. The instructor's credibility can make or break even the best course. In some organizations, for specific topics, an outside trainer will not have the impact of an internal trainer. If the salespeople feel that an outsider who has not been in their position will not understand the real-life process, he or she will not be effective. On the other hand, some organizations or topics may lend more credibility to using an outside trainer. If an internal trainer is trying to present a new selling model that the audience knows he or she has not implemented in the field, the trainer will not have credibility.

It is important to have a salesperson on the team when conducting the needs assessment to represent the audience and to provide insight into who should teach the program.

The time frame is another consideration with the choice of instructors. If you have a tight deadline and the completion of the training will require more trainers than are available internally, you will need to find a middle ground. You may need to immerse the outside instructor into your selling environment and build the course to counteract any loss of credibility. You may also consider pairing an outside trainer with a senior salesperson to teach the course. This will provide the content and training expertise, as well as the real-life examples for the participants' environment. If you choose this route, make sure you leave enough time to train both the external trainer on your environment and the internal resource on the training course and objectives.

THE BUYING PROCESS

Whether you decided to outsource the entire creation of a six-week initial sales training or to look for a single person to help build job aids for a four-hour course, you will have to manage the outsourcing process to bring the project to a success. A small project may call for a simpler process; you may include the search for suppliers, a request for proposal, and a request for quote into one step. You may also send the request to only one or two people or firms. No matter the size of the project or process, the concepts and information in the steps are the important takeaways; this information is key to ensuring success.

According to a survey conducted by the Outsourcing Institute, the top ten factors for successful outsourcing are:

1. Understanding company goals and objectives
2. Strategic vision and plan
3. Selecting the right vendor
4. Ongoing management of the relationships
5. A properly structured contract
6. Open communication with affected individual/groups
7. Senior executive support and involvement
8. Careful attention to personal issues
9. Near-term financial justification
10. Use of outside expertise

Of the items listed above, we discussed those related to defining the vision and plan, including the affected group and top executives in Chapter 6. Now let's look at the remaining items. It is important that all of these items are defined and followed during your project.

DEFINING YOUR REQUIREMENTS

The first step in the buying process is to define your requirements. Requirements will fall into three categories:

1. Supplier requirements
2. Internal requirements
3. Project requirements

Supplier requirements. The following list of what to look for in a supplier may not include all the factors you feel are important, or may include some that do not apply to your situation, but these are the basic areas considered in most situations:

- *Size.* Do they have the resources to deliver your requirements?
- *Years in business.* Do they have experience and are they credible?
- *Expertise.* Do they offer the expertise for your objectives, selling model, industry, etc.?
- *Past clients.* Do they have experience with other clients like your organization? Do they have a strong customer base?

Internal requirements. This list includes organizational-specific information that will aid the supplier in responding to an RFP or be used to make a choice on suppliers:

- *Selling model.* Do you have a specific selling model a supplier must work with? This may influence you choice of suppliers.
- *Environment/culture.* What is your environment or culture and how will this impact the choice of a supplier? Are there specific organizational practices that must be communicated or addressed?

Project requirements. This list includes all items that define your project and outline the outcomes, objectives, and work:

- *Project outcomes and objectives.* What are you trying to accomplish and what do participants need to learn?
- *Scope of work.* What tasks will be expected from the supplier? You need to be specific about what the supplier will complete and not complete.
- *Time frame.* When is delivery expected? When must the course be ready for delivery? If delivering, when is the last class to be delivered?
- *Budget.* This is for internal purposes only, but you must be clear on the budget for the entire process including delivery.

Of course the process of evaluating suppliers is not completely objective; there is a subjective aspect to every evaluation. You will often give more credence to a supplier you've used in the past or to one referred by a colleague. You may run into suppliers with which you learn during the RFP process that you have a personality or cultural conflict, and thus have a difficult working relationship. It is acceptable to have a subjective aspect to the evaluation. You may even choose to include some of these as your requirements.

In the survey in Figure 7.3, respondents were asked to rate different criteria regarding their consideration in making a decision. The results showed that there are many considerations, both objective and subjective.

LOCATING APPROPRIATE SUPPLIERS— INITIAL RESEARCH

Next you will want to identify suppliers who meet your overall requirements. You can locate suppliers by talking to colleagues in other companies, researching through the

FIGURE 7.3 Criteria Considerations

Percentage indicates number of respondents selecting:	1 Never a consideration	2 Rarely a consideration	3 Sometimes a consideration	4 Often a consideration	5 Always a consideration
1. Recommendation from someone outside your organization	0%	0%	29%	55%	16%
2. Recommendation from someone in your organization	0%	0%	19%	68%	13%
3. Industry experience	0%	6%	19%	45%	29%
4. Price	0%	10%	19%	39%	32%
5. Project-specific expertise	0%	3%	10%	42%	45%
6. Size of vendor organization	6%	52%	16%	26%	0%
7. Seeing example of their work	0%	0%	7%	34%	59%
8. Client list	3%	19%	42%	23%	13%
9. Intangibles (attitude, flexibility, rapport, responsiveness)	0%	0%	10%	52%	39%

Internet, using industry or professional organizations for resources, or finding suppliers that have been used for other projects within your organization. The outcome of this step should be to have a list of suppliers to send your RFP.

There is no hard number to define how many companies to research but typically you will research 10 to 15 suppliers with an eye toward narrowing the results to no more than five to which to send out the RFP. In some cases, sending the RFP may have already been completed. You may have a few suppliers that have been used in the past or with whom you have a relationship. If you are in a specific industry or geographic region, there may be a few top suppliers. In any case, make sure you have a variety of suppliers, including a few new ones, so you can complete your due diligence and gain various perspectives.

In narrowing the list of suppliers, perform a high-level review to ensure that each meets your supplier requirements and can address your project requirements. This can be completed by reviewing the supplier's Web site, having a conversation with the supplier, or by sending an official request for information (RFI). A high-level review of your project and the expected outcomes, as well as the basic work you are expecting to have the supplier complete, is essential.

Reviewing up to 15 suppliers may seem daunting, but in practice it can be a quick process. You may find from researching Web sites or having a quick conversation that many suppliers who made your list do not meet your requirements. It is helpful to create a checklist like the one in Figure 7.4 to use for rating each supplier.

CREATING A REQUEST FOR PROPOSAL

With your list of potential suppliers narrowed to around five, you will develop an RFP to learn more about the capabilities of the suppliers and what they suggest as a solution to

FIGURE 7.4 Supplier Checklist

Criteria	Expected Response	Supplier 1	Supplier 2	Suppler 3
Supplier requirements	_____	_____	_____	_____
Size	_____	_____	_____	_____
Years in business	_____	_____	_____	_____
Content expertise	_____	_____	_____	_____
Industry experience	_____	_____	_____	_____
Past clients	_____	_____	_____	_____
Project requirements	_____	_____	_____	_____
Experience with our expected outcome	_____	_____	_____	_____
Expertise in our needed services	_____	_____	_____	_____

your requirements. This document should be complete and detailed because your requirements set forth need to be clear so all suppliers respond appropriately. Putting the time and effort into the RFP up front will aid in the contracting steps and in the creation of a statement of work.

There are many books and courses on how to complete the sections of an RFP, but let's look at a few key areas. If you need additional help in creating the RFP, you may want to consider additional resources. Your organization may have a set format for the RFP, but likely includes the sections listed in Figure 7.5.

EVALUATING POTENTIAL SUPPLIERS

Typically the process of evaluating potential suppliers will include these six steps:

1. Send RFP to suppliers.
2. Discuss with supplier to clarify.

FIGURE 7.5 RFP Format

1. Introduction

a. Organization overview

An overview of your company, services or products, and departmental information, if necessary.

b. Project overview

This should include outcomes and high-level description of work to be completed.

c. Evaluation process

This section will include:
- Process
- Schedule
- Contact information

You may include a demonstration or presentation as part of your process; some firms prefer to receive a written RFP response and then request a presentation from a few firms. This will depend on your needs and preferences.

d. Guidelines

- Confidentiality
- Use of this RFP
- Assumption of costs (supplier assumes costs to respond)
- Other legal details

2. Requirements or requested services

a. Internal requirements

Taken from what you outlined in the previous step; should be very detailed.

b. Project requirements

Taken from what you outlined in the previous step; should be very detailed. What are you asking them to complete?

3. Response format

The response may be requested in a written form, presentation, or both. Make sure you define how you prefer to have the suppliers respond.

a. Organizational overview

Supplier should give an overview of their company including size, years in business, clients, address, contacts, etc.

b. Services

Supplier should outline their mission, vision, and types of services provided.

c. Qualifications

Supplier should state, based on their understanding of the requested services, why they are qualified.

d. Proposed solution

Supplier should state their understanding of the requirements and how they propose to meet those requirements.

FIGURE 7.5 RFP Format *(continued)*

e. Pricing and payment terms	This is an optional section; some companies prefer to have a separate request for quote (RFQ). You may ask for pricing and terms in the step if desired.
f. Additional information or considerations	This section provides the supplier an area to make any additional comments on their services or qualifications.

3. Receive responses or hold presentations.
4. Evaluate responses.
5. If not done previously, request a presentation to review the response.
6. Create a final list.

After sending out the RFP, you will want to create an evaluation form. This form should look similar to the one used when locating potential suppliers but include all of the requirements and more detail (see Figure 7.6). It is often helpful to create a separate sheet for each supplier to record and rate their responses and then have an overview sheet to summarize the ratings of each supplier (see Figure 7.7). After creating the evaluation form, be sure that all project team members who will be included in the evaluation understand the form and how to use it.

After you evaluate the RFP responses, you should have the potential supplier pool limited to your top three. One supplier may stand out and make the final decision easy, but often there are multiple suppliers that can meet your need. This is where the subjective aspect to the decision-making process comes into play. You may have a gut feeling about one company, or find one to be extremely easy to work with. Whatever your feelings, you should be able to rank your top few.

FIGURE 7.6 Supplier Evaluation Form

Criteria	Expected Response	Supplier 1 Response	Rating 1–5
Supplier requirements	_____	_____	_____
Size	_____	_____	_____
Years in business	_____	_____	_____
Content expertise	_____	_____	_____
Industry experience	_____	_____	_____
Past clients	_____	_____	_____
Project requirements	_____	_____	_____
Experience with our expected outcome	_____	_____	_____
Expertise in our needed services	_____	_____	_____
Fee vs. budget	_____	_____	_____

You might consider inviting more than one supplier to the contracting phase to ensure a speedy process in case the contract cannot be finalized with your top choice.

Again, this part of the process may vary by organization, and your company may have an established process.

The top ten factors in vendor selection, according to the Outsourcing Institute's annual survey, show that at times the final deciding factor can be one outside your requirements. The results listed these as the top ten factors in vendor selection:

1. Commitment to quality
2. Price
3. References/reputation
4. Flexible contract terms
5. Scope of resources
6. Additional value-added capabilities
7. Cultural match

FIGURE 7.7 Overview Sheet

Criteria	Expected Response	Supplier 1 Rating	Supplier 2 Rating	Supplier 3 Rating
Supplier requirements	_____	_____	_____	_____
Size	_____	_____	_____	_____
Years in business	_____	_____	_____	_____
Content expertise	_____	_____	_____	_____
Industry experience	_____	_____	_____	_____
Past clients	_____	_____	_____	_____
Project requirements	_____	_____	_____	_____
Experience with our expected outcome	_____	_____	_____	_____
Expertise in our needed services	_____	_____	_____	_____

8. Existing relationship
9. Location
10. Other

CREATING A CONTRACT

Now that you have selected a supplier or suppliers who can meet your outcomes and requirements, you must create a contract for the work. The contract must include two sections: the legal considerations and a statement of work (SOW). Most contracts only include the legal language, but the SOW is important because it will outline, in detail, what is to be completed, how it will be completed, and the due dates. The more detailed the process, the less opportunity for problems to occur during the implementation phase. It is important to approach this part of the process with a sense of urgency.

There are many contract templates available and your organization should have a standard. Never use the contract from the supplier; always use your own. When completing the contract, remember that this is a prenuptial agreement and not a love letter; you need to be tough and outline all expectations in detail. One of the most common and costly mistakes is trying to be nice and accommodating to "start the relationship on a positive note." This thinking can cost you in the long term and you must outline all expectations to ensure the best for your organization.

Even if you are purchasing an off-the-shelf program, be sure to be thorough in the contracting. It is important to detail what can be changed or customized and what must remain intact. Ensure there is a clear understanding of the copyright and ownership of the material. Cover yourself so that if you do make changes or use the material on your own, there are no legal implications. If the supplier will be customizing an off-the-shelf program to meet your needs, you will want to have a more detailed and complete SOW. In this situation you should proceed as if the supplier was completing the entire project.

The SOW section of the contract must be derived from requirements and outline in detail the work to be completed. Performance should also be outlined and it is critical that it is linked to SOW. It must include:

- Internal resources responsibilities
- Supplier responsibilities
- Deliverables and dates
- Payments, linked to deliverables if possible
- Delivery and communication approach
- Project structure and timeline
- Performance standards, including rewards for exceeding or consequences of falling short
- Any metrics used to evaluate performance (meeting dates or course evaluation results)
- Dispute resolution process
- Change control process
- Copyright and ownership of materials

BRINGING THE SUPPLIER ON BOARD

Once the vendor is selected and the contract—including a statement of work—is signed, you are finally ready to get to work. It is important to get the project started off well and maintain the relationship throughout. The first key is to begin the project with the vendor with an appropriate kickoff meeting. Treating this meeting with importance will encourage a more productive relationship. Many companies view bringing a supplier on board as simply bringing in the hired help and do not spend the time or dedicate the energy to making this an important moment. Put in the time and effort. Treat this supplier as you would a new employee. Make it a big deal and put some planning into the process.

Include all team members in the kickoff meeting and make sure there is a show of executive support. Make the vendor feel welcome.

There are two main areas of focus for the meeting: people issues and business issues. For the people issues, introduce everyone on the team and define their roles. Review the company history, culture, policy, procedures, and so on. Introduce the vendor to key people in the company and department, not just the project team. This can include the accounts payable department or whoever will be involved in documenting hours or expenses. This can be very important and help build a strong relationship. Also think of daily logistical items or computer issues—anything and anyone who may be a key person to know—and communicate these in the meeting. The people side of the meeting should ensure that the vendor feels welcome and comfortable in your company.

The business issues are also important to review as you kick off the project. You should have spent a lot of time and energy outlining these in the statement of work, but you should review them again at the meeting. Be sure to cover roles and responsibilities, set clear expectations, and review critical milestones, dates, and the communication process. There are many other details that can be reviewed, but the key is to make certain that everyone has a clear picture of what needs to be completed.

The results of the survey conducted by Renie McClay provide some good insight into what you should do and how to avoid some pitfalls.

Tips:
- Provide your supplier with very specific requirements and go to see some examples of their work. Watch a workshop they present before making a decision.
- Make sure they clearly understand the objectives of your project before you begin.
- The vendor should research and know about the business.
- Make them a partner. Invite them into your culture.
- Always have an internal point person who is held accountable for the performance of the outside resource.
- Make your expectations clear, and have written roles and responsibilities, deliverables, and timelines.
- Have a project kickoff meeting so expectations are clear from the start of the project. Have a detailed project plan to include resources required from your company as well as the vendors and deadlines.
- Always identify, up front, who will own the product. If you pay for the development, you should own it, *not* the vendor.
- Don't be afraid to ask for financials with small firms when large investments are being made.
- If you are asking for something original, ask for references to show that the vendor can produce something other than a retooled version of their existing product.

In bringing the supplier on board, and during the entire engagement, do not forget to refer back to the design process presented in the previous chapter. Depending on what section of the project you are outsourcing, the vendor may help you identify the information, but always use and refer to the training design process detailed in Chapter 6. As shown in Figure 7.8, make sure to define each step and build upon it as you move forward.

MONITORING THE PERFORMANCE OF THE SUPPLIER

The last step in the supplier management process is to monitor the supplier's performance and act appropriately to ensure you receive the solution and quality you expect. If you have completed all of the previous steps well, you will have defined and communicated your outcomes, requirements, and expectations to the supplier multiple times and in multiple formats. This should help ensure that you receive what is outlined, but the truth is that there is always a chance that things may go off track. Your SOW should have outlined how performance would be monitored, and now it's time to put that plan into action.

While managing the relationship and performance during the development of the program, complete the following steps:

1. Monitor performance against the statement of work on a regular basis.
2. Review the performance and clearly state your expectations.
3. Meet on a regular basis to review progress. Be open and honest. Give both positive and negative feedback.
4. Recognize superior performance or going beyond expectations as you would for an internal employee.
5. If the vendor is not living up to expectations, be sure to communicate this and propose a solution.

FIGURE 7.8 Course Design Process

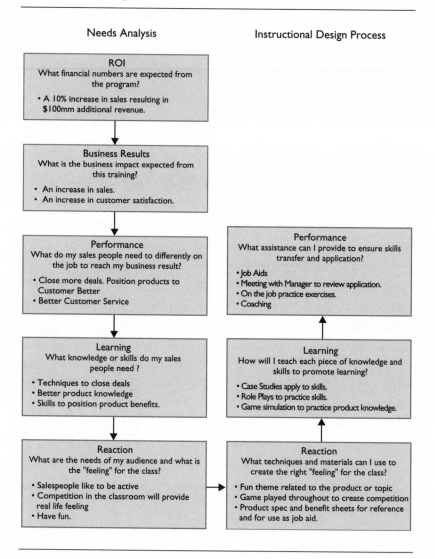

6. If the vendor is not living up to expectations and will not change to meet expectations as defined, don't be scared to terminate the contract. Point out where they are falling short according to the statement of work. It is better to end a nonproductive relationship than keep it going.

The final step in any project is ending the relationship or closing out the contract. If it was a successful project, be sure to credit the supplier's work. When ending the project be sure to receive all of the information collected and materials produced by the vendor.

SUMMARY

Now you've seen the specific steps and templates that can be used to help determine what to outsource and how to outsource effectively. Remember that you must complete your due diligence in each step of the process, and be sure to follow the course design model discussed in this chapter and Chapter 6. Define your program and requirements before discussing the project with suppliers, and ensure the supplier is following a detailed process to meet your objectives. Remember the basic process for outsourcing offered in this chapter:

- Define your requirements.
- Locate appropriate suppliers.
- Create a request for proposal.
- Evaluate potential suppliers.
- Create the contract.
- Bring the supplier on board.
- Manage the performance of the supplier.

To make sure you have a complete understanding of the above process, and that you can use it in any situation, I suggest copying this outline into a document, reviewing the chapter, and adding what you feel are the most important learning points for each bullet. Note what is important and how you will complete the step in your project. Keep this outline handy so you can refer to it whenever you begin a new project.

CHAPTER 8

Making Sales Training Fun, Interactive, and Educational

RENIE MCCLAY, Sales Training Utopia, formerly of Kraft, Novartis, Pactiv Corp.

The intention of this chapter is to focus on defining how to reach the learning objectives while limiting the amount of instructor lecture time. We will give you ideas of how to include fun and interactive ways to teach material. Let's be clear here. This is *not* for the purpose of having fun in a class (heaven forbid!), but for the purpose of keeping learners engaged and maximizing their attention and learning. I will admit I have more fun if things in a class are lively (both as an instructor and as a participant). If you object to the concept of "fun" in training (it is an "f" word, after all), please substitute the word engaging. I am not looking for reasons to bring a hula hoop into the classroom. Is it possible there could actually be a business purpose for using interaction to keep learners engaged? Let's stay open to that.

In Chapter 6, a learning process model was presented with three steps:

1. Introduction to material
2. Guided practice
3. Individual practice

Because the two steps involving practice tend to be more interactive and involve application of the knowledge and skills, this chapter will offer techniques to make the introduction to the material more fun and interactive, but it will also offer some ideas on how to vary the methods of practice.

The introduction to the material does not have to be one-way communication from the instructor, as many people believe. The idea that participants cannot learn or understand unless new information is first explained to them is fundamentally wrong. People acquire new knowledge and skills every day, and they do this through their own research and experience.

Think back to a class you took in high school or college, or even a professional course you have attended in the last few years. My guess is that it included a good amount of up-front lecture. What do you remember? How effective was this class at teaching you a new knowledge or skill? You may remember little from the class.

Now think about the first time you used Word or Excel, or even the last time you purchased a new car or a DVD player. How did you learn to use Word or Excel, or learn the features of your new car or DVD player? Did you attend a class? Probably not. We learn by trial and error, or by using such resources as manuals, the Internet, relatives or friends, and help menus. We had a reason to learn and used our skills and abilities to overcome the challenges. This is how we should approach training classes and meetings. People are capable; they learn new skills and achieve their goals every day. Do not sell them short in the classroom.

The first key to making your sales training more effective is to use a variety of techniques to introduce learners to the material. And we must not forget to have them apply their newfound knowledge so it sticks with them. Remember, the objective of your sales training is not to teach product knowledge, but to teach how to use product knowledge to sell.

Don't just create a fun way to share the information, but ensure it will then be used back on the job. Do not forget the application of knowledge in your attempt to be creative in presenting the material.

We know people are more engaged when training is fun and interactive. Humans (and most salespeople) are social beings, so the social aspect should be included in the classroom. This chapter offers creative techniques to make training more interactive, social, and fun while still being educational. These techniques can be used in any stage of the learning cycle. Many can be an alternative to lectures, while others are great ways to have fun when offering guided or individual practice.

THE BENEFITS OF MAKING LEARNING FUN AND INTERACTIVE

Making your program fun and interactive will not just provide a more enjoyable experience for the participants, but it will lead to greater learning. The truth is that we learn best by being active. According to adult learning principles, we learn by processing information, linking it to previously held knowledge, and by applying the new knowledge. All of this is also more effective in a social setting. So designing your training to include fun activities and social interaction will lead to a more successful and educational program.

LEARNING STYLES AND THEIR EFFECT ON LEARNING

I am an experiential learner. Becky Stewart-Gross referred to this as a "learn by doing" person in Chapter 1. I know as trainers we should stay neutral to learning styles and include them all. I must confess being a kinesthetic learner is frequently a pain. Most college classes were not taught for my learning style. (We now know many corporate classes are not, either!) I found out for myself that I needed to highlight the text, develop my own outline of the chapters, have someone quiz me, and attend all labs available. All around me, people were attending lectures and remembering what was taught. My sister breezed through college with little studying. As a result of attending lectures, she answered the questions correctly on the test. I thought she was really smart. Today, I know she *is* really smart, but I can be more lenient with myself, knowing that I can get to the same place; I just have to do it in a different way. Not until I got into training did I understand the larger learning picture. I found it very interesting learning about the audio and visual learners and then contrasting those with my own hands-on learning style.

So, I definitely have a personal conviction about interaction in a classroom. Showing text on PowerPoint slides will help some people in the audience. A verbal explanation will help others. A great model will help others. But the key is that an activity will solidify the learning for all types.

Some of the interactive methods for training in this chapter will be familiar to you. Hopefully some will be new ideas or a reminder of something you have heard before. I wish I could tell you I was the inventor of these awesome methods. Many of them I have seen over my last 17 years of training. I was fortunate enough to have been introduced to the Professional Society of Sales and Marketing Training early in my career. I have seen many training methods demonstrated there at national conferences and at sales trainer trainings over the years. I give my peers much of the credit for these methods. As we do in training, we see something, tweak it, pass it on, and all of a sudden there are many variations and they are all good and work. Thanks to my peers for generously sharing their methods and successes over the years.

FIGURE 8.1 Energy Levels

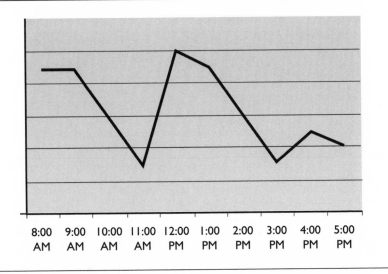

| 8:00 | 9:00 | 10:00 | 11:00 | 12:00 | 1:00 | 2:00 | 3:00 | 4:00 | 5:00 |
| AM | AM | AM | AM | PM | PM | PM | PM | PM | PM |

ENERGY LEVELS AND ATTENTION SPAN

Energy levels and attention spans vary during the day. Training experience tells us a participant's energy level follows a flow similar to the one shown in Figure 8.1.

People start the day with a lot of energy and this usually lasts for the first hour or two. Energy levels and attention spans then quickly fall as lunchtime approaches. At lunch people have the highest energy levels. Why? Because they are physically active and having fun. Energy then takes a dip after lunch as our bodies digest our food. This drop continues throughout the afternoon until we gain a small burst of energy in anticipation of going home.

This is important to remember because we have to ensure that we design activities and movement into low points, and that we can ruin a great opportunity of naturally high levels with a sedentary activity, such as an extended lecture. It's a mistake to put long lectures at the high points, thinking that

FIGURE 8.2 Attention Span Equation

$$\text{Attention Span of the Individual} = \frac{QP}{IM} \times \frac{FCB}{CF} \times \frac{CS}{CD} \times \frac{DR}{SF}$$

QP = Quality of Presentation
IM = Importance of Material
FCB = Frequency of Coffee Breaks
CF = Caffeine Factor
CS = Comfort of Seat
CD = Classroom Dynamics
DR = Darkness of the Room
SF = Sleep Factor (which may have something to do with the alcohol consumption the night before)

people will have the energy to withstand the time with no activity. Many classes begin with a long lecture to introduce the material, and then include a long lecture after lunch. The result is a lower high point in the beginning of the day and then an even lower level after lunch.

So how do you make sure that our participants stay engaged in our class? Take a look at the equation in Figure 8.2.

Okay, so the equation is more fun than scientific, but it does offer a glimpse into some of the factors to consider when designing training. While frequent breaks will aid in energy levels, the real solution is varying activities and focusing on the attention span of individuals.

Learning professionals know and scientists have shown that most people have an attention span of 15 to 20 minutes. Some say that it's even worse, citing the nine-minute rule—the amount of time there is between television commercials. Everyone differs, but whatever the exact number, we should be aware of the concept. That means we should change something every 15 or 20 minutes. This doesn't just mean limiting lecture time to 15- to 20-minute increments (though this is often the interpretation of the rule); it also refers even to interactive activities. A 45-minute or hour-long group activity may also result in a reduced attention span. If you have an extended activity, interrupt it with a break or a quick review of progress, and use the interruption to add variety and restart the attention span clock.

It's important to remember that it's not enough to just change the style of lecture (where in the room the instructor stands, using a new A/V method or topic, etc.), you must change the training methodology. Participants need to be able to change how their mind is working, to move around in order to get the blood flowing. The blood flow does not require physical exercise, but can be encouraged simply by splitting the participants into groups and having them move to different areas of the room.

One frequent mistake is to carve up lectures into 20-minute increments with brief activities in between. While this is better than having a long lecture, the repetitive nature of the cycle will lead to the same loss of energy level. Think about the following two-hour lesson:

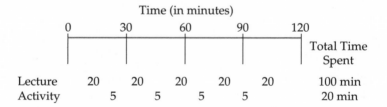

While this does offer a break in the lecture and include activity, over the two hours there are still 100 minutes of lecture (83 percent of the time) and only 20 minutes of activity (17 percent). Energy levels may not be as low as with a 90-minute lecture followed by a 30-minute activity, but participants will still wilt.

Another frequent mistake is to think that an instructor demonstration is not a lecture. Many classes, especially system classes, have an overview lecture followed by a demonstration. This can be 90 minutes to two hours combined. Designers of such classes may think that this level of variety in the type of activity will result in increased energy and learning, but the truth is that the participants still have not interacted and have remained sedentary.

Many other mistakes are made, such as considering group discussion as an interactive activity. While this is more interactive than lecture, it still does not get all participants active and should not be considered a break from lecture. While we could keep listing mistakes it is more important to offer solutions.

CONSIDERATIONS

Before discussing ways to make training more interactive, fun, and educational, take a look at some factors to consider when designing activities—an organization's style, the audience, and the trainer. Some activities may not be appropriate in some circumstances, and could alienate participants.

ORGANIZATION AND AUDIENCE STYLE

While companies and people often don't like to admit it, each one has a culture and expected way of doing things. We may want to introduce fun and a variety of activities, but doing so may not be acceptable to the organization or audience. Be cautious and try not to implement too many new activities in a session. We can still limit the lecture and make training interactive and fun, but we have to choose our methods wisely.

Companies and individuals can be thought of as falling somewhere on a continuum from dignified and reserved to animated and fun (see Figure 8.3). A 100-year-old drug company will differ from a ten-year-old dot-com. It is also true that an audience of engineers or accountants will vary from a group of salespeople. And because employees are often drawn to the culture of the organization, or they alter their style to work within the organization's culture, it is typical for the individuals and companies to fall close together on the continuum.

FIGURE 8.3 Personality Continuum

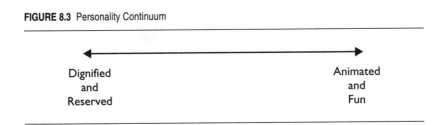

We must know our audience and design programs for them. This is not to say we shouldn't push the company or participants out of their comfort zones; this is often very effective, but we must be cautious and not try to implement too many changes too fast.

TRAINER STYLE AND SKILLS

Not all trainers can facilitate all activities. Trainers can fall along the same continuum—they can be dignified and reserved or animated and fun. Skills of trainers also differ. Some are great presenters, while others are great facilitators. It takes a mix of personality and skills to be effective in delivering any methodology.

Where possible, select the instructor only after defining the experience you wish to create for the participants (see defining reaction in Chapter 6). This will allow you to create the class you want for the audience first and not have to design to the instructor. It is possible to stretch the comfort zone of the trainer, just as you can stretch the comfort zone of the audience. But I wouldn't expect to totally transform either the trainer or the audience.

METHODS

Now that we have discussed why it is important to include interaction and fun in your training, as well as some of the points to consider when designing it, let's turn to specific activities you can incorporate into your program.

First, drop any preconceived ideas that a lecture is needed at some point during the program. It's true the instructor may need to provide information, but there are times you can do so without the use of any lecture. Open your mind; be creative; lecturing is not the only way.

In Chapter 6, Mike Rockelmann offered an example of a lesson without any lecture. It included:

- Identifying the customer situation
- Describing the product features
- Describing the product benefits
- Using information to position benefits to meet customer needs

Even without the lecture, the key objectives of having a technique to define the customer situation and identify product features and benefits were achieved. The elements of the class—including activities, teamwork, real-life scenarios, research, competition, and the Disney theme—were included. The trainer could have lectured on process to identify the customer situation, the features and benefits of the products, and how to link the two, but instead used social and fun activities that had participants applying the information at every step. Participants will remember these activities and how they created the answers when they return to the job.

Mike Rockelmann shared with me another example that really drives home the point that there are alternatives to lectures. It involved training for a product labeling and marketing group at a major pharmaceutical company. The course was one in a three-day-long program designed to teach the group the FDA laws and regulations relating to the labeling and marketing of drug products, and it was one of the lowest-evaluated courses in the program. The original course was designed and delivered by a vice president within the group and involved a three-hour lecture with 150 PowerPoint slides. Mike convinced the vice president to try a new method and allow him to cofacilitate the course. The new course outline included:

15 minutes	Overview of the course, learning objectives, and why it is important
30 minutes	Divide the class into three groups
	Hand out the laws and regulations and a different current drug label and marketing material to each group
	Have the groups identify where and how the laws and regulation were applied in the drug label
30 minutes	Groups present findings and discuss laws and regulations.
15 minutes	Instructor reviews laws, regulations, and major learning points.
30 minutes	Groups take a hypothetical drug that had been used as a theme in all courses and create a label and marketing materials in accordance with the laws and regulations; points are awarded for the best materials that follow all rules.
45 minutes	Each group presents their label and marketing materials. The participants and instructors review to ensure they followed all rules. Instructors rate the material.
15 minutes	Review of key learning and questions

Notice that the class involved little lecture or instructor-focused activities. Almost all of the learning was completed and presented by the participants. It also included a competition and a theme used throughout all courses. After the new format was implemented, the evaluation rating rose dramatically, and it became one of the most fun and effective courses.

Take these two examples as a starting point in considering the kinds of methodologies you can incorporate into your program. They are meant to open your thinking and increase your reception to a new way of training. While lectures or variations of lectures may be needed at different points, you should also trust that the participants are capable of learning on their own and that they can draw the main learning points from materials just as well as the instructor. In fact, having participants draw out the learning points and the instructor review them is more effective because the participants have created the information for themselves instead of passively receiving it.

Now let's look at some additional alternatives to lectures and other activities that can be used in your training program.

LECTURES THAT DON'T LOOK LIKE LECTURES

Sometimes you need to present content, but it just doesn't lend itself to some fun little game. Some of the following activities are still instructor-led, but they offer interaction so that participants must think instead of being passive learners. They can be used in the place of lectures, or to support a lecture.

- *Expert panel* (see Additional Resources at the end of this chapter for a sample agenda). Have knowledgeable people come in to discuss the topic. They can answer questions and offer different viewpoints. When should you use this? When entering a new industry or market segment; with executives at a national sales meeting; with product management during a new product rollout.
- *Use the Socratic method to draw the information out of the group.* That is, question the participants and use their answers to your questions as the basis for asking another question. The idea is to lead the participants to the point you're trying to make, to make them think things through. They apply the information for themselves,

linking it to previous knowledge as you lead the discussion with questions.

■ *Do a "chalk talk."* Diagram the process or concept in such a way that the listeners are following the evolution of the concept visually as well as hearing it. For an extra twist, you can have the participants come up and draw out the diagram as you discuss.

■ *Audio or video.* A video is a lecture because of the lack of interaction. Years ago, videos were frequently used to open or close a session. Some Olympic athlete or successful coach would talk about motivation that all you have to do is want it bad enough and work hard and you'll achieve it. It had nothing to do with the content, but it was flashy and made us feel good. Companies are trying to find a more direct tie to content for videos these days. And the videos are closer to 8 minutes than they are to the 20-minute videos of long ago. It is possible to use a recorded situation to present a topic or idea, stopping regularly for discussion. The audio is still lecture, but it is done differently. It should not be overdone or it gets monotonous. It can be done with flair that is often difficult to do in a live training environment. Recordings can look or sound like a newscast or an interview. It can involve personalities from the organization (leaders, management, or team members), which helps to increase interest.

■ *Provide an outline of your notes to the group.* Indicate which material is prerequisite or fundamental to the understanding of the subject and which can be taken in any order. Have the group prioritize the secondary list, and convince you—if they can—that they don't need the prerequisites.

■ *Let participants read the material and answer questions.* Then go immediately into questions and exercises. Any of the exercises listed in the next sessions can be used to test understanding and then discuss to clarify material.

- *Put an idea on trial* (see Additional Resources at the end of this chapter for an example script). This activity presents and explores an idea in a structured way with which most people will be familiar, through television and movies if not by firsthand experience. Using a judge, prosecutor, and defense attorney, you will examine both sides of an issue.
- *Debate.* Two individuals (or teams) each take on a side of an issue and present both sides to the group in the form of a formal debate. (See Additional Resources at the end of this chapter for an example script.)

REVIEW GAMES

You can start your program with a question-and-answer game or use it as a follow-up review. This can be a great way to begin a module if you believe the participants have base knowledge of the topic. It acts like a pretest in which you can then discuss each point and offer more information to correct misperceptions or fill in information gaps. But do not use such activities if the participants cannot provide any answers, as it will unmotivate them. Review games at the end of a session can be an effective way to test understanding and increase energy.

Any game that we have played or seen on TV can be the model for this activity—*Who Wants to be a Millionaire, Jeopardy,* Trivial Pursuit, card games, or even Candy Land. It can be low tech, such as a board from an actual game with customized questions, or high-tech with the use of PowerPoint or software programs such as Gameshow Pro (can be purchased at *www.learningware.com*). Plain board games can be purchased from companies like Trainer's Warehouse (*www.trainerswarehouse.com*). Questions can be straight product facts, key benefits, or customer problems/scenarios. Keep the information relevant to the topic. If you have the budget you can incorporate an audience response system to track how learners are doing. Review games work very well to reinforce product information (including highly technical information, see Chapter 10). (See Additional Resources at the end of this chapter for instructions on how to create a card game.)

Historical timeline. A variation of a card game is to use cards to put information in a time sequence. I have used this to discuss company history in new-hire orientations. Give new hires prework that includes a summary of the company history to read before they come to class. Put posters on the wall with decades written on them (you can do this online as well). Make cards of historical facts of the company, with no reference to dates.

Distribute the shuffled cards between the participants. First have each individual put their card(s) on the decade poster (or decade timeline) in which they think it belongs. Next, have the group look it over. Let them discuss and as a team arrange the cards as close as they can to the correct history as they remember. Finally, give them a summary of the history, written in paragraph form. Let the group make any corrections that are needed. When all the cards are in the right place, have the group summarize each decade for the company. This can be an entirely learner-directed process and is an alternative to a death by PowerPoint presentation reviewing the company history. See Additional Resources at the end of this chapter for an example.

GROUP TEACHING

Group teaching is another method that can be used in place of a lecture, or afterward to help participants apply knowledge or see its application. If used in place of a lecture, provide the needed materials to the group that will teach the lesson, including guidelines on use of flip charts or an activity to help teach. Assign teams to research topics and present them to the group, adding only critical items that were overlooked. My rule is that the whole team goes up front to present, even if they don't all have speaking parts.

This method works well when discussing competitors. Each team can research one of the organization's competition (brochures, Internet, product samples reviews). They can compare product lines, quality, and sales forces, or identify strengths and weaknesses.

One thing I love about this is the physical movement. Participants can do this anywhere, and will often end up on the floor with a laptop or a flip chart. I love activities that bring people out of their seats and into different places or rooms.

SCAVENGER HUNTS

Ever go on a scavenger hunt as a kid, walking through the neighborhood looking for a paper clip, a cinnamon stick, yesterday's newspaper? Looking for things is a great way for people to get to know resources. A scavenger hunt on an Intranet or in a corporate headquarters is a good way for people to start learning their way around and how to find things. You can send the group out to evaluate sales techniques at stores, in the hotel shops, or that night at dinner. Many companies use this method to check out competition, or to look at products at retail. The key is to provide a list of items to locate based on the program's learning objectives and content. It is interesting to have participants come back and present their findings to the class and include any interesting anecdotes. See Additional Resources at the end of the chapter for specific examples of scavenger hunts (in a corporate headquarters and on an intranet).

CASE STUDIES

Case studies are a widely used and effective way to teach key concepts and skills and can be used to begin or end a session. Case studies in the beginning of a session can create interest in the topic and offer a way to judge the knowledge of participants. After presenting a case study, you can then offer participants a new way to think about the situation, and then have them apply the new model or way of thinking to the case study and see the difference. This helps link a new way of thinking to an old process.

Case studies are effective because they bring a real-life scenario into the training class. They also take the learning to a higher level because participants need to understand and apply the knowledge. Case studies are beneficial because they:

- Promote thinking
- Are largely a participant-directed training methodology
- Are generally nonthreatening to participants
- Build on the experiences of the learner
- Let people see the issues
- Are cost-effective because you can write it once and use it over and over
- Can be customized to the organization needs; can have different versions for different divisions or job levels if needed

There are some disadvantages to case studies as well. While a lecture may require minimal preparation, writing case studies takes certain skills and time in order to be done well. They are also more time-consuming to run. The learning is often greater, but sometimes time is a factor. Case studies can also take participants off the intended learning path if they begin to argue about the details or how they interpret the case.

You can use a case study for a variety of reasons:

- Practicing a newly learned skill or putting together everything that has been learned during a workshop
- Progressively adding more complex information to a situation
- Problem solving

Information on developing and using case studies, used with permission from SMT, is at the back of the chapter in Additional Resources.

ROLE-PLAY

Role-playing is a tried-and-true method and it is also a powerful sales training tool. It allows you to give a good demonstration and then let participants practice doing what they have just learned and seen. It is one of the only ways to simulate a live account call. It works well because people can build their learning: learn step one and practice, learn step two and practice steps one and two, learn step three and practice steps one, two, and three.

Important benefits of role-playing include:

- Repeated practice
- Immediate feedback
- Chance to correct behavior
- Incremental learning
- Can be repeated with many different skill and knowledge objectives
- Can learn without the stress of doing it on a live account call

Common areas to use role plays are:

- Interpersonal skills
- Communication
- Manager coaching
- Problem solving
- Selling or negotiating

Are there downsides to role-play? I believe there are. Someone freezing in a role-play or being embarrassed can have lasting effects on the individual and the class can have a long memory of it. It doesn't just affect one person. Also, it isn't necessarily a good indicator of performance in front of a customer. There are instances where someone excels in performing a role-play with peers, but isn't listening in front of a customer. And the reverse can be true. Someone can be nervous when role-playing in a classroom situation, yet when they are in a familiar place with a customer they know, they can excel.

Role-play remains a staple of sales training, because it has the power to simulate the buyer-seller interaction that takes place on the job. However, it is exactly because of that power that role-play can be so stressful. There is a continuum of stress in the various types of role-play available to the trainer, as illustrated in Figure 8.4.

Most salespeople carry more anxiety around traditional role-play in classroom sessions than they do around a call on their toughest customer. Role-playing in front of a class is like being under a microscope. Having management in attendance, and/or a camera, makes it worse.

Many companies are refusing the videotape anymore. No one wants an old video of a new salesperson—overpromising what a product can deliver—lying around in a closet somewhere. Companies don't want any possibility that such videos can end up in front of a judge. As a result, many pharmaceuti-

FIGURE 8.4 Stress Continuum

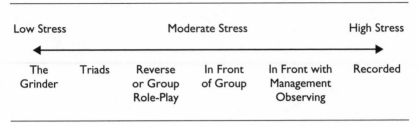

Low Stress		Moderate Stress			High Stress
The Grinder	Triads	Reverse or Group Role-Play	In Front of Group	In Front with Management Observing	Recorded

cal and insurance companies have already banned recording role-plays. I don't think this is a bad trend.

However, many companies still videotape and conduct grueling new-hire training, because of legacy. Sales managers who went through stressful training and had to pass demanding tests, feel "if I had to do it, so should you." It becomes more of a test of character than training.

Or perhaps you have heard, "If they can handle the stress in front of the room, negotiating with a sales manager, then I know they can handle the stress with the customer." This is hazing, not training.

The principles of adult learning state that the learning environment should be supportive, not stressful. The triad, grinder, and reverse role-play techniques outlined below tend to be low-stress versions, particularly when they are done "bedlam style"(everyone doing it at the same time, generating a lot of noise or bedlam). "Players" feel hidden by the action of the whole group. It's like having a private conversation in a noisy, crowded restaurant. You are actually more alone than you are in a canoe in the middle of a lake, where sound travels well (and you never know who may be listening). For our purposes here, I am referring to these as role-plays. In a class, I would never refer to the R-word. I say we are going to practice what we have learned, or I will call it skill practice or application exercise.

Role-play variation—triads. A triad works just the same as a large group role-play but splits the participants into groups of three. One person is the buyer, one plays the role of the sales person, and one observes to give feedback. Limiting the group size takes some of the anxiety out of a role-play. You can then have the groups switch roles so everyone has to participate. These small groups also allow for everyone to participate and observe in a shorter amount of time. Allowing for "do overs" (calling a time out during the role play to think through or change something) lets people truly learn and adjust as they go—a great way for people to practice and build skills.

Role-play variation—the grinder. Despite its name, the grinder is another low-stress form of role-play. I learned this method from SMT. People stand in two lines facing each other. One is the buyer and the other the seller. They role-play (generally for two minutes), buyers give one minute of feedback, and the sellers "grind" to the left (move to the next buyer, the person at the end of the line goes to the beginning). Now they are facing a different seller and they do it again. Feedback again. Grind again. Feedback again. Grind again. Switch roles and repeat three (or more) times.

It is important to do a grinder three times.

1. The first time they are getting used to the process.
2. The second time they are getting real benefit from the feedback.
3. By the third time they have likely incorporated new ideas for improvement.

I'll give you a tip from personal experience. Make sure you have the instructions really solid. This is hard for people to visualize from verbal instructions. So let them prepare (if required), get them in lines, verbally tell them what will happen, and then demonstrate it. This can be done with really large

When to Use the Grinder

- "Canned" sales presentations

- Overcoming objections

- Closing techniques

- Benefits of a product

- Introducing themselves or the company

- Practicing questioning

- New product release

groups (at a national sales meeting, for example). It is tricky to manage (sometimes people need to stop in the middle of a conversation and move on), it is loud, it is energizing. Try it, you'll like it!

Role-play variation—reverse role-play or group role-play. In a reverse or group role-play, participants are not in front of the room; they can participate from their seats. The reverse role-play has the instructor playing the part of the salesperson (better be pretty fluent with the selling or negotiating model!). The trainer needs to act on his or her feet and respond to what the class presents. The class can act individually or in groups. The class has the scenario and one person or group starts. The instructor responds and it moves to the next person or group to continue the scenario. Another way of doing this is to have the groups take turns coaching the instructor on what to say in response to what the customer says.

The group role-play follows the same logistics but the participants play the role of the salesperson. Someone acts as a customer and the individual or group must respond. A facili-

Suggestions for Taking the Stress Out:

- Start with a series of grinder or group exercises and then graduate to triads. Because the stress level is lower, the focus will be on skill building.

- While triads are going on, notice reps who play their sales role very well. After they are done, in private, ask if they and their partner would be willing to demonstrate their sales call to the rest of the group. Chances are, they will gladly accept and will do well.

- Ask for other volunteers to demonstrate techniques they used or particular situations they were modeling.

- Always allow the "salespersons" to critique their performances first, followed by the "customers" and then any observers. Most sales reps are their own harshest critics.

- Give guidelines to the buyers and observers roles to ensure success and playing fair.

Guidelines for a Successful Role-play

To make any type of role-play successful you need to have a good scenario. Make it realistic and provide enough information to begin the discussion. Do not provide too much information or it may lead to a quick ending.

When running the role-play ensure all participants have a "play fair" mentality. Have a discussion on what is expected of the person playing the customer. The customer should not make the situation too difficult or too easy. Be careful, people get carried away so the trainer must jump in when necessary.

tator carries on the scenario to the next individual or group. A variation of this is to have a seller in the hot seat and his or her group behind the seller. At any time the group can coach the salesperson, or someone else can step into the hot seat. You can have some great fun discussing the responses and what went well or might be improved. I think these methods can actually create a great learning environment.

SIMULATION

Generally, a simulation is simply a variation of a case study or role-play, but the skill can be taught or applied through the use of technology. This may be a computer system to input an order or complete research, setting up a phone call in which the salesperson works through the call on the phone, or working through an entire sales cycle to see the results of pricing decisions. For dos and don'ts of simulations see Chapter 11.

IMPROVISATION

One example of a technique that is wonderful for practicing sales training skills but often is overlooked is the use of improv. This is one example where the content does not even have to relate to the topic, because the skill practiced is still in line with the end objective of selling. A salesperson should be able to think on his or her feet and react quickly. Practicing improvising can improve this skill.

Participants can learn the product knowledge, practice it in some activities, and then participate in an improv session either related or unrelated to the content. A good debrief followed by a transition on how those same reaction skills can be used in selling will lead you perfectly to a practice exercise in which they combine the product knowledge and selling skills.

I had the pleasure of studying with Second City, the world-famous improvisation group. After completing their curriculum, and doing a number of shows, I saw many similarities between being successful improvising as an ensemble and being successful in business. Salespeople improvise every day, on every call. Trainers improvise every day, on every presentation. There are some fundamental improv principles that, if followed, would create more productive teams:

Here is the caveat: Be careful about trying this at home! Ask for help from trained professionals! Improvisation is a skill, a muscle to be toned, just like presenting and facilitating. Some people aren't successful their first time facilitating a group. Many aren't stellar their first time presenting. Improv demands a safe environment with people supporting each other. In the Additional Resources section at the back of this chapter, I have included some basic and "safe" improv exercises that you will likely feel comfortable using in training situations.

As with many exercises, it is all in the debrief! Choose improv activities that support your objectives for the event. The purpose for many exercises will be:

- Practicing thinking on your feet
- Practicing real listening
- Practicing accepting what your teammate says, without judging

In most brainstorming or innovation sessions, people's roles should be neutralized. Every person's ideas are valued regardless of job level. And there are similarities to brainstorming ideas that seem impractical or out there can lead to the next big thing. Judgment and cognitive weeding out can come later! Early on, encourage ideas to flow. If you ask participants what the relevance was of this activity, they should be able to state it.

The facilitator should demonstrate and participate along with the group. Don't ask them to do things you are not willing to do. No one should be forced to do improv in front of a group. You can set up a safe environment and let people participate if they choose. If it is going on bedlam-style (several doing it simultaneously), it is generally safe.

WHOLE GROUP MOVEMENT

As you incorporate some of the discussed methods, see where you can get people out of their seats. Divide into groups and have them move to different tables. Put a flip chart on the wall and have people brainstorm or do their exercise there. Encourage people to move around. Plan a reason to move to a different place in the room. The change of scenery is good, and it is energizing to get up and move.

HOW TO DETERMINE WHICH METHOD TO USE

There is no one real answer to which method is the best to use for a given situation; it will vary based on content, participants, time, and instructor ability/style. The best approach is to be creative and try different methods. If you don't have access to the audience for some practice, grab a colleague or two and do a run-through. That will help ensure success when you do it the first time.

Remember, the first key is to open your mind and be creative; don't ever say a lecture is the only way to teach a section. When being creative, don't forget that all activities should support the class objectives. Don't just add an activity to add an activity. Be sure that it is appropriate, tied to the objectives, and that you understand why it is being used. And if you need to do a lecture in a traditional lecture style, make sure it is darned good!

The test for knowing if it is the right method is to be ready to respond to the following scenario: What if the VP of sales or the CEO came into the room in the middle of a very competitive Jeopardy game or when people are tossing an invisible bowling ball around the room? Can you explain the learning value very concisely and convincingly? "This will add energy" is probably not enough. You should be able to articulate things such as:

- Before this activity they did X, which accomplished X objective. After this activity they can do X plus Y.
- This activity is stimulating creativity.
- The team is practicing listening to each other.
- This review game is reinforcing what they learned yesterday.

When choosing a method, the first question to answer is if you are teaching knowledge or a skill. Knowledge is easier to learn than a skill because application of a skill first requires knowledge of the subject. If you are teaching a skill, you actually need to teach or ensure knowledge first. Remember to follow the three-step teaching model: (1) introduction to material, (2) guided practice, and (3) individual practice, incorporating activities for all three. You may first need a method to teach the knowledge and then continue with the application to make it a skill. One example of what appears to be knowledge but is actually a skill is the teaching of product knowledge; you are teaching knowledge, but the end objective is to have them apply the knowledge when selling (a skill).[3] (See Figure 8.5.)

HOW DO YOU KNOW IF IT IS SUCCESSFUL?

The number-one success criterion of any training is that participants have the knowledge and skills intended. Can you say that you have met all of your objectives? Did the partici-

FIGURE 8.5 Determining If You Are Teaching Knowledge or Skill

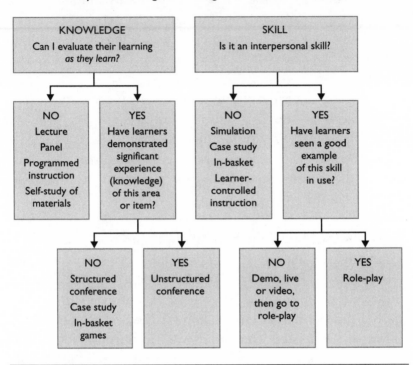

Are you in the stage of building KNOWLEDGE or SKILL?

KNOWLEDGE	SKILL
Can I evaluate their learning *as they learn?*	Is it an interpersonal skill?

pants model the intended skill in the class? If yes, then you have been successful in that most important aspect. However, it is also important to create a fun, interactive, social, and educational learning environment so that people want to come back. You can rate your success in this area on the reaction of the participants. The easiest way to gather success information on this aspect is to use an after-class survey. To judge your success in this area, ask:

- Did you know what you were supposed to learn or be able to do in this session?

- Did this session keep you interested or engaged, and provide the chance for you to apply the content?
- Do you feel you have learned the knowledge and skills intended?

And to determine if your class was worthwhile and fun, ask:

- Would you recommend this class to others?
- Do you look forward to coming back for the next session?

It is certainly not a requirement for learners to have fun in a learning environment. That would never be my reason for adding an exercise. I do, however, want them to be engaged.

SUMMARY—WHAT CAN WE DO?

So, did we find any legitimate reasons to vary our training methodologies and perhaps even design engaging methods in our training? I sincerely hope so! There are certainly people who see training as serious business and who see fun as something to be avoided. I am not evangelizing to them. I respect that there are different styles and that all can be effective.

I have presented tools here for your use, but just because you have new tools doesn't mean they will immediately work well. Keep these tips in mind:

- The first time you use something, plan it well. Practice it. Consider in advance the participants style, obstacles, or potholes that might come along.
- Know your audience. Choose activities that are a good fit and use variety.
- Try it once with a test group before you take it to your target audience. Try it at home with neighborhood kids.

Make a run-through with a couple of colleagues or people you trust. It is good to practice verbal instructions. It is good to see whether written instructions support the exercise. Where appropriate, have written as well as verbal instructions.

- Don't do an exercise for the purpose of doing an exercise. Have a purpose; have a point. Make the connection so learners know why they are doing it. Better yet, let them explain why they just did it.
- Provide highlighters, Post-it notes, and fiddlers (Koosh balls, stress balls, or something for active bodies to handle) in a classroom to assist fidgeting participants in connecting with content.
- Leave time in class (traditional or online) for participants to list a-ha moments and link those to something they know.
- Let participants know why you are using different methodologies; remove the "curtain" so they can see that different methods help different people. People learn by seeing, hearing, and doing. We have all styles in the room, so we will teach using different methods to respect each person in the group. You may find you don't like some of the methods, but it will likely be helping someone in the room.

It is my sincerest hope there are choices you see here that you can try. Remember, just because I drink Tang doesn't make me an astronaut. Many of these approaches take planning, and they need to be used in the right places at the right time for the right audiences.

ADDITIONAL RESOURCES

EXPERT PANEL

- Give panel questions in advance. (Ask the audience to submit questions, if appropriate.)
- Have a moderator (required skills are intense listening and playing the role of "host"; moderator can be a lead panelist if needed).
- Prep the panel members as to what to expect (the agenda).
- Introduce the panel members and include their bios as they relate to the topics.
- Moderator asks a question and then lets panel members answer the question.
- Moderator asks the next question; panel members answer.
- If there is disagreement or lively discussion, let members address concerns or ideas.
- Take questions from the group live.
- Moderator repeats the question, unless a microphone is used in the audience.
- Moderator ends discussion with closing comments.

JURY TRIAL

This can be done in person or in a synchronous online class.

Preparation
- Roles: judge, bailiff, defense attorney, prosecution attorneys, witness for the defense, witness for the prosecution. The rest of the audience can be the jury.
- Give time for the attorneys to talk to their witnesses.

Execution (Sample script)

Bailiff: All rise. Court is now in session. Honorable Judge Susan presiding.

(The judge comes from outside the room wearing judge's robes (or black tablecloth) and/or white wig, looking serious or comical, holding a gavel.)

Judge: Welcome to the Court of Sales Professionals. This is the case of the questionable product. Bailiff, has the jury been impaneled?
Bailiff: Yes, your honor.
Judge: Who are they?

(Bailiff points to the jury, the whole audience or an identified couple of rows of people.)

Judge: Opening comments. The jury is going to hear statements from the defense on the advantages of The Good Guys product line, which is being challenged by the competition. Consul for the prosecution is seeking the death penalty for Product Line X. Your job is to hear the testimony and decide on the merits of Product X for yourself. If you are convinced beyond a shadow of a doubt that Product X is guilty as charged, you are to find it guilty and recommend a sentence. If not convinced beyond a shadow of a doubt that Product X is a worthless product, you should enter a verdict of not guilty. Ladies and gentlemen of the jury: Do you understand your charge?

- Prosecution's opening comments
- Defense's opening comments
- Prosecution calls first witness
- Defense cross-examines
- Defense calls first witness
- Prosecution cross-examines
- Prosecution's closing arguments

■ Defense's closing arguments

Judge: Closing comments. Ladies and gentlemen of the jury, the evidence has been presented on the legitimacy and value of Product X. Your job at this time is to render a verdict on the validity of this product. You are being asked to decide the guilt or innocence beyond a reasonable doubt. I am going to poll the jury at this time as to the guilt or innocence of this product. Jury, please raise your hand at this time if you agree with the prosecution and think that Product X should be put to death.

(Judge records hands.)

Those who feel not guilty?

(Judge records hands.)

The decision of the jury is final. Pound the gavel.

Now, as we have heard before, it is all in the debriefing. Find out from the audience what salient points came out pro and con.

This is a fun way to present ideas, but it can get long. You can limit cross-examination to one or two questions, and consider giving a time limit to each attorney. The first time you do it, I would try and keep it to 20 or 30 minutes. If people are into the roles, and salespeople often are, it can go pretty long. I love using people from the audience for roles where possible.

It works well as a review of the previous day's content. (Learners can pour over the salient point while preparing for the trial.)

DEBATE

Here is a "not ready for prime time" debate method for training purposes. You will need three people: moderator, proponent, opposition.

- Moderator reads debate issue
- Opening remarks in favor
- Opening remarks opposed
- Opposition responds to the proponent points
- Proponent responds to the opponent
- Closing comments from each

You can have the audience vote on the conclusion. You can have a panel of judges decide the outcome. You can have a scripted conclusion, reviewing the main points and reinforcing the learning. Debrief after to get participants reactions.

Watch out: If there is a predetermined outcome, do not use this method. This method helps identify and bring out points from both sides. If there is a right answer, it is best to just present the right answer.

CARD GAME

How many ways can you split up a topic? How much can be learned by putting things back together again that have been split? "Shuffling a deck" of mixed items that were once together is a simple process and can reinforce lessons on processes or important combinations of elements. Here's how to do it:

1. Determine the skills or knowledge area. Examples:
   a) Selling the benefits of Product X to customers with different needs
   b) Following a prescribed call procedure in detail
   c) Matching feature, advantage, benefit
2. Divide it into its component parts. Examples:
   a) Five different customers with five different sets of needs; 10 or 15 product benefits that could help each customer in appropriate combinations

b) The ten-step call procedure and the many tasks that are to be accomplished in each call

3. Write all the component parts on card-shaped sections of card stock. Print and cut.
4. Shuffle all the cards to mix them up.
5. Have participants sort them. Have a discussion about the various combinations.

Notes:

- The project is best done in groups of four or five, where people can see all the cards laid out.
- In groups larger than five, you will need a set of cards for each small group.
- The main content of the lessons should be taught before the game. For example, in 2a above, participants should be given examples and work through benefit/customer combinations, and in example 2b, participants should be aware of the ten-step call and its components. This is critical, because the game is just one more way to teach complex subjects and cannot be a substitute for adequate instruction. Also, if the material is not understood before the game, the game will become extremely frustrating.
- There should always be a follow-up discussion at the end of the game. While challenging questions are good, there should be no ambiguity about the "right" answers, once you explain them.[1]

SAMPLE TIMELINE

1950s

1951 Started making spaghetti sauce and pasta in mama's kitchen
1959 Started selling at the corner grocery store

1960s

1962 Gained first major account and sold in supermarkets

1967 Purchased a manufacturing facility and became Mama's Sauce and Pasta

1969 Made variations of the basic spaghetti to include linguine

1969 Created a marketing department; company slogan was "Just Like Mama Made"

1970s

1971 Acquired a noodle company and began manufacturing macaroni and bow-tie pasta under the brand Noodles for Dinner

1973 Added flavored sauces to the line (marinara, meat sauce, pepper-basil flavors)

1974 Expanded the line to include oils and seasonings

1975 Hired the first sales force and took the product lines national

1979 Had the first national sales meeting

1980s

1982 Had the first sales contest

1985 Was the number-one–selling pasta sauce nationally for the first time

1986 Company went public

1988 Introduced the Just Add Meat boxed dinners

1989 Company slogan was "Just Like Mama Used to Make"

1989 Downsized the sales force and used brokers

1990s

1990 Expanded sales to Canada

1993 Created a Web site of 10-minute meal ideas

1997 Hired back the sales force

1997 Brought the Allitalian brand from Europe to the United States

1998 Sold the Just Add Meat boxed dinners

1998 Built a West Coast production facility

2000s

2000   Created account teams

2001   Record-breaking sales for oil division

2004   Introduced a Pasta Fast entrée line

ONLINE SCAVENGER HUNT

Have participants find information from the company's intranet site, such as:

- Who is the VP of finance?
- What is the current stock price?
- How many SKUs are in the storage bag product line?
- What product lines are for sale in Canada?
- Where do you access the expense reporting?
- What is the phone number for customer service?
- How many regions does the company have?
- What is the order minimum for a printed deli storage bag?
- How do you order product brochures?

CORPORATE HEADQUARTERS SCAVENGER HUNT

This one is great for orientation to a new building. Possible tasks include:

- Get a cup from the cafeteria.
- Get a business card from customer service.
- Find out from what high school Bill Sodes graduated.
- Get a business card order form from the copy center.
- Determine your region number for expense reporting purposes.
- Bring a sales brochure for the newest product rollout.
- Get an autograph from someone in marketing.

- Get a company pen from the company store.
- Get a company envelope from the mail room.

CASE STUDIES

This material is from SMT. In preparing case studies, consider these purposes:

- To allow participants to apply knowledge to a realistic situation
- To generate informed discussion around an issue
- Problem solving

Write down your learning objective (what you want participants to get out of this exercise). What do you need to create a case study?

- The case study formula
- The skills to be taught
- The industry/business vocabulary of the learners

To create your case study, follow these steps:

1. State the problem.
2. Select a setting that is not an exact replica of the work environment and characters who will not be recognized. You are trying to eliminate distractions or sidetracking.
3. Give sufficient background information to make an informed judgment.
4. Pose the problem as a question.
5. Write directions and discussion questions.
6. Write facilitator notes (what points trying to make).
7. Pilot and revise the case study (it can be just a few people who understand the audience, but don't present it to a live audience without testing it).

As your case study comes together, ask yourself these questions:

1. Is it too detailed?
2. Is there appropriate detail level and enough time?
3. Is anything distracting (sounds like my account, too close to industry)?
4. Is the dialogue clear?
5. Are directions clear?
6. Is the facilitator prepared?

Is the case too difficult? (The more complicated it is or the more "twists" you include, the more opportunities you give for it to be argued or interpreted.)

IMPROV EXERCISES

Giving credit for improv games is always a tough thing. I have seen and done most of these at Second City. There are many improvisation groups and most games are variations of something done someplace. I give credit to other creative improvisers for much of this content; my contribution is to write it into a usable format. If you want more exercises to choose from, I recommend *Playing Along,* by Izzy Gesell.

Mirroring. Participants face each other and mirror the actions of their partner.

Audience: Any size group; paired up.

Why use it: Listening, accepting, supporting, team building, concentration.

What to do:

- Have participants face one another. Ask partner A to begin a slow physical action (hand making a circle, head moving from side to side). Partner B should try to mirror (not anticipate) what partner A is doing. There is no verbal communication in this exercise.

- After a minute or so, ask the pairs to change who is leading and following sometime during the next 30 seconds (without verbally discussing the handoff). Change the lead again with no signals. Facilitate working as a team, so observers can't tell who is leading and who is following and only the pair knows when the handoff happens.
- This activity may require a demonstration from the teacher! Make sure they understand that this activity is about seeing what your partner is doing, accepting that action, and mirroring the activity.
- This activity is about giving and receiving. The important thing is to have a balance and be able to lead or follow depending on the needs of the situation.

Debrief: What are keys to success here? Having slow movements that your partner can follow. Not trying to trick the other person or make it hard to follow. What can we learn from this exercise and apply to how we relate to each other in real life?

Counting as a team.

Audience: A group of 8 to 15.

Why do it: Working together as a team, listening to each other, concentration.

What to do: Have participants stand in a circle, facing out.

- We are going to count as a group from 1 to 21.
- The goal is to get to 21.
- Each person can only say one number at a time. No one can say two numbers in a row.
- Anyone can speak at any time.
- Only one person can speak at once.

- If two people speak at the same time, we will stop and go back to one.
- Someone starts with one.

Don't let them discuss a strategy of how to do this. They should not speak other than to say a number. If the game takes too long, coach them about remembering the goal and what is the easiest way to get there. Facilitate for listening. You are trying to work as a team to get to this number. Ways this might be accomplished are going in a sequence around the circle or making a signal before they speak the number or emphasizing the first syllable they say to signal the others they are speaking.

Advanced version: Forbid them to go in a certain sequence. Or have volunteers lay on the floor in a random pattern and close their eyes.

Debrief: What was frustrating here? What was helpful? How did you decide whether or not to say a number? What were you listening for?

Sell this!

Audience: Groups of 3 to 5.

Why do it: Creative thinking, listening and accepting peers' ideas, working together as a team.

What to do: Brainstorm a list (or come with a list prepared) of fictional product names and give one name to each small group.

Give each group 15 minutes to come up with the following:

- What the product is/does
- A celebrity spokesperson for that product
- A jingle or acting out a commercial

Each team presents their "product" to the large group. For example, "Our product is Can Can and it is a new motivational diet drink. Our celebrity spokesperson is Oprah Winfrey. Our jingle will be 'Maybe diets didn't work in the past, but now you Can Can.'"

Facilitate acceptance. This doesn't have to be funny (although it often is). The point is for groups to work together and support each other's ideas.

Examples of fictional products are Bling, Bling; Orange Blast, Hidey Ho, Kookie, Cool Colors, Notables, Darl Doodles, Heat Up, Can Can, Alabaster, Lemon Zestier, Born To, Deluxe Portion, Ganglion, Blue Laze, Lucky Lew, Phony Phylum, Beach Core. Or use terms that are meaningful to your industry. Fictional names should refer to something that doesn't exist.

Talk to me.

Audience: Any size group, people working in pairs.

Why do it: Listening, accepting, supporting each other.

What to do: Two participants have a conversation without speaking in any real language. Instead they use a made-up language and must convey meaning through tone and gestures.

- In pairs, ask participants to start a conversation using only gibberish (the facilitator should demonstrate this). Gibberish is a nonsensical, made-up language.
- They should focus on having a conversation that makes sense to them (i.e., they should know what they are talking about).
- After several minutes, ask the pairs to disclose what they are talking about. See if the partners agree.
- Switch partners and have them try it again.
- Ask for volunteers to do it in front of the class. Ask the audience what they think the pair was talking about?

Variations: Let them hold products or industry props. Add a translator who describes to the audience what each person is saying. (All three speak the same language, but only the translator also speaks English.)

Debrief: What clues did you see that provided insight into what the person meant? Who was really successful and what made them good at this (speaking matching sounds so one doesn't sound like Russian and the other like a tribal language; responding to the previous statement so it sounds conversational)? Is there any application of this exercise to communicating in the real world?

Playing catch.

Audience: Any size; broken into groups of 6 to 10.

Why do it: Accepting, working together as a team, listening, adding energy.

What to do: The group will play catch with invisible balls.

- The facilitator tosses a "ball" to someone. They continue to play "catch" around the circle. Facilitator explains, we will continue to play catch, but it will get more complex.
- Start over. Toss a volleyball to someone and say "volleyball." The ball you toss should be the size of a volleyball. Have them continue to toss the ball and each time they toss it, they say "volleyball." Then toss a beach ball to someone else and say "beach ball." (Change the size of the ball you are throwing.) The group should continue tossing the beach ball and calling it by name. So now two different balls are being tossed around the circle at the same time. Add additional balls, things like footballs, tennis balls, bowling balls. Watch the size and weight of the balls. Each time the tosser says the name of the ball he or she is throwing, so the receiver knows which ball he or she is catching.
- If a ball gets lost, start over with one ball again.
- The group is doing great if they can keep track of one ball for every two people (five different balls for ten people). They are amazing if they can increase that number.

Debrief: What is the purpose of this exercise? What was the key to success here (getting eye contact when you throw a ball to someone and stating clearly what ball it is, catching the same size and weight ball as being thrown, focusing with no distractions, throwing the ball to someone who is open, always throwing to the same person so he or she expects it)?

RECOMMENDED RESOURCES

- Professional Society for Sales and Marketing Training, *Trainer Talk, www.smt.org*

ADDITIONAL READING

- Izzy Gesell, *Playing Along* (Duluth, MN: Whole Person Associates, 1997)
- Jean Barbazette, *Instant Case Studies: How to Design, Adapt, and Use Case Studies in Training* (San Francisco, CA: Pfeiffer, 2003)

Creating Effective Product Training

DIANE M. BOEWE, Drake Resource Group

While selling skill training is an essential component of your sales training curriculum, it shouldn't be the only component. Great selling skills aren't going to overcome a deficit in product knowledge. Educating sales professionals on your products is the fundamental building block to the later selling skills training. Time and resources devoted to product training will contribute to increased sales and return customers. Knowledgeable sales professionals who can answer their customers' questions have an advantage over those who can't.

Customers expect sales professionals to go beyond traditional selling tactics. Hearing about features and benefits in isolation of real-world application does not meet their needs. They want and need to hear about product characteristics and advantages that connect with their industry and corporate needs. They look to sales professionals to solve their problems and/or relieve their pain.

Devoting time and resources for product training can often be a hard sell to management, but taking the time to incorporate this component into your training will help your sales professionals be able to meet their customers' needs and reach their full potential. This chapter will focus on the key principles necessary to develop an effective product training component for your sales training curriculum.

Let's explore some important facts about adult learners to lay the foundation. Andragogy[1] is one theory of adult learning that attempts to explain why adults learn differently than other types of learners. Andragogy makes the following assumptions about the design of learning:

1. Adults need to know why they need to learn something.
2. Adults need to learn experientially.
3. Adults approach learning as problem solving.
4. Adults learn best when the topic is of immediate value.

While there are a number of different specific theories of adult learning,[2] many of their key principles are the same as listed above. See Figure 9.1.

Adult learners usually approach learning differently than younger learners,[4] they

- are more self-guided in their learning;
- bring more, and expect to bring more, to a learning situation because of their wider experience—and can take more away; and
- require learning "to make sense"—will not perform a learning activity just because the instructor said to do it.

It's also important to remember that different people learn differently. As was mentioned in Chapter 1, there are three learning styles:

1. *Visual learners.* They process new information best when it is visually illustrated or demonstrated using:
   - Graphics, illustrations
   - Images
   - Demonstrations

FIGURE 9.1 Adult Learning Principles

Adults –	Therefore they –
See learning as a means to an end rather than an end unto itself.	Must know what is to be gained and must see progress.
Bring considerable experience with them.	Wish to speak, participate, and contribute to proceedings.
Prefer to be active versus a passive mode.	Should be given ample opportunities for active participation.
Have a here-and-now bias.	Want a focus on current issues rather than the distant future.
Are accustomed to being self-directing.	Want facilitators to work *with* them rather than direct them.
Want the focus on real-life problems, tasks, and opportunities.	Prefer a strong how-to orientation to avoid restlessness.
Have a strong need to maintain self-esteem.	Desire courses that enable a high probability of success.

Adapted from "30 Things We Know for Sure about Adult Learning" by Ron and Susan Zemke[3]

2. *Auditory learners.* They process new information best when it is spoken, as in:
   - Lectures
   - Discussions
3. *Kinesthetic learners.* They process new information best when it can be touched or manipulated, such as:
   - Written assignments, taking notes
   - Examination of objects
   - Participation in activities

To develop training for your adult learners, not only do you want to keep the adult learning principles in mind, but you also want to keep the three different learning styles in the forefront. Providing information that addresses each of these learning styles helps ensure that you reach all of the individuals.

Those adult learning theories that emphasize the importance of experience and self-direction are quite relevant to

FIGURE 9.2 Matching Instructional Methods to the Product Training Elements

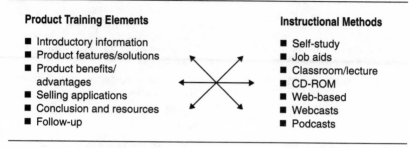

Product Training Elements	Instructional Methods
■ Introductory information	■ Self-study
■ Product features/solutions	■ Job aids
■ Product benefits/	■ Classroom/lecture
advantages	■ CD-ROM
■ Selling applications	■ Web-based
■ Conclusion and resources	■ Webcasts
■ Follow-up	■ Podcasts

sales training. Sales depends on human interaction and training that prepares individuals to handle the unexpected challenges of human interactions is especially successful. While training can provide a foundation and key knowledge, it simply can't prepare an individual for all the real-world situations he or she will encounter while dealing with people.

Based on these principles, my instructional design education, and my corporate education experience, I've incorporated the following philosophy while designing and developing training. Learners need to *hear* it, *see* it, *feel* it, *practice* it, and *do* it. I find these to be essential in all training, but particularly in product training. Let's explore the key elements of product training and some practical ways to incorporate these principles.

As the simple graphic in Figure 9.2 demonstrates, you can mix and match instructional methods with each component. Using the surveys provided in Chapter 1, you can identify which methods best suit your learners.

INTRODUCTORY INFORMATION

To set the stage for any educational program, you'll want to lay the foundation for your learners to provide a big picture explaining why this topic is important for them, where they're going to begin, where they're going to end, and how they're going to get there. This introductory information helps your learners see what's in it for them and how this will be achieved. It eliminates the fear of the unknown, provides the adult learners with the self-direction they desire, and sets the framework to best assimilate the new information.

Here are some real-world examples of how you can provide this introductory information.

NEWSPAPER

I created a newspaper-style newsletter for telecommunications professionals that was delivered through interoffice mail the week before training was scheduled. Each column in the paper provided key foundational information about the class agenda, the types of activities we planned to do, the history of the products, and a Dear Mr. Wire column that addressed frequently asked questions. We also provided a contest for the readers. We asked them to find certain products in their office and/or department and bring them to the class. This approach gave us the opportunity to provide not only text information, but also product graphics for learners. The contest also gave those tactile/kinesthetic learners a chance to get some hands-on experience with the products.

E-CARD E-MAIL

I created an e-card (electronic html card) that was sent via e-mail to learners providing the foundational information. This format allowed us to incorporate many Web site links that allowed the learners to truly direct what they learned and when. It also allowed us to incorporate sound and animated graphics to touch the other senses.

SLIDE SHOW

Using PowerPoint, you can create a visual slide show that you can send via e-mail to learners. The slide show can incorporate your agenda, objectives, product overview, history, etc. This method also allows you to provide links to existing resources. By providing links to learners, you prepare them to be able to answer questions they have in the future by giving them access and direction to resources.

WEBCASTS

The use of Webcasts for delivering information allows a good deal of flexibility and reusability. You can develop a program, deliver it live, and record it for future use. Using the Webcast for introductory information allows you to provide the introductory information and interact with your audience. The recorded session can then be delivered again, whenever needed. One example of this was done for a Fortune 100 insurance company for which I consulted. The organization was introducing new proprietary software to be used by the entire sales force. It created the Webcast and used it on four separate occasions in its pilot program. When the Webcast was finalized, it was recorded and was used as the program was rolled out around the country.

PRODUCT FEATURES/SOLUTIONS

This section of your product training provides the nuts and bolts of your products. It gives you a chance to provide learners with the features and background specifications of your products. While this information may seem unimportant, it does provide important background information to prepare your sales professionals to answer the questions they may be asked by some of their customers. It also gives them the information that allows them to feel confident about your product and being able to think for themselves and on their feet when in front of a customer.

For some of you, your product line may be so extensive that it would be impractical to include every product. I'd suggest that you incorporate the information for your best-selling products and then direct your learners to this information for your other products. Some of your sales staff may not look at it initially, but should they be asked a question by a customer, they will know where the answer is and will be in a position to let their customer know, with confidence, that they can easily access the information and get back to them.

Below are some examples of how product features can be provided to your learners.

PRODUCT BOOKS

One client I worked with had a fairly extensive list of products and they wanted their sales team to have as much information about the products as we could provide in a realistic fashion. The primary goal for this product information was to provide as much information about the products before the sales team attended classroom training to maximize the use of their time in the classroom and their time out of the field. They also wanted learners to have this information in a format that would allow them to access it as they needed it, and to be able to refer to it in the future. To accommodate this we created self-study guides for each product. The format for the guides was the same for all the products to help learners know where in the guide they could find the information they wanted. The guides included text in a bullet-style format and graphics, so as not to have paragraphs and paragraphs of text. We also provided self-check questions at the end of the guides to provide a hands-on approach.

CD-ROM REFERENCE

One very large client I worked with wanted a library of product information for their team. They wanted this to be developed in an electronic format so it could be updated frequently and cost-effectively.

We created this resource in a true library format. When individuals inserted the CD-ROM into their computer a very elaborate graphic of a library appeared on the screen. The bookshelves in this library were full of books, one for each product. The user could click on the book and through the use of animation, the book came off the shelf and linked them to a table of contents that contained a list of the product information. At the time of the development of this product training, the organizations intranet was still in development, which is why it was originally created in a CD format. Several years later, I heard the library was moved to the intranet and the advances in technology allowed them to incorporate sound and many more text links than were originally included.

CLASSROOM ACTIVITY—WHAT'S MY PRODUCT?

We created an activity titled "What's My Product" which was used by a client in a weeklong sales session. At the end of day one, each learner was given three products in a brown paper bag. As a homework activity, they were asked to learn as many features of their products as they could and they were not to tell anyone else what products they were given. The next morning, the instructor gave everyone in the room a score sheet. The score sheet contained a list of all the client's products and then a blank line next to each. The blank line next to the product name was to be used to write down the person who had that product in their brown bag. Rotating around the room, the instructor asked each person to share one feature about each of their products. After this first round, no one was able to write down a name next to the product, as was expected. The facilitator used this rotation activity a couple more times throughout the day, when a change of pace was needed. At the end of day one, a few names were written, but not many and the instructor noticed that some of the individuals in the room were purposely sharing vague and somewhat meaningless details. The second day, the instructor changed things a bit and instead of individuals sharing features with the class, he rotated around the room and allowed people to ask questions of others about the products they had in their bag. Again, using this technique throughout the day to change the pace, learners were asking questions of one another. The learners became quite competitive and the instructor learned that on night two almost everyone studied more about their own products as well as all the other products so they could ask and answer specific questions to find out who had what product. By day three, learners were really enjoying the activity and asking when they could do this throughout the day. The end result was that learners really knew more about the company's product features than we had imagined. Due to the competitiveness and fun nature of the activity, the learners directed themselves to learn about the products.

JOB AIDS/QUICK REFERENCE GUIDES

According to Rossett and Gautier-Downes, "A job aid is a repository for information, processes, or perspective that is external to the individual and that supports work and activity by directing, guiding, and enlightening performance."[5] In most cases, job aids and quick-reference guides support training. They provide information for the learner to use on the job. They are designed to allow learners to reference information such as processes, procedures, or other important facts.

Some common job aids are:

- Steps to execute in a software application
- Checklist of supplies or materials
- Consultative questions to consider before meeting with a customer
- Product specifications and/or detailed facts

PRODUCT BENEFITS/ADVANTAGES

As you can imagine, this is a central focus of your product training, and unfortunately in some organizations this is their entire product training. As we discussed earlier, this component is critical, but in isolation will only allow your sales force to touch the surface and won't allow them to reach their full potential. This section provides your team with the benefits and advantages of your products—the reasons your customers want and need you. It provides your sales professionals with the information they need to solve their customers' problems and/or relieve their pain. It's critical in this section that you use the language of your customer. The verbiage and terms you use will be the verbiage and terms your salespeople use when speaking with their customers.

I like to begin the development of this section with the customer focus, putting myself in the role of the customer to provide the direction and framework. Some questions I ask myself are:

- Who are my customers? What role(s) do they have?
- What are the needs of the customer?
- What are the customers' problems? What pain are they feeling?
- What can I do to meet their needs?

- What products do I have that will meet their needs and/or solve their problems?
- What products do I have that will save them money, time, and resources?
- What solutions can I offer that will relieve their pain?

These questions and answers will help you define the parameters, goals, and objectives of this section.

The product book example and the "What's My Product?" classroom activity can both be modified to include advantages and benefits. Here are some additional examples that you can modify to meet your needs.

BOARD GAME

One client I worked with had a very young adult sales staff and they requested that our session be driven by fun and interactive activities. To address the demographics of this audience, we created a board game. We developed a board game that was similar to the Parker Brothers game Sorry!®. We color-coded the squares, which corresponded to different questions. One category was customers' questions, such as "We are currently experiencing [*insert problem*], how can your [*insert product name*] help me?" Another category provided product names for which the player had to list three of five advantages. If features were given instead of advantages, the player moved back the number on the dice.

POST-IT GAME

This activity was delivered in a classroom setting when originally developed, but was later modified for a Web-based course. Using large poster boards with one product name on each, teams were given 11-inch-by-7-inch pieces of paper, each containing different advantages and benefits. Teams were given a specified amount of time to tape the benefit/advantage sheets onto the correct product board.

When the game was adapted to an electronic course, the participant clicked and dragged advantages/benefits into the correct product block.

ELECTRONIC TRIVIA

While working on a Web-based course for a group of very competitive sales professionals, we decided to incorporate a score-based activity throughout the entire 90-minute course. At planned intervals throughout the course questions would pop up about the advantages of a variety of products. Users were given a question with four multiple-choice answers. The participant chose their answer and their score was tracked and shown in the bottom right corner of the screen.

WEBCAST ACTIVITY

Using the survey/question feature of a Webcast product, participants were presented questions throughout the session and they could answer them confidentially. At the end of the session, the facilitator pooled the answers and used the activity to review key advantage/benefit points about their products. Again, in this instance the majority of the questions presented were questions that would be asked by customers.

SELLING APPLICATIONS

Now that your learners have the foundational information, they understand your products' features, and understand the products' benefits and advantages in the eyes of their customers, it's time to pull it all together and apply it to real-world selling situations. As you probably know, role-playing is often used at this point. It provides your team with the practice they need, the feedback they desire, and the opportunity to make mistakes in a safe environment. As we discussed earlier, adult learners learn by doing and that includes making mistakes.

In addition to the standard customer/salesperson role play, here are a few variations that can be used.

WEB-BASED SCENARIOS

One course created for telephone sales professionals used audio and graphics to model real-life phone calls. The screen was a picture of a desk, with a telephone, note pad, and file drawer. The learner clicked on the phone when it rang and an audio recording presented the learner with a situation. The learner was then presented with four choices on how to verbally respond to the caller. They were also asked to type notes on the notepad and click on the items they would pull from their file drawer. Based on the verbal response chosen by the learner, a series of additional audio pieces would begin. When the scenario was over, the learner was provided with a score for their verbal responses, a score for their file drawer selections, and a reminder of the items that should have been typed on their notepad.

WEBCAST SCENARIOS

Using the example just provided, the same could be done via the survey and question features provided in most Webcast software packages. Using a Webcast would allow for more personalized feedback for each learner, as well as the opportunity for other learners in the session to learn from their colleagues.

CONCLUSION AND RESOURCES

As with all training sessions, it's important to close your session by pulling the pieces together, reviewing your goals and objectives, and highlighting, one last time, key points. It's also very important at this time to provide your team with resources to open the door for future learning and questions.

This section is generally delivered verbally by the instructor or written in bullet points in paper-based courses.

ONGOING FOLLOW-UP

This component is most often overlooked or cut when budgets get tight. Unfortunately, this can be a big mistake. Too often, training is considered an event, when in fact it's a process. It is very difficult for any person to be able to assimilate all the information provided in a course or session into real-world application. Knowledge objectives can be measured and accomplished in a training event; however, skills must be reinforced in the work environment to be developed. The use of a follow-up component can maximize this transfer of knowledge into skills.

According to a study conducted by the Xerox Corporation on skills training, 87 percent of the desired skills change was lost without follow-up coaching. The implication is that no matter how good the classroom training is, the effectiveness is lost without on-the-job reinforcement.[6]

Here are a few examples of follow-up components:

- *E-mail.* Instructors can write one e-mail and personalize it to each participant reminding them of key points, as well as asking specific questions about their on-the-job performance.
- *Phone calls.* Follow-up phone calls can be delivered to each person individually or group conference calls can

be set up to allow the entire group to come back together at preset times.

- *Podcasts.* Information can be delivered to participants as audio files, reminding them of key points, scheduled follow-up conference calls, and/or follow-up Webcasts.
- *Job aids.* Job aids can also be used for follow-up, either sent electronically or by regular mail.

SUMMARY

Product training is a foundational piece for your sales training curriculum. It helps provide your team with the knowledge and resources to reach their full potential. Using adult learning principles, instructional design principles, and varied approaches to meet the different learning styles of your sales team will allow you to impact the largest number of people effectively.

RECOMMENDED RESOURCES

- M. Knowles, *Andragogy in Action: Applying Modern Principles of Adult Education*
- Sharan B. Merriam and Rosemary S. Caffarella, *Learning in Adulthood*
- A. Rossett and J. Gautier-Downes, *A Handbook of Job Aids*

CHAPTER 10

Tech Talk—Teaching Technology to Sales Professionals

LUANN IRWIN, LAI Associates, formerly of Kodak

Your Learning, Anytime, Anywhere. That's the Kodak Americas Academy "Sales Training Utopia." The academy provides the learning needed to be successful in a sales position—using a variety of learning methods—so salespeople can do what they need to do, when they choose. Working with customers is top priority for sales, of course, and training's job is to make them the most capable and best-informed sales professionals, without taking their time away from selling.

When you are presenting technical topics to sales professionals, a flexible approach is critical because some learners need more time than others and have different levels of knowledge or skill coming into the learning experience. If you miss learning the basics on a technical topic and aren't already confident in your knowledge, it can be very hard to catch up. Many people give up or avoid technical training because it is frustrating and embarrassing not to "get it" right away. It reminds us of our early school days and how hard it was with certain topics—all of our old emotions are aroused. This means that some of our students who enter a course or program already have "baggage" or an "attitude." On top of that, we are often the messengers of a new system, software, or product that replaces something they have been comfortable with and requires them to learn many complex tasks very quickly. It becomes even more challenging if we are changing something very dear to them, such as the way they are paid (new sales compensation system) or making them learn about one technology (e.g., digital photography) when their expertise and lifework has been in another (e.g., film—a Kodak example).

HOW *NOT* TO TEACH TECHNOLOGY TO SALESPEOPLE

Sending a mandatory requirement memo with time and date for participation in training is a sure way to get people angry and certainly does not provide the best learning environment. It is especially important to introduce concepts and skills in carefully crafted communications, instead of just putting the training out there. We'll talk about some examples of how this can be done to engage and excite your learners and have them asking for more.

GETTING STARTED

What are your organization's goals and sales targets for the future? Aligning the training with the organization and identifying what targets training can help to reach are steps that provide focus and credibility to the training. This can be done by collecting all of the information possible and then conducting a needs analysis to help prioritize learning projects. Interviews and surveys are methods that provide information to create your strategy. At Kodak, we found it helpful to create our own learning and development team. Vision, mission, strategy, and goals that were used in our introduction to key managers, who then could provide their expectations and learning needs in an interview. These interviews, of course, can be done over the phone or by computer, as well as in person. If you need to interview international managers and sales professionals, you can obtain cultural and language support through books or Internet information to avoid cultural missteps or insults. Choose a theme or overarching concept for your programs that can be varied and useful for introductions throughout the year. Ours was "Your Learning, Anytime, Anywhere." This was developed by reviewing corporate goals and marketing, as well as considering our own training team's vision and mission for providing learning solutions. Because of cost restrictions and the need to reduce travel, we decided to focus on our learners' need for convenient, quick, excellent, but cost-effective learning opportunities and resources.

The next major focus after finding out what *the business* needs/requires for learning and skills is to determine what *each person* needs to learn for his or her own success and productivity. This can be done through a capability assessment. Start by talking to the sales professionals and asking them, "What do you need to learn to be successful in your job?" Tell them what management's expectations are for learning, and ask them to validate the competencies and skills. This gives you their input and ideas, as well as their engagement in the development of their personal learning plan.

To "triangulate" (approach the needs assessment from a third angle), review all of the current literature and benchmark with colleagues to find out what sales professionals need to learn and what the most successful sales professionals already know how to do. After talking to a few representatives, begin dialogue with the sales management and the sales professionals. For example, you can ask a small representative team to be your training advisory board and then share what the board recommends with all of the sales management and the sales representatives to get their input.

Here is a summary of a process that can be used for assessing and aligning training:

Organization Vision/Goals/Targets →
Management Expectations of Sales → *Sales Professionals'*
Learning Needs → *Training Plan*

As needs become identified, you can develop a plan for providing learning solutions. This plan should be communicated, updated, and available electronically to all stakeholders on an ongoing basis. For us, the Americas Academy became the vehicle for communication, design, registration, delivery, and evaluation of learning.

DESIGNING LEARNING SOLUTIONS

As you begin the design of learning solutions that will result in sales force excellence, you define the learning objectives—what participants will be able to do at the end of the learning experience. For example:

- The students in training for the new sales promotion tracking system will be able to use the system to accurately track all sales promotions.
- They will be able to describe the system to others.
- They will be able to use data entered into the system to identify the most successful promotions that have been implemented.

For each objective, list all of the critical learning points, steps required to achieve each learning point, and the information needed to complete each step.

Then, as in any good training program, determine the best methods to deliver the training.

Typically, you want to help learners understand the "big picture," that is, the overview of the system and how it fits with other processes, procedures, and work tools. Step-by-step procedures for completing key tasks are provided in small modules or learning topics that can be illustrated, demonstrated, and easily reviewed to reinforce the learning. For most technical training, hands-on experiences help people remember because they can actually enter data into a test environment on a system software and/or actually use the product or service that they will need to learn to sell.

If you are training learners to use a new system, software, or product, provide them with:

- System/software/product overview
- Step-by-step procedures
- Demonstration
- Practice

Assessing learners' knowledge and experience levels can help provide them with the "fast track" to learning. For example, if they can already describe the system and what it does, they can "test out" of the overview and go directly into the skill development learning modules. They also should only be required to take the learning modules that they are expected to use as part of their job. Once they can explain the steps to complete a task, they should be required to perform the task with accuracy (you choose the criteria level; e.g., 90 percent correct for noncritical tasks or 100 percent correct for critical tasks). Pre- and post-training testing can be intimidating to learners of technology, but can be presented as an opportunity, in a non-threatening way, such as completing a quiz to see if the individual should start in Level 1, Level 2, or Level 3 (basic, intermediate, or advanced).

There are many ways to design the training. If you are designing it, make sure you have access to the newest technical information and design the program so that it can be instantly updated because technical topics change constantly. If you have technical experts who are available and reliable to review and critique training drafts quickly, then you can keep on top of the changes. If you are a technical expert, that is even better. Sometimes you need to purchase the technical expertise or design from external technical experts. In that case, you need a really good relationship and contract for the design elements that you require for excellence. For example, you have purchased new software to record sales and customer information, and the company that created the software has experts who can conduct the training. You should create an agreement as part of the software purchase contract that includes costs and the time frame within which they will develop and deliver the training to ensure successful transition to the new software.

There are also many elements of design that you may want to consider, such as:

- How will the training be announced?
- Is it required training or voluntary?
- Has management been briefed on the need for the training?
- Is management in full support of the time it will take for their salespeople to complete the training?
- Will management help communicate the need and support the attendance of their employees?
- Is management required to use the system, software, or product themselves?
- Has management been trained?
- What is management's reaction to the system, software, or product?

Other questions include:

- How will the training be implemented? The answers to this question will influence your design. For example, if everyone can't come into the same location on the same dates and time, you need distance learning as part of your design. If everyone does not have access to the same computer configuration, there may be technical issues that will increase their frustration. The design will need to allow for variations. For example, online training is designed and available, but salespeople who travel and have home offices may not be able to stay online long enough to download or take the training so storage devices such as CDs or DVDs could be mailed to them to ensure smooth implementation. This needs to be known before designing the program, because it will influence how the program is designed.

- What are student learning styles and preferences?
- Does each person like to learn in groups or alone?
- Is the person new to the job or very experienced?
- What do they already know about the system or product to be learned?
- Are they in close proximity or dispersed throughout the nation and other countries?
- What languages are required for translations?
- What is the timeline for learning?
- How can students be prepared to learn most effectively?
- How can the new learning be reinforced, practiced, and evaluated?
- How can I incorporate activities to engage learners and reinforce their learning?
- What are all the elements of the training that can be designed to ensure success (e.g., prework, pretesting, job aids, simulations, case studies, practice sessions/scenarios with feedback opportunities from experts, contests, recognition).
- Can learning be achieved by using simple methods like PowerPoint or does it need to be authored in software that provides more interaction and graphic appeal?

- Do students have certain days or times that are the best for them to learn when they are not required to be in other meetings?
- Do they have scheduled sales meetings that could be used for training?
- How can you get their hands on the system or product to be learned?

It is especially helpful, when designing technical training to include ways to create a learning community (LC) or learning partners (LP). The learning community is an environment that you create to ensure that each person feels guided, supported, and successful at learning complex skills. Members of LCs or LPs will feel like they are all learning together, helping each other learn, and willing to enjoy each other's success in learning each module, section, task, or skill. This allows each person the comfort to ask any question and get help along the learning journey. Even if there are different levels of expertise, every person is encouraged to share their knowledge and concerns as they travel together along the path to competency in the topic they are studying together. This can be done while students are together in a classroom and when they are on their own in their locations, using phone, e-mail, mailings, Web conferencing, etc. Learning partners are two-person teams determined by allowing them to choose their own partner or assigning partners (randomly, by location, or level of learning need). They provide opportunities for each partner to practice and learn with another student. Technical training can make learners feel isolated and "stupid" if they cannot grasp certain knowledge or skills. These learning support systems, such as LPs, give people an opportunity to gain capability and to vent their frustrations, if needed, throughout the learning process. LPs should be brought together with the larger group for group discussion of their learning, an opportunity to ask questions of the experts, and recognition of their accomplishments achieved along the learning path or map.

You can create a learning path or map that helps each student to continue on track and feel a sense of satisfaction at certain points throughout the process. This increases the environment for motivation to complete their learning. A learning path or map, such as the example in Figure 10.1, can be created by listing all of the key tasks that will need to be learned in the best order for easy comprehension. Each learning module needs to build more competency at a steady pace for the learner to understand and practice, starting with the most basic or the first task required for performance success. A short quiz or exercise should be designed at the end of each module to ensure mastery of the current skills before moving on to more complex skills. This provides sufficient foundation and satisfaction on an ongoing basis as well as a sense of adventure while the learner travels toward their final destination of completion.

Making the learning experience fun and engaging also helps to keep participants involved. More information on this is included in Chapter 8. Training can be engaging, even if it is a technical topic. Making telephone skills teaching opportunities into the format of a radio program in which two trainers banter back and forth to share knowledge adds some spice and variety to the learning process. Creating videos and CDs/DVDs with demonstration and light humor provides a break to the normal presentation techniques that can be designed into the overall learning experience.

Job aids and learning projects help reinforce the learning. It is important to consider creating these in the design phase, if they are appropriate for the topic to be learned. Job aids, such as the example in Figure 10.2, provide quick, clear, attractive summaries of the steps required to complete tasks successfully. Learning projects can be designed similar to job aids (e.g., you can hold the steps in your hand in a neat little

FIGURE 10.1 Systems Tools for Success (STS)

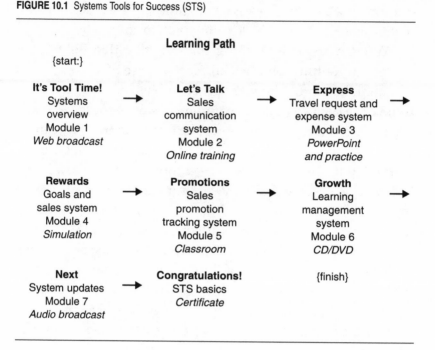

Learning Path

{start:}

It's Tool Time!		**Let's Talk**		**Express**
Systems →		Sales →		Travel request and →
overview		communication		expense system
Module 1		system		Module 3
Web broadcast		Module 2		*PowerPoint*
		Online training		*and practice*

Rewards		**Promotions**		**Growth**
Goals and →		Sales →		Learning →
sales system		promotion		management
Module 4		tracking system		system
Simulation		Module 5		Module 6
		Classroom		*CD/DVD*

Next		**Congratulations!**		{finish}
System updates →		STS basics		
Module 7		*Certificate*		
Audio broadcast				

brochure), but they require the learner to take action to complete each assignment. This can be laid out in a step-by-step/checklist format, telling the learner what actions to complete. For example:

- Go online and order the product or service that you are going to be selling and record your reactions to the ordering process.
- Once you receive the product (or use the service), notice the packaging/marketing and record your reactions as you take the product components out of the box (or use the service).
- Review the quick set-up guide and follow the directions.
- Practice using all of the features of the product and record your reactions/questions.

This information (and practice) provides hands-on learning and feedback regarding frequently asked questions (FAQs) that need to be included with the product or service that is being sold.

During the design, you are focusing on each learning objective and identifying all the learning components that must be in place to help the student achieve the objective. Then you go on to the next objective and create a new module, chapter, or section to complete the learning required for achievement of that objective. Objectives must be written with specific achievable wording so the training can be designed to ensure that learning can be observed, tracked, and enabled to the level of competency required.

For each task to be learned, complete a task analysis (steps) and task breakdown (details of steps, materials, equipment, knowledge, skills, and tools required for successful task completion). The level of competency required needs to be clearly stated (e.g., 90 percent accuracy on tasks A, B, and C). The learning and practice should build the student's ability to achieve this step-by-step.

Once you have ensured that each objective can be achieved by your design, you should look for an overall theme or concept to help learners get the "entire picture" of what they are accomplishing with each module and what they will achieve by the end of the entire learning experience (including prework, postwork, and performance assessment).

Technical training needs to be designed in a logical, clear flow of modules and tasks that build to total the capability needed.

If you are designing a classroom experience, you need to include all of the classroom logistics to make sure that any equipment being used for technical training is in full working order. If you are designing virtual or remote learning experiences, you must include logistics requirements for a successful learning experience in a variety of possible settings. This takes a lot of

FIGURE 10.2 Sample Travel System Job Aid

System Logon: ↓	Step 1: Enter name and password Step 2: Select tab "Request"
Making Request: ↓	Step 1: Choose travel location Step 2: Choose travel dates Step 3: Enter reason for travel (e.g., customer visit)
Making Reservations: ↓	Step 1: Choose/reserve airline flight Step 2: Choose/reserve hotel Step 3: Choose/reserve car
Entering Expenses:	Step 1: Gather all receipts Step 2: Enter expenses for air, hotel, car, meals, tips Step 3: Itemize details as appropriate (e.g., taxes) Step 4: Check and recheck totals for accuracy Step 5: Submit expenses for payment/reimbursement

research regarding the conditions under which students will be taking the training, such as ensuring the computer specifications are consistent on each person's computer, each person has comfortable phone headsets for long sessions, etc.

This can all be determined as you complete the initial needs assessment and are involved in your design by continuing a dialogue with the potential students and the experts who know the system, software, or products/services that will be the focus of the training.

Here is an example of the Americas Academy training designed for Kodak:

- The Americas Academy (for the United States, Canada, Latin America, and South America) was introduced to the sales management and sales representatives by the vice president and directors as the vehicle for learning by using e-mail introductions and schedules as well as a Lotus Notes database for registration, program information, and reference (recordings and copies of presentations).

- New product (e.g., cameras and printers) and service (e.g., Kodak Gallery photo collection, sharing, and printing) training sessions are introduced monthly and are held at the same time and day each week—a day that is most convenient for the sales force.
- Sessions are conducted by the experts using Web conferencing software and phone conferencing.
- Hands-on sessions are set up in various locations for practice labs (technical "playgrounds") and feedback (by coaches) on the products.
- Technical documentation is provided in a common database accessible to all learners.
- Online training and demonstrations are available to all learners (designed at different levels of capability from basic to advanced).
- Product CDs/DVDs are available for review.
- Advertising and marketing materials are available for review.
- "Radio broadcasts" and "tech talks" are held on an ongoing basis to provide more details on products as needed.
- Evaluation surveys, observation of demonstrations/ performance, and sales achieved are all used as measures of success of the training resources provided.

DEVELOPMENT

Once you have the content of what the sales representatives need to know, you can "storyboard" each module. This is an ongoing layout of each topic and how it will be conveyed—similar to a comic strip—where you place graphics and information in a clear flow that brings the learner from the simple concepts to the more complex tasks to ensure they are learning at a reasonable pace. As you develop the modules, you can insert checkpoints (quizzes) to see if the learners have grasped the concept or task before they go on to learn the next one. This also provides opportunities for accelerated learning by giving students a chance to go to the next level of learning as soon as they are ready. Try to develop a simulation (practice) of the task that the learners can perform. This can be done by asking them to complete the steps in the task and providing immediate feedback to them, as well as additional information, as needed.

It is important to have potential students try out the modules ("developmental test") before any authoring is done to finalize the training in the least costly stages of the process by piloting the training with typical students who are willing to provide feedback to improve the development of the training. All of the pieces are brought together to complete the sections and the entire learning experience and are then polished/enhanced for clarity and appeal.

Mindi Tripp, regional sales trainer for ChoiceOne Communications, has shown me some terrific examples of training materials her company developed to train its sales force. The examples are so user-friendly and easy to read that you could probably use them without a training session. Each task is clearly laid out in a step-by-step manner, using bold type for key reminders, bullets, carets, white space on the page for readability, and screen shots of the view of the system that is being learned. When these views are provided, with step-by-step directions for what to do next, the button is circled or the field has an arrow pointing to it so the learners immediately can see what they should be doing on the system. These tools provide materials to be used when learners are practicing in a class, as well as great reference for them to use after the class. Successful technical training provides the learners with enough practice to be able to do common tasks and the references to use for more complex tasks so they don't have to remember everything. It will be easy for them to look it up when they need to and quickly perform the necessary task.

It is important to create a layout for the materials that is inviting and easy to use by including a lot of white space on each page, legible type, and consistent elements such as titles and icons to keep the learner oriented at all times. It is especially easy in technical training for a learner to get lost in jargon, terms, or acronyms, so you need to make him or her feel comfortable that the learning is on track to success at all times. Consistent use of terminology, spelling out acronyms, providing an outline of the learning steps, and a glossary of terms are all ways to make the learner feel more supported and competent. This speeds and reinforces learning by reducing stress and making the learner successful on a continuous basis. The learner should be provided with tools to feel in control of the learning process, such as guidelines, choices, the ability to stop and restart without having to go through what has already been learned, an opportunity to advance to the next level of information if he or she has already obtained the knowledge and skill to go on, and the ability to ask questions, participate in discussion, and provide feedback throughout the learning experience.

Materials should be edited and reviewed by others who have not been deeply involved in the development (we sometimes are "too close" to our own work to notice mistakes). Materials should be field-tested with typical potential learners to ensure they are understandable and complete. They can be developed for different levels of learners—novice, intermediate, and expert—so that less-experienced learner will not get "lost" in the quantity of information and experts will not get "bored" but will feel challenged and more advanced than they were when they started the training.

Key questions to ask and answer for the development of training include:

- Do I have enough graphics, tools, and charts to help the learner complete the necessary steps for performance?
- How will the materials be produced and duplicated?
- How will the materials be distributed?
- How will the materials be maintained and updated (version controls)?
- How will the materials be tracked and archived so the most recent version is always available to the learners?
- Who "owns" the material (i.e., copyrights, rights to modify or change them)?
- Who has the responsibility to update the materials and how often?
- How do we assure technical accuracy?
- What reference materials and support can be provided for the learners (e.g., online tutorials, help desk support, references, check sheets, job aids, updates, discussion sessions, or an electronic performance support system that provides instant electronic access to answers for the most commonly asked questions)?

DELIVERY

If you have designed and developed all of the materials for classroom delivery, or virtual delivery, and they have been tested and piloted with potential learners who can provide detailed feedback, you can prepare for delivery. Once the program is ready, you can conduct train-the-trainer sessions to ensure consistent, high-quality delivery every time the program is presented. If the learning solutions are virtual, you need to make sure that you are providing help—both online and in person, or by phone (help desk)—so that learners can obtain immediate help. This prevents frustration and keeps the learners on track to completion of the training. Brainstorm and list all of the things that have to go right to ensure high-quality instruction and place these items in a checklist to make sure they are all in working order before each learner starts the learning experience (see the example in Figure 10.3). Then list all of the things that can go wrong and develop contingency plans to ensure that the learning will continue even if something goes wrong. This includes having experts and technologists available to make certain that equipment, systems, and software are working or can be immediately worked around. Any "workarounds" should be practiced and be "transparent" to (unnoticed by) the learners.

The important thing to attempt is a constant, steady flow of learning that is uninterrupted. Any breaks in the learning have to be designed into the program so they are at the appropriate stopping points, leaving students refreshed and reinforced rather than confused or frustrated. Practice, practice, practice. Every concept, movement, transition, and response should be practiced so the event looks flawless and you only have to deal with extreme out-of-the-ordinary events (such as what to do if there is a fire drill right in the middle of some highly technical information presentations).

Len Kellogg, technical specialist from Xerox, shares some dos and don'ts from his experience of teaching equipment technology to salespeople:

- If learning is done in a classroom environment, remove all pagers, cell phones, and BlackBerrys/PDAs. Try to eliminate as many interruptions as possible.
- Schedule breaks and messaging into your lesson plan.
- If managers aren't required to attend, or if the learning session will take place before or after a sales team meeting, keep all sales managers out of the learning session. Doing this will help all the trainees feel more at ease, elim-

FIGURE 10.3 Sample Session Delivery Checklist

❏ Classroom is reserved.

❏ Materials have been reproduced.

❏ Management knows who is participating and is supportive of the program.

❏ Participants have been notified, registered, and confirmed in the program.

❏ Participants clearly understand why they are participating in this program.

❏ Participants are at the right level of capability for the presentation (they won't be overwhelmed with the complexity or bored with the program).

❏ Classroom is set up for maximum learning (e.g., location of presentation).

❏ Materials have been delivered.

❏ Materials have been checked to make sure they are complete and enough copies for each participant are available.

❏ Equipment is in the classroom.

❏ Equipment works and has backup just in case.

❏ Trainer has prepared and practiced the program presentation.

❏ List of participants includes information about each participant that helps trainer to know how to focus the learning levels and presentation ("know your learners").

❏ If virtual delivery is involved, equipment has been checked to make sure it works in the learners' locations.

❏ Delivery materials are available and working (e.g., markers, easels, name tags/cards, pens, computers, projectors).

❏ Software has been loaded and tested on all computers and equipment.

❏ Learning environment has been enhanced to support the learners.

❏ Refreshments are available.

❏ Directions and any necessary passes for entry have been ordered, cleared, and received.

❏ Systems log-in and passwords are obtained/available to ensure everyone can participate.

FIGURE 10.3 Sample Session Delivery Checklist *(continued)*

❑ Senior management support of the training is obvious (e.g., manager introduces the training).

❑ Break equipment is available (e.g., phones and computers to check messages during breaks).

❑ Introductory information is well prepared and posted (e.g., agenda with times indicated for each section and each break, what to do in case of emergency or if participant needs help).

❑ Perform trainer introductions and introductions of everyone in the session; trainer controls the flow of the session to ensure maximum learning.

---

inating any pressure the trainees might feel having a manager present. This gives trainees the opportunity to ask questions they might have but wouldn't have asked if their manager were present. It will also get the *same* message out to everyone by eliminating the manager's input. No matter how hard you try, someone will always ask the manager present a question, and the manager's answer could open up other areas that you are not prepared to address in this session.

■ Provide follow-up reminders to reinforce skills that have been learned by giving quick-reference tools (brochures/cards) and sending a monthly/quarterly e-mail to the participants with updates, reminders, or tips.

The timing of training delivery is critical. Don't deliver the program until the students will actually be able to use and practice the learning, that is, just before the system, software, or product is introduced.

EVALUATION

There are several aspects of evaluation to consider:

- Did the learners learn what they were required to learn? (Conduct testing.)
- Can they perform the tasks to the level of performance required for their job? (Provide observation checklists.)
- Can they explain and demonstrate what they have learned? (Track performance.)
- What are the results of the training (e.g., increased sales, decreased costs, increased customer satisfaction, increased performance)?
- How did the learners like the experience?
- Is senior management pleased with the results of the training?
- Was it worth the time and money invested?
- Is there a better way to provide the instruction?
- Did the learners feel they learned a lot?
- Did they enjoy the process?
- Are pre- and post-training testing necessary to prove improvements?
- Did you enjoy designing and delivering the program?
- Was productivity increased? By how much?
- What has been the payback on the investment (gains minus costs)?
- Are follow-up programs necessary?

You can provide a variety of ways for learners to easily and quickly give you feedback regarding their experiences with the training. Surveys, e-mail addresses, and phone numbers all provide opportunities for you to find out if what you have created is really working. Revisions can be made as good evaluation feedback is received to further enhance learning and provide insight into what else is needed for the learners to be successful. Continuous improvement and updates are important parts of this process. (See Chapter 12, "Measuring the Impact of Sales Training.")

SUMMARY

Technical training often has more complexity and detail than sales professionals care to have. If you can break the content up into meaningful chunks of information, delivering each in a systematic, consistent, and clear way and check for understanding on a continuous basis, the learning experience will be successful. Pre- and postsession work should be considered for learning complex technologies.

Presession work is important. It sets the stage and can have additional benefits. For example:

- Prereading can show needed support from management (e.g., letter of invitation from their manager explaining why it is important to attend).
- Prereading/prework provides foundation learning that brings everyone up to the same level and saves valuable time when together in the session.
- Pretest/quiz assesses learners' level of understanding/ skill before entering the program. If pretest results show that there are learners with several levels of expertise who have to be in the same session, design ways of grouping learners so that the same levels are together or so that one or two experts are on each team or subgroup for practice sessions.

Postsession work is critical to reinforce technical learning ("use it or lose it"). So it is important to provide postsession exercises or quizzes/practice problems that have to be completed two weeks after the training session is completed. These postsession actions are required before the learner can obtain a certificate of completion. Anything that can be effectively learned by reading or doing online or on a CD before or after the session will save valuable time when students are together. Certainly any knowledge about the system or product should be provided ahead of time. This gives less-technical students more time to learn the information and prevents people from coming together to just get information that they could have learned more quickly on their own. Sessions that include all learners together should be reserved for advanced information and practice. This way costs are kept to a minimum and the students' valuable time can be respected.

When delivering the training sessions, keep the delivery approach light and informative, using more opportunity for interaction, practice, and breaks than in nontechnical training. Try to be creative and clever but thoroughly test each presentation ahead of time to ensure it has clear, crisp information as well as being enjoyable to receive.

The sales technical training Utopia is an environment where learners are excited about participating in training and look forward to and request learning experiences, as needed. In this Utopia, learners are skilled and capable of performing their required tasks with excellence. Managers visibly support training, expect participation, reinforce learning, and request additional training as needed. The organization shows that it values training enough to provide sufficient budget and resources to design and deliver high-quality training at a reasonable cost. Sales are up, costs are down, customers are satisfied, and the sales force knows that they are fully capable of being successful.

CHAPTER 11

Developing Strategies for Sales Training Technology Selection

WILLIAM MAGAGNA, Dade Behring

When it comes to the use of technology for sales training, most people can agree on the end goal: to effectively and efficiently develop a sales professional to successfully sell product. How that gets accomplished is where opinions diverge.

From traditional technology choices such as CDs, DVDs, and Internet portals supplying an array of software products and collaborative communication tools to more recent trends such as text messaging, podcasts, and blogs, the array of technology choices to deliver your sales training curriculum are staggering. Companies today must embrace a myriad of technologies for sales force training in order to stay competitive in diverse, competitive, and global markets.

However, this raises many questions concerning the hardware, development time, user acceptance, reliability, technical support, updates, effectiveness, and costs. Training professionals and those experienced sales professionals charged with sales training development and delivery must have tools to make decisions on what technologies will most effectively and efficiently deliver their sales training curriculum.

Fundamentally, I am of the opinion that learning to be good at selling product is really no different than learning to perform well at any complex task. What I mean by *fundamen-*

tally are the components, design, and implementation of the instructional design model that will make the difference in the measure of effectiveness and efficiency and, eventually, the selection of technology to design and deliver your training. Here the term *effective* means to what extent the trainee learned what was intended. *Efficiency* is a measure of the time, money, and other costs that went into the training effort. It is important to balance efficiency and effectiveness to come up with the best training solution. Unfortunately, many sales training organizations may start out with a very important but overlooked disadvantage: organizations often rely on expert sales personnel to provide leadership in the area of sales training curriculum decisions, design, and delivery with little or no professional instructional design support. The old adage, "He who does knows best," is very true. However, it doesn't mean they can provide sound instructional design in the development and delivery of a sales training curriculum that allows for the knowledge transfer of their years of expertise. This results in common pitfalls, all of which compromise the training initiative. The incorrect choice of technology is just one of those pitfalls. Let me explain.

In my discussion with very successful sales trainers here at Dade Behring, they eluded to the fact that most times, very successful sales professionals have a very difficult time describing what they do that makes them successful, not only in their overall efforts but in individual situations themselves. That is, they find it difficult to deconstruct their tasks into distinct components in a manner meaningful to a novice that can then be captured in a curriculum. On the other hand, inexperienced sales professionals seem to be able to list a far more comprehensive set of attributes, actions, and knowledge they feel are key to becoming a successful sales professional. Although this may seem like a paradox, it's actually quite common among experienced (expert) and novice professionals in virtually every profession.

From my own experience, I can recall working with my grandfather in his garage when I was a teenager. He was what could be called an expert mechanic, and, of course, I was a novice. Because of the disparity of knowledge and experience between the two of us, learning anything was always a challenge. He would ask me to replace the carburetor and I would hesitate for a moment and then ask how to do it. His answer was simple, "Take the old one off, and put the new one on." Sales training, and the use of technology to accomplish that training, faces a similar challenge. That challenge is the need to overcome the very flat knowledge base that experts possess, and develop a more procedural and tiered learning curriculum that novices require in the most effective and efficient manner.

A natural result to this dilemma is one of the oldest forms of learning known to humans—the story. Renie McClay shows us some great ways to engage learners in Chapter 8, and some of those will work with technology as well. We need to remember, though, that long ago humans were telling other humans stories, and from those stories, no doubt learning a behavior without ever even engaging in it. And thus, much of what I have seen done in sales training has become essentially storytelling. I have seen several excellent examples of this used with various forms of technology, and without a doubt it is a very effective learning tool. Problem-based learning, scenario critique, and intelligent coaching are examples of these training packages.

Over and over again, I hear at conferences and around the instructional design campfire how difficult it is to teach "soft skills" with technology. It seems that the last bastion of technology-driven training resides firmly within this realm. I'm really not very sure what the term *soft skills* actually means when it comes to sales training and I suspect many in the training business don't either. Sure it's used to refer to employee actions, conduct, mind-set, and so on, and that's fine, but I'm not buying that when it comes to sales training. I believe when it comes to sales training this term *soft skills* is used to describe those nebulous functions some possess but can't self-articulate very well, yet these functions result in being successful out there selling product.

Ultimately, the question really is whether training professionals can choose and implement technology to teach the problem-solving skills necessary to develop sales professionals. The answer I come up with is, if done right, most definitely yes. But before we get into the actual technology uses I have experience with both at Dade Behring and elsewhere, we should first briefly outline the initial design work that goes into helping us decide what technology platform to choose for our training.

Over the years, a mountain of research has been compiled on how people learn. Adult learners in particular are an interesting bunch; however, I argue, not much different than any other age group. That is to say, how they learn to be great salespeople is very similar to how adolescents learn to be good part-time employees, or seniors learn their volunteer work in retirement. To use instructional design lingo, they all must at any given time while performing recruit the needed facts, rules, and procedures to solve problems. How they learn all these is basically the same.

I am a firm believer in very concrete curriculum requirements for all people when it comes to learning. Though individual differences do exist among the population in regard to age, gender, and culture, people learn in very predictable ways. What I have found to be much more unpredictable is the technology you choose and the platform you use to deploy your training.

Without risking an intellectual debate, and to somewhat oversimplify for the sake of this discussion, I characterize learning as a chunking process by which the information-processing model takes in stimuli and networks it in both semantic and nonsemantic ways. In other words, either the learner will acquire knowledge and remember or will retain the stimulus for, at best, rote recall. The latter means that decay quickly sets in. How people network that stimulus into knowledge is a matter of never-ending intellectual debate, but I feel it is a measure of motivation, intelligence, experience, and curriculum. All trainers must face the reality that of the four, they have the most control over the last one—curriculum design.

How any novice progresses to functional, proficient, and eventually expert can be attributed to a form of incremental learning called scaffolding. Scaffolding is simply constructing framework of knowledge from where the learner is to where you want them to be. The size of the step and amount of information required to get there is commonly referred to as the zone of proximal development and is a measure of good instructional design. Keep in mind that people seem to learn the most complex tasks, such as being a successful sales professional, with a mix of cognitive and hands-on learning in a constructivist environment. That is, learners will construct their own knowledge base in a manner that is most meaningful and relevant to the chunking process for them.

That means there must be adequate processing time. Contextual activity and practice must be built into the learning to allow for this, and properly applied technology can provide that. However, a story told for the sake of pointing out a specific sales issue has trouble meeting these requirements regardless of the sophistication used to deploy it.

Therefore eliciting and breaking down into the levels of learning each task from the experiences and actions of a true expert is a cumbersome and difficult task. This is commonly referred to as "task analysis." Many tools are available for task analysis, and most instructional systems design (ISD) professionals can provide sound implementation of them to accomplish this.

The initial key component to the design of instruction, and subsequently the selection of the appropriate technology to transfer that knowledge, is the thorough analysis of the knowledge required to achieve the performance goal. Ironically, though it sounds simple enough, this is where many training initiatives for sales professionals begin to weaken. This effort is referred to as task analysis, and from that effort a media (technology) selection taxonomy is developed.

In essence, you are taking a complex goal and deconstructing all the tasks required to achieve that goal. The process is not easy or quick. However, cutting corners at this juncture will almost always compromise instructional quality.

Essentially, the result of the task analysis becomes the first component for the selection of appropriate media (technology) for the sales training effort. I like to refer to this analysis result as the identifying and labeling of the tasks in terms of "level of learning." Identifying levels of learning provides the sales training program with a fundamental baseline of all the critical tasks a successful salesperson does to perform well and sell product.

Regardless of whether the goal is for students to learn the new software they need to run their sales activities, promote a new line, renew an old contract, displace a competitor, or whatever, keep in mind, as mentioned earlier, certain very predictable things happen when people learn. And technology is just the tool for those things to happen, not the method. That is to say, technology is not a means to an end. Let's take a look.

STEP ONE: LEVELS OF LEARNING

Once high-level tasks are identified, training professionals need a simple yet effective set of definitions to assign to the result of the broken-down tasks of successful sales professionals. For this need, I prefer using a simple four-tier approach to classifying all tasks. The lowest and most basic level of learning is *facts*. Although volumes of educational research will define and describe a fact and its relation to learning, in the simplest of my own personal terms, facts are discrete objects that can stand alone (using the word *objects* creates another problem, but we will deal with this a bit later). For example, a basic fact for all sales professionals at Dade Behring is the throughput (how much work an instrument can do, usually measured in an hour or a workday) of each diagnostic instrument. It is a basic object that can stand alone—"This model can do X amount tests an hour"—nice and neat, as well as essential to any sales negotiation.

The second level of learning that builds on the list of identified facts is a *rule*. Again, in simplest terms, two or more facts linked together form a rule. For example, by rule, one instrument is faster than another. "The throughput from this instrument is X and the throughput from that other instrument is Y and therefore the one instrument is faster." So, in order to truly understand the rule, one must know each fact.

The third level of learning is the *procedure*. Two or more rules linked together form a procedure. For example, by rule, one instrument is faster than another, and by another rule, one instrument is more accurate than another. The client expressed to the sales professional that accuracy is the primary concern of the lab, so what should the next action be? That action could be described as a procedure. A more realistic context, in the sales world, is the classic example of a procedure—"If I say or do this, then the client will say or do that and then I will perform accordingly."

The top level of learning is *problem solving*. Two or more procedures linked together form a problem-solving strategy. Any time a sales professional has contact with the client, he or she is in a problem-solving mode. The sales professional is drawing on multiple procedures, rules, and facts to formulate the correct problem-solving strategy in what can most likely be a real-time, high-pressure environment.

For thousands of years, apprentice modeling has been very effective in scaffolding the inexperienced and uneducated in the ways of a given profession. If you want to be a mechanic, go work with one, and if that mechanic manages to put up with you long enough, you eventually become a great mechanic. The same could be said for sales professionals. The problem is that it's not very efficient, meaning you're paying that newbie to be schlepped around by a heavy hitter in the field.

Shrinking the time from novice to expert is what sales training, or any other profession, is really all about. The correct application of technology can either help or impede, which leads us to another dilemma: this is by far the most difficult level of learning to accommodate in terms of technology, but it can be done. I will discuss this in more detail later in the chapter.

STEP TWO: IDENTIFY THE TYPE OF TASK

Now that you have conducted a task analysis and identified the levels of learning, as well as the coinciding knowledge required to meet each task, you need to identify what type of task it is. Again, striving for simplicity without sacrificing quality, I usually recognize three task types.

The first is *cognitive*. This is a task that resides in whole within the individual's information-processing capacity. It is a "mental" task and requires no physical action. Rote recall, deduction, and complex reasoning are all cognitive tasks. Note that all tasks, regardless of levels of learning, can reside within this type of task.

The second type of task is *psychomotor*, which is really a 25-cent word for a type of task that requires physical action. Again, levels of learning can reside within this type of task. In most cases, purely psychomotor tasks happen without any type of precognition. The individual simply performs the task with little cognitive deliberation.

Finally, there is what I refer to as the *omni task*. This type of task requires a complex mix of cognitive and psychomotor functions working together to achieve a result. Although difficult to imagine, I believe that all levels of learning can reside within this type of task as well.

STEP THREE: LIST THE TYPES OF MEDIA

Because the focus of the discussion is on technology, forms of media, such as paper, need not be addressed. Traditionally, the terms *technology* and *media* are used somewhat interchangeably in training circles. I don't know if I agree completely with the practice, but in the context of this discussion we will. Identifying the types of technology is really a lot like creating a list of tools you have available for the instructional designer or training professional to reach into the technology toolbox and pull out. A comprehensive list would include everything from standard desktop collaborative tools like e-mail and Web browsers to software and hardware that allows for the development of any optical media–delivered packages. This sounds simple enough but often within today's diverse organizational environments no such clearinghouse of available technology options exists, or if it does, many training professionals may not know about it. The key is to gather the stakeholders and compile a list of such tools that exist within your organization and others you think you might need.

REVIEW OF CURRENT TECHNOLOGY OPTIONS

The hierarchy of current technology can best be defined by the following list in order of simple to complex:

- *Static content.* This is usually in the form of text and graphics typically represented within Web pages, CD, and other optical delivery. Easy to develop and quick to deploy with multiple platforms for development and delivery, it can be self-directed or paced. Although paper-based is the usual choice for this medium, optical media are sometimes used. With this training it is difficult to track progress, and difficult to distribute any updates.

- *Dynamic content.* This is usually in the form of text, graphics, simple and complex animation, video, and voice. Multiple platforms for development and delivery are somewhat easy to develop. It can be self-directed or paced instruction, and is usually delivered with a portal or other optical media.

- *Interactive courseware I.* Characterized by courseware that requires minimal interaction by the trainee, this is usually in the form of navigation or mouse-click responses. Often in the form of Web pages and optical media storage, this form usually contains minimal animation, audio, and virtually no video. It can be tracked and scored, but rarely is.

- *Interactive courseware II.* A more complex technology delivery platform, it requires the user to engage far more with the tool, and usually requires a more complex mental tasking. It is usually in the form of case-based and problem-based scenarios delivered in various forms of media requiring the user to interact in an appropriate way and forcing the trainee to recruit a mixture of experience, intelligence, and knowledge to complete the curriculum. It can be costly to produce and deliver, and typically contains less than four media events and user interactions per learning objective.

- *Interactive courseware III.* The most complex of technology-driven learning environments, it requires constant learner interaction to progress through the curriculum and consists of both cognitive and psychomotor tasks that reside at all levels of learning. It usually consists of software simulations, problem-based scenarios with multiple outcomes, decision trees, situational awareness, and flexible hypertext to formulate opinions and strategies. This type of courseware usually engages the learner with more than six media events and user interactions per objective, and it contains multiple learner interactions, randomized remediation, review loops, and constructivists learning objectives. By far, this is the most costly to design and deliver.

STEP 4: CONSTRUCT YOUR TAXONOMY

Now you are ready to construct your taxonomy in a way that best fits your company's needs. Construction is simply a matter of listing all the broken-down tasks (learning objectives), the levels of learning, types of tasks, and correct media that are available or attainable that fit with the best measure of effectiveness and efficiency. Remember your target is to break down the complex goal or objective into all the different tasks, isolate the components of those tasks, identify the level of learning for each component and the type of task it is, and finally, select the technology to deliver the learning.

Questions to ask before selecting technology:

1. Should it be synchronous or asynchronous? Will the student(s) and the instructor/curriculum be engaged at the same time?
2. Will it occur in the same place or different places? Will the students be together in the same room or different locations?
3. Should it be self-paced or directed? Will the curriculum be directed by the technology at a given pace, will the student control the flow of learning, or will it be a mixture of both?
4. Should it be measured or unmeasured? Will the learner be measured? How often and to what extent will it drive the curriculum flow?

All of these concepts and the questions they pose describe how technology is chosen in broad definitions. Most technology-based education falls into these categories. And these questions must be answered before curriculum development. The answers to these questions should always be driven by sound instructional design, and a drive for a balance of effective and efficient outcomes. In most cases, a mixture of the strategies and technology will be employed to reach all learning objectives. Rarely will a single curriculum, single strategy, and single technology choice meet all objectives.

In regard to sales trainees, for example, will the sales professional be alone or in a group? Will the sales trainees have access to technology? Will their progress or achievement be tracked or measured? These questions and many others must be asked and, more importantly, answered prior to any training plan development. Often when it comes to training efforts, before any analysis, the project director declares something like: the training will be an hourlong computer-based training (CBT) followed by classroom instruction that will last two days. Most instructional designers immediately would have reason for concern.

The final component to the technology choice is what I consider the litmus test of any learning environment, and that is: does your curriculum and the technology chosen to distribute and deploy it accommodate all the necessary events of instruction? The answer to this question is often no. Below is my list of the nine questions the curriculum designed and the technology chosen must answer:

1. Does it gain and hold attention?
2. Does it probe and assess prior knowledge?
3. Does it clearly inform the learner of the objective?
4. Does it present the instruction and conform to quality visual literacy?
5. Does it allow for questions and feedback?

6. Does it allow for rehearsal?

7. Does it measure their progress and achievement?

8. Does it allow for remediation?

9. Does it allow for mastery learning?

If the answer to any of these questions is no, then a review of the curriculum and the technology chosen must occur. Omitting any of these events invites potential issues and may compromise your training effort. I have seen quality curricula where some components are left out, but not many. Remember, the technology or tool used to deploy the training is only as good as the curriculum design.

SUMMARY OF TECHNOLOGY AVAILABLE AND SOME EXAMPLES FOR THE SALES TRAINING PROFESSIONAL

THE CD/DVD STAND-ALONE AND BLENDED-LEARNING SOLUTION

This technology has reached a point where the average modern desktop or laptop computer can maximize the tool. Optical media can stand alone or be run in conjunction with paper, instructor-led, or portal-delivered instruction. This type of technology has a tremendous amount of flexibility with the inclusion of audio, video, and graphics, and can deliver interactive material, and be student-driven or paced instruction. This technology is fairly mature and technically sound, so it is not a difficult venture to get off the ground.

It also allows for infinite practice and can be customized easily for different audiences within your sales force. Some packages we use at Dade Behring to develop our CD/DVD–based material include applications that are part of the Asymetrix Toolbook, Macromedia, and Adobe software suites. We use this heavily at Dade Behring for prelearning workshops, just-in-time job aids for remote users, competitor positioning platforms, advanced supplemental training, and refresher workshops as a follow-up to in-class training.

Disadvantages include that, for the most part, it is static content and static content always presents the learner, and even more so the developer, with serious constraints because once placed on a CD, the content is difficult to update, pull back, and in some applications remove from the laptop hard drive. In the past, this has created version control problems for us at Dade Behring, and questions about whether the learner has the most up-to-date training.

It's also costly in terms of time and effort to produce, maintain, and distribute, but most of all, to update. Tracking of training attendance and performance is also an issue, as well as ongoing user feedback and support to allow for mastery learning. This is a constant struggle because accountability for the sales force in regard to training is not where it should be.

Other issues we have had at Dade Behring include providing the sales force with copious digital training materials on CD for review and learning prior to attending update or new-product launch training, only to find out that less than a third of sales professionals ever took the time to review the training, the rest coming to the meeting unprepared. Similar experiences have occurred with new-hire sales professionals in certain niche markets as well.

PORTAL-DELIVERED CONTENT

This technology currently occupies the lion's share of the training curriculum for sales training. This is probably due to the plethora of software packages out there that leverage the browser-based delivery virtually every PC has. Portal-delivered content is ideal for conveying everything from basic product knowledge to product positioning, information dissemination, collaborative learning, enterprise software functional and navigation simulation training, communication and collaborative learning environments, and high-end soft-skill simulations and random-response scenario-based role modeling.

Examples include interactive Web pages, online e-learning communities, business maintenance help tools, cognitive flexible hypertext environments, chat rooms, instant messaging, communities of practice, customer outreach platforms, and formatted e-mail communications.

Software we use at Dade Behring to support these environments includes packages based on HTML, Flash, and Java to deliver interactivity, 3-D animation, audio, video, and graphics. Another component to the e-learning continuum is the learning management system (LMS). Sometimes referred to as the learning content management system, an LMS is designed to track attendance, measure performance, and provide for content organization of curriculum.

Another example is the in-application help support Web links to just-in-time job aids, performance support, intelligent tutoring, mentoring, and communication communities of best practices for sales professionals to draw the information, training, or learning they need when they need it. This is especially critical for newly trained sales professionals who find themselves out there in the field and in need of help fast with a specific issue or situation and have little or no time to sit through a traditional training package of which only a small component fits their needs.

One product used at Dade Behring to meet our browser-delivered training need is Flash software. Although there is a serious commitment in terms of license costs and training professionals to become proficient authors, in our situation, it has been a very worthwhile expense. This technology allows the sales training staff to quickly develop Web pages that are the foundation of a blended-learning solution for customer and sales training. With this learning model, technology is used to prepare new hires for the classroom experience, track their progress, and ensure entry-level knowledge prior to coming to the classroom training. Additionally, once sales professionals leave the classroom, these tools provide a link to them wherever they are in the field. For the mature sales force, it is a constant one-stop shop for news, events, best practices, and lessons learned. The technology works well with our Siebel sales platform to help gain a 360-degree view of the sales force and customer interaction.

Another example of portal-delivered content is leveraging from what the majority of sales professionals know how to use to transfer knowledge to the sales community as best practices, critical information, and training. What we have found is that almost all sales professionals have a fairly proficient understanding and working knowledge of PowerPoint and can use this tool to transfer knowledge when giving a presentation to a sales audience. We decided to leverage this proficiency and add some instructional design tools, such as knowledge capture flowcharts, PowerPoint templates that include branding platforms, instructional cueing, directions for the recording of audio and video, and the protocols for storage and quality that go with it. Finally, we invested in an application from Macromedia called Breeze that converts the PowerPoint content by building a Flash player frame around the application and all imported supporting media and quickly and easily distributed that training via an e-mail message with a link to the training, and basically turned the sales trainers loose. The result has been a huge success for us in terms of both quality and quantity of training events that are being delivered to the field. The product derived could best be described as real-time updated Web pages with interactive engaging content that could be easily developed, tracked, measured, and stored within our e-learning online university. This allows for professional development, certification, and better knowledge management of a diverse and geographically challenged sales force.

Training the sales force for functional and navigation use of such enterprise applications as Siebel, SAP, and PeopleSoft is another example of portal-delivered content. Both new-hire and existing user updates are accomplished via a Web browser with a simulation of the software, through which the sales professionals experience the business procedure in the software, are allowed to try it themselves, and finally test their own knowledge with infinite practice. Research shows that companies that operate both SAP and Siebel are 60 percent more profitable than companies that do not. However, implementing an enterprise system such as Siebel from scratch into the sales force presents several challenges for training.

Simulation technology seemed the best method for us to meet these training needs. We even went one step further to imbed this training into the live application for real-time job aids should the users find themselves performing unfamiliar business procedures. The effort was extensive, but has paid for itself every time we have a new hire or update to software.

The ultimate goal is mastery learning throughout the training continuum of preclass, classroom, and on-the-job performance without the risk of contaminating the production software. For these and similar learning applications, Dade Behring has invested in a tool called On Demand to meet our continued training needs for software applications. It has become our global standard for any software training and simulation. All training is hosted on our Web page and can be also accessed on a CD if needed.

Some disadvantages of these and similar technology tools are that they all require a substantial investment in terms of time, expertise, and money to develop, manage, and support. In particular, the recording of quality audio and video is always a challenge. Most companies will hire an outside firm to shoot or record these components of the training to save time and money, although we have not found much savings because of the need for constant updates and changes. It was cheaper for us to learn and master the capability. Additionally, the availability of an Internet connection—via modem, DSL, cellular, wireless, or whatever—with sufficient speed and bandwidth to deliver the curriculum is at times a limiting factor for the remote sales force. Another challenge is investing the time and effort in establishing proficiency in authoring software applications such as Flash, and object-oriented packages such as On Demand, Toolbook, and others. Keep in mind that without the employment of sound instructional design, as with any tool, these tools are only as good as the curriculum, and so quality is important to justify the investment. There is great information in Chapter 6 on designing training using sound instructional design principles.

NEXT-GENERATION BLENDED SALES TRAINING: SIMULATION, PODCASTS, AND BLOGS

The maturation of a new wave of online applications and tools, such as blogs, podcasts, online gaming, and wireless and mobile technologies, is just now beginning to find its way into sales force training curriculums. I feel that, other than for entry-level knowledge, these tools have a more limited application for the novice salesperson than they do for the seasoned sales force out there pounding the pavement. It's important to keep in mind that these are tools for delivering a digital message in terms of graphics, animation, video, or audio along with text, and support a blended (using several methods) approach. They can be designed to be synchronous (everyone online at the same time) and deliver dynamically changing content, therefore providing for real-time changing interaction within the organization. These tools represent an interesting and intriguing frontier as a new learning delivery format, and I'm sure future uses have yet to be explored and developed. Below is a summary of these tools followed by some dos and don'ts put together by Anders Gronstedt, of the Gronstedt Group.

- *Podcasts.* Thanks to the iPod-driven phenomenon known as "podcasting," reps can now listen and learn while driving to work, walking the dog, or riding the subway. The radio-style format of a podcast can be used to reinforce sales skills and share breaking news while reps are on the go.
- *Blogs.* An internal sales community blog serves as a forum for free-flowing conversations. It's an engine for sharing experiences from the front lines across the sales organization without inundating reps with e-mail. They can read the musings, rants, raves, insights, and opinions of their peers and weigh in on conversations about pressing issues that will help them better do their jobs.
- *Sales simulations.* The value of online simulations is that they replicate sales situations but can be played out without the risk of failure. Airplane crashes don't hurt nearly as bad in a flight simulator as they do in real life, and it's likewise more cost-efficient for salespeople to make mistakes in a simulator than to deal with the fallout of customer defection and lost productivity associated with on-the-job training.

The Dos and Don'ts of New Technology

The Don'ts of Podcasts:

- Don't treat podcasts as time-shifted lectures; they need to be carefully crafted "edutainment" shows that sound more like a talk radio program than a training session.

- Don't take a course approach; make it a regular program.

- Don't hide the podcasts in your learning management system; make them available on a blog to transform the podcast into a two-way, listener-driven medium.

- Don't expect your reps to use their own players; give them each an iPod.

- Don't put out audiobooks and other generic content; custom-develop the podcasts for your organization; generic off-the-shelf programs only work for generic off-the-shelf companies.

- Don't trust your in-house training staff with the development of podcasts unless they have professional radio and podcast background.

The Dos of Blogging

A sales community blog is one of the most effective platforms to facilitate *real-time conversations* in far-flung sales organizations. It's an online focus group, a whistle-blower hotline, a bully pulpit, a suggestion box, and a knowledge management tool. A marketing or sales leader will write personal entries in this online journal and invite sales reps' comments and discussions. Here are the dos of blogging:

- Comment on recent wins and losses and provide insight and helpful sales tips.

(continued)

- Write on breaking developments about which reps need to know.

- Recount conversations with reps, customers, and product developers.

- Link to other useful resources (internal and external) and offer context for news, competitor announcements, product releases, and more.

- Facilitate sharing of information between reps; they're the true experts in what works, and this will be an opportunity to share experiences and learn from each other.

- Have fun! Don't take yourself too seriously.

The Dos and Don'ts of Sales Simulations

Sales reps from a growing number of companies are getting valuable hands-on training with a new generation of online sales simulators. Virtual scenarios help them role-play the entire sales cycle. They get scored as they go and receive feedback from an online coach.

Dos:

- Do make it competitive; post a high-score list.

- Do make it lively and interactive with sound, video, and computer-generated characters.

- Do make it look more like a video game than an e-learning course.

- Do launch the simulations with a big splash, play them at the kickoff meeting, and advertise them with banners on the intranet and plugs in senior management communications.

(continued)

Don'ts:

- Don't focus the simulations on product presentation unless you want to turn your reps into talking brochures; focus on asking the right probing questions and identifying customer needs.

- Don't make them boring; use as much humor as your HR department will let you get away with.

- Don't buy off-the-shelf simulations if your sales force is larger than a few hundred.

Dos and Don'ts provided by Anders Gronstedt, PhD, president of Gronstedt Group, *anders@gronstedtgroup.com.*

SUMMARY

Choosing the best technology for your organization's sales training should be driven by these components:

- Your media selection taxonomy with the deconstructed task of scenario-based sales professionals
- A thorough analysis of the current technology tools your organization has available in its toolbox
- A thorough analysis of the curriculum design model, including the questions concerning delivery and events of instruction

Your organization must seek a well-defined path that ensures that the measure of a training initiative's potential success is one that is driven by a balance of both instructional effectiveness and cost efficiencies. There is always a level of maturity that goes with the level of expertise/knowledge and the formation of curriculum. For example, a sales professional who has been successful and has years of experience might not require the same training curriculum as a rookie when it comes time for a new-product launch. Likewise, that level of maturity among sales professionals should also reflect the selection of technology.

Measuring the Impact of Sales Training

GARY SUMMY, Motorola

Training professionals have been in search of a way to identify, measure, report, and receive credit for the ROI of the initiatives we champion. From the first time Donald Kirkpatrick introduced his four levels of training measurement in his book *Evaluating Training Programs* (American Society for Training and Development [ASTD], 1975) through Jack Phillips's work in *Measuring Return on Investment* (ASTD, 1994), which took the discussion to five levels with attempts to clearly define ROI (return on investment), we have been like Arthur's knights in search of this Holy Grail that will return our Camelot to glory. One of the things we attempt is to change the perception from cost of training to investment.

ROI—THE QUEST

While the quest is admirable, is the effort worthy (or even attainable)? ROI is an extremely useful metric when applied to capital purchases, investment options, and other expenditures and alternative uses of capital. But is it really appropriate for sales training? Can it or should it be applied to learning? I often hear from my colleagues focused on other training-related disciplines that I have it easy because sales training is simple to measure. Did salespeople sell more after training? It would seem to be an easy metric to capture and prove our results. Or is it?

Looking at the overall topic of measuring training departments, including sales training, there are two areas that every department leader must address: operational excellence and business impact. *Operational excellence* refers to our efficiency and the effectiveness of the transactional aspect of training. Historic training metrics apply to the operational aspect of training departments, measuring such things as cost per student, training days or hours delivered, pretest and posttest results. *Business impact* is all about our ability to create a positive effect on the metrics that matter to our clients. In other words, did the training actually make a difference to the business? My intent is to leave the operational measurements alone and focus on evaluating sales training programs in terms of business impact.

Let's look at some classical dilemmas in the evaluation of sales training. Many things affect the measurement of sales training impact, not the least of which are deciding which metrics are most appropriate to use. We know that simply looking at increased revenue (gross sales) is not always the best measurement. For example, gross revenue may increase, but how about net revenue? Selling more at lower margins with a higher cost of sales is probably not the long-term goal of most businesses, and if we measure only that aspect, what have we proven? However, if the corporate objective for a given period of time is market share (often at the expense of margin), it could be a more reasonable measurement to consider. Of course, this implies we have selected revenue as the market share metric instead of the myriad of other metrics like units shipped, units in the pipeline, number of active customers, and a host of others.

We want to be sure that whatever we attempt to measure (and hopefully the focus of our training content) is appropriate to the corporate objectives. Negotiations training with a focus on margin improvement, in the middle of a campaign for market share improvement at virtually any price, may not be a mutually supportive choice of engagements. It is like serving salty peanuts to a person dying of thirst. Under the right conditions peanuts are desirable, but what you are providing not only fails to meet the most urgent needs, it may actually have a negative impact on the current objectives.

For the sake of argument, let's assume we are in alignment and the expected outcome of our offering is designed to address the needs and objectives of the business. We deliver our training, the smile sheets are all top box (they loved the doughnuts), and three months later the business metrics we have targeted show positive improvement. Life is good and we have proven our value. Except then marketing steps in and makes the case that it was its amazing new promotion or literature—not the training—that made a difference. In the meantime, finance tells us that the market growth during the measurement period would account for most of the financial gains, and the strategy gurus claim it was their insight on the markets and customers to target. And just when we think everyone has joined the "grab the credit" melee, in comes the competitive intelligence group to confirm two of our major competitors suffered significant shortages of materials in their supply chain and were unable to meet some delivery commitments, so no one can claim credit.

Because we work in a dynamic and changing marketplace with competitors, suppliers, market forces, and sometimes natural disasters and other phenomena all having some impact on results, how can training take credit for specific ROI gains and come up with a return on investment figure? With so many things potentially (and actually) having an effect on the performance of a sales organization's financially related metrics, it is difficult to claim, much less validate, a true ROI for sales training. I realize there are organizations that claim to measure true ROI for training and I applaud their effort, but in my experience it is difficult to accurately assign responsibility for the returns. I remember a measurement project some years ago when we indicated we would be looking to provide an ROI number to sales management. They all smiled, applauded our efforts, and wished us luck. Then as we were leaving they told us they would be interested to see our results, but that no matter what number or ROI we would claim, they would not accept it because there are just too many variables. While we may be dealing with some obvious organizational metrics in sales numbers, we have little, if any, control over all the variables. So how do we sort out the variables and show that it was the training that made the difference? I promise to address that issue, but there is something we need to do first.

I am sure that occasionally we each have our difficulties communicating with others. Often the difficulty is more acute when our interaction involves someone close to us, perhaps on our team, in our company, or all too often with our clients. When that happens to me I am frequently reminded by people: "You teach this stuff, why don't you use it?" Too often I have taken shortcuts and not used the active listening skills, feedback tools, and the genuine interest in the other person I know I should employ. I assume I know what they want to say before they say it, or my behavior does not really foster a mutually respectful engagement. I know better, but still I persist. As sales trainers, it is my belief we do not always pay attention to the content of what we deliver and fail to practice what we preach. One of the cardinal rules of *consultative, solutions, customer-centric*—or whatever description you use—selling is to find out the business drivers and key issues of the client. If we are unable to demonstrate how our "solution" will have a positive impact on the priorities of our client, we are at risk that funding will go to someone or something else. Should we not do the same when we begin to justify our value to our clients?

IDENTIFYING METRICS

Step one in measuring the impact of sales training is to engage the client and find out what metrics matter to them. Ask probing questions to determine how they are measuring these key factors now. You might learn they want you to show improvement in an area where no viable current metrics exist. Frequently, I have found situations where a client wants to show improvement in areas such as call-to-close ratio or cycle time, only to find out they have no current metrics, but they know that whatever it is now, it should be better. How do I show improvement if we don't know where we are now? When no baseline exists, it is impossible to validate positive or negative movement. The lesson is never promise impact, or attempt to show improvement, if there is no starting position. You may move the needle, but how will you know, conclusively, the amount or even the direction of movement. The degree of impact of where you finish depends on where you started.

Without question, we must begin with the client and the client's priorities. The caveat is that, as with a call on a senior executive, this is not purely a "discovery" call. We should have a good idea of what these critical metrics might include. Here are some examples of potential metrics of value to our clients and where a baseline may exist:

- Funnel speed or sales cycle time
- Level of relationships (top to bottom)
- Breadth of relationships (horizontal across business units and departments)
- Call-to-close ratios
- Number of "units" shipped or in the pipeline
- Mix of "units" shipped or in the pipeline
- Product-to-service mix
- Revenue generated
- Revenue mix across product/service lines

- Margin/profit generated
- Margin/profit mix across product/service lines
- Sales (fiscal or numeric) of targeted product/service lines
- Sales mix (fiscal or numeric) of targeted product/service lines
- Sales (fiscal or numeric) in targeted markets
- Sales mix (fiscal or numeric) in targeted markets
- Repeat customers (same mix)
- Repeat customers (new products)
- New customers
- Number of new opportunities added in the pipeline
- Size of transactions
- Breadth of transactions across products/services/markets
- Time to first order or revenue (new representatives)
- Time to "breakeven" (new representatives)
- Customer satisfaction (surveys and comments)

In Chapter 4, Bob Rickert gives you ideas of metrics to use when developing your business case. Be careful of the metrics you use there because you will likely need to report on them after the fact. Think about how you will impact the organization and use those metrics to sell the idea as well as to report back on the results.

This list, along with metrics appropriate to your business environment, should form the foundation of your discussions with your sales leadership. Don't use the whole list, but pick the top three or four. They may already be defined in your company's business plan and objectives. If not, use your general knowledge of your company and its goals to identify those metrics that reflect the priorities of your sales leaders. You are now in a position to validate whether your understanding of key metrics is the same as if they would set priorities. If they push back, you have opened a dialogue. You can use your basic "handling objections" skills to understand the disconnects and get their list of priorities. Experience tells me most people will be glad to edit your list (if it truly represents insight) but are less likely to create the list for you. In the same way we coach our salespeople calling on a C-level executive to have a clear understanding of the clients' issues, starting your dialogue by asking what are the top three performance issues they need to address demonstrates a lack of understanding of the priorities of your client and could significantly affect your level of credibility. Worst case, you may not be invited back and you become a commodity. To move to business partner, you need to engage your client on their terms and bring insight and solutions unique to your perspective of their issues.

The list contains business and sales metrics, not training metrics. The key is to focus on what is critical to your client, not to you. Traditional training metrics (operational) are things like cost per student day/hour, number of people trained, positive smile sheets, or improvement in pretest/posttest scores (which by the way only measure potential capability, not performance). Once we know the key metrics our clients view as critical we can begin to explore how to measure them and how to link our efforts to positive changes in the metrics. A key thing to mention again is that while our clients may identify key metrics they want to see change, they may not have any data on that metric at the moment. If you don't know where point A is, how will you know if point B is better or worse (or the same) as point A, or the magnitude of any change. It is worth repeating to be careful not to get caught up in proving positive impact on something not currently defined.

ESTABLISHING THE LINK

Let's assume we have clearly defined metrics identified and sufficient baseline information exists for us to move forward. We need to begin to look at the direct link between the content we will deliver, the skills and behaviors that will be developed, the results expected when those skills and behaviors are effectively implemented, and the value potential of those results. The most effective model I have found to identify that linkage was developed by Robert O. Brinkerhoff, EdD, currently professor emeritus at Western Michigan University and a principal consultant for Advantage Performance Group. The model is the Impact Map.[1] Dr. Brinkerhoff has written several books on the subject of the impact of training and how to measure results and I recommend you pursue his models in greater depth. Several books are listed in the reading list at the end of this book.

I will outline briefly the concept of the Impact Map, but recommend you get the information and application directly from his books or specific training that is available from Advantage Performance Group (*http://www.advantageperformance.com*).

In essence, you first need to identify and validate that what you are delivering will address the business issues and associated metrics of your client group. An Impact Map uses a matrix to develop direct line of sight between training content and business goals and objectives. The brief example in Figure 12.1 might fit into a standard program in negotiation skills.

As noted in the example, we create a direct link between the knowledge and skill content of the training effort and corporate goals. Left to right we see that the skill is for participants to develop a plan and strategy for the inevitable concessions that are part of any negotiation. One of the critical actions that must happen in the process is to know what options are available for you to concede or trade. When the knowledge is applied or the skill performed appropriately, the result is to ensure you receive value in return for giving value. The impact (and this is the specific metric) is an improvement in profitability for the negotiation. Finally, if profits go up, so should net revenue.

FIGURE 12.1 Example of Impact Map

Knowledge and/or Skill	Critical Actions	Key Results	Business Unit Goals	Corporate Goals
Develop a concession plan and strategy	Develop a list of negotiable options and desired returns for trading	Never give anything without getting value in return	Meet profitability targets	Grow revenue

We can validate this by using a right-to-left analysis. We need to grow revenue. One way to do that is to improve our profitability on the deals we close. In order to improve profitability we must ensure we don't give away value without some commensurate value being realized. In order to get something in return for what I give, I need to understand both what I have to offer and what I want in return. The basis for being able to engage in that action step is the skill of developing your plan and strategy for concessions. Using the Impact Map model with managers helps them see the direct link between the training initiative and the on-the-job impact they can expect. This is also an excellent tool for managers to use with their direct reports that will participate in the training ensuring everyone knows what will happen and what is expected.

With the Impact Map model, we create (and validate) the direct link between what we deliver and the metrics we are measuring. If there is no link, are we delivering appropriate training? Without a direct link between the capability (knowledge and/or skill) and performance (actions and results) we are trying to influence, how can we expect to demonstrate what impact we are trying to achieve?

A problem in this scenario results from all the other variables beyond our control as trainers. Negotiation skills and net revenue or value per deal/transaction may improve and sales teams may meet the profitability targets on a deal-by-deal basis; however, if we are engaged in fewer deals or deals of a smaller magnitude, total revenue may not be impacted in the desired direction. We have proven ability to impact individual transactions, but total revenue, even net revenue, may still not achieve overall corporate goals. The issue is not our negotiating ability, but perhaps our selection of opportunities to pursue or the ability to feed the sales funnel to ensure we are expanding the potential revenue opportunities. We do better at what we chase, but we may not be chasing enough to meet the total revenue targets. Therefore, it is essential you get agreement and commitment on exactly what you are measuring and attempting to impact up front, and an understanding of what may be out of scope (opportunity selection or funnel management in this example). If this agreement on the targets and metrics is not established in the beginning, we may find we have delivered and measured skill improvement in the areas we targeted, but our value is not seen as significant. However, we may identify skill gaps not previously recognized as an issue, demonstrating the need to analyze the total environment versus isolated perceived deficiencies.

On the plus side in this scenario, if we have truly engaged in a total performance improvement discussion with our clients, we are in a position to demonstrate that impacting sales effectiveness is not the result of a single class or intervention but of a total analysis of the sales environment in which our teams must operate. Earlier I mentioned the issue of getting credit for our impact, given all the variables involved in measuring sales performance. Using Impact Maps and the corresponding analysis of success and nonsuccess scenarios helps us to clearly identify the factors that influence the results. This is the next step in the process developed by Dr. Brinkerhoff, called Success Case Method.[2]

MAKING THE CASE FOR SUBJECTIVE ANALYSIS

Let me pose a question. Which is a more valuable metric, objective data or subjective analysis? Most people believe that "hard" or objective data is the more valuable and I would not disagree that this type of information can make a compelling story. On the other hand, is it possible that this type of data might be misleading at best? It might even create a false or inaccurate analysis of the true situation. Many things go into ensuring that so-called objective data and metrics actually measure what is intended or that the results truly depict the veracity of the circumstances. When first becoming aware of this potential issue related to objective data, I did a Web search using the phrase "how to lie with statistics" and Google identified over 50,000 results. It is possible to maneuver the statistical response based on what you measure, when you capture the data, how you capture the data, and a variety of other techniques.

Take for example an end-of-course questionnaire that captures the participants evaluation of the value or impact of the course to their on-the-job requirements. This is often used in an attempt to produce "objective" data that shows the course has on-the-job impact. This is not "objective" data, but is a numerical value that is easy to compare and gives the impression of objectivity. I have also seen this type of question used as part of the validation of the elusive ROI calculation, using the results to point to direct links between training program and job impact. However, a program potentially could receive excellent responses immediately after the session with participants responding that they see a direct link to their ability to perform on the job. Based on the questionnaire, the case is made that the participants recognized the value and potential for impact. Often these surveys are done immediately after the session or within 48 hours using Web push technologies. However, the same survey taken three months later may have a totally different set of results. In this case, the "objective" data may appear to support the fact that the intervention had (or in reality appears to have the potential to have) impact on job performance.

Let's look at it from a personal perspective. Assume you have an opportunity to attend some training that will impact your career skills and opportunities. You do some research and identify a program that, based on the participant surveys using a 5-point scale with 5 being most definitely, the average score on the question about whether the program will have a significant impact on your job performance and expanded career opportunities is 4.7. Would you consider attending? Would you spend your own money? The data certainly looks good and the participants have clearly identified the value of the program.

In further research, you discover the questionnaire was administered on-site at the end of the program and was available online for 48 hours after the session ended (on a Friday). You learn that one of your most trusted friends from another company attended the session and you call that person to discuss the program. You mention the survey results and would like this trusted friend's personal opinion. She tells you she rated the program a 5 when she completed the survey. Sounds good so far; I'm probably ready to send the check. But then she tells you that after getting back to her real job she realized that while there was a lot of good information, the training really didn't develop actionable skills that transferred to the job, and the training provided no tools to implement the learning or ways to reinforce the content. In retrospect, it was nice stuff to know, but nothing that could be put into practice. Her advice? "Don't waste your time or money." What information is more credible and personally valuable to you, the "objective" and numerically expressed survey results, or the opinion of your trusted friend?

While "objective" data is valuable and compelling, it can often be trumped by subjective data based on the source and how it is presented. Although clients tell you they want objective validation of a program's value, do they ever use subjective information to make decisions? As you think about the value or weight of subjective versus objective metrics, have you ever been asked to deliver a program based on any of the following reasons from your sales managers?

- Read the consultant's book
- Talked to another colleague that "swears" by the content
- Hired a new "hot shot" who "swears" by the program
- Listened to a 60-minute Webinar/commercial and it sounded good
- Met with a salesperson from a training company who bypassed you and "made a compelling case"
- Actually believes the information in the brochure or e-mail they received?

Subjective information has perhaps more of a role in our decisions or evaluations than we would like to admit. How often do we discuss with sales professionals that customers make decisions based on personal reasons and use objective analysis to validate the subjective choice of suppliers? The same is true for the evaluation of the impact of the solutions we deliver. So how can we bring them together to make a compelling presentation of our value?

COMBINING OBJECTIVE AND SUBJECTIVE ANALYSIS

Used in conjunction with Impact Maps, a methodology for evaluation I have found useful is the Success Case Method developed by Dr. Brinkerhoff. It uses both an objective survey process and an in-depth interview format to uncover the more subjective analysis of the impact. I will review the basic process and approach, but recommend that if this approach makes sense that you investigate it further. It represents a methodology that works to bring both objective and subjective evaluation to the process. My intent is not to train you on the methodology, but introduce you to the approach.

The basic process builds on the Impact Map process where we establish a direct link between the program content and the business objectives and metrics. Essential to this process is working with your clients to ensure your Impact Maps represent the same view as your clients, the specific metrics you are trying to measure are of value, and the acknowledgment of the other variables in play. This up-front analysis and agreement ensures our measurement process is of value to the client and represents their expectations.

With Impact Maps in place, we build a brief postsession questionnaire designed to identify those participants who have been successful in applying what they learned, and those who were not successful (but not necessarily failures). We need to identify situations of both success and nonsuccess from our postsession survey data. As much as possible, your survey should be limited to five questions or fewer (other than demographics you may want to capture) and phrased to capture specific examples directly related to the critical actions and results defined in the Impact Map. Questions are related to uncovering who has applied the skills of the program and the level of success related to the desired results. An open narrative opportunity to explain or provide an example is useful to determine where the most robust stories exist in both the success and nonsuccess populations.

Using the results of the survey, the next step is to identify a representative sample group in both the success and nonsuccess groups. This is not a huge group, but enough to get good stories. Because we will be doing follow-up interviews, we need to identify each survey participant. You should identify up front that because you will be contacting some individuals for further information it is necessary to capture the identity of each participant. You should be very clear on this aspect of the survey. It is recommended that you also confirm that this information will be used only by the evaluation team or department and that no data or information will be linked to specific individuals. If you find it could be of value to identify a specific respondent, you should do so only with his or her knowledge and consent. Survey participants must feel confident in their ability to provide honest responses without fear of repercussions, especially for the nonsuccess situations. Your own policies and procedures around disclosure should be reviewed and discussed with your appropriate human resources or legal departments before proceeding with the data collection.

It is vital that you select only individuals who fall at the extreme ends of the distribution—both the highly successful individuals and those indicating no success in the application. Generally select about twice as many success stories versus the nonsuccess pool. As part of the Success Case Method you learn an interviewing process and use that approach to discuss and capture the stories of both success and nonsuccess cases. The idea is to capture robust information that very specifically identifies the elements of the training that were responsible for success and minimize the effect of other variables. It is through this process that you separate the variables and focus on the impact of the application of the skills on the outcome.

You are able to report, from credible sources, exactly what impact was realized and, more importantly, what elements of the training program were directly responsible. The application of these elements was the difference between the top performers and both the nonsuccess and midrange populations. The nonsuccess group provides both you, as a training manager, and the sponsoring management teams a clear understanding and awareness of what factors inhibit success. You use real stories about real accounts and opportunities from credible sources within your own environment. It is a compelling message with built-in credibility. Sources to learn more about this process are found at the end of this chapter. Whatever process you use to capture the results achieved by program participants, the question you must answer is have I really measured the impact of our training? Does a training program really create impact? Let me raise the question of what training professionals can truly influence.

As Brinkerhoff explained in *High Impact Learning* and expands on in his new book, *Telling Training's Story*[3], our domain is capability. Performance (that has impact) happens on the job. The best training in the world, not performed on the job, realizes zero impact. This is the domain of the manager, coach, or perhaps a mentor and happens in the real world, not a classroom, a virtual environment (virtual environments reap virtual results), a role-play, or a case study analysis.

MEASUREMENT IS A SHARED RESPONSIBILITY

Let me close by stating that in my opinion, training, in isolation, has no impact. Training on any topic or via any delivery mode, when done properly and with good instructional design, will ideally develop skills and improved capability. If we have analyzed the current *as is* and desired *to be* situations and addressed the appropriate skill gaps to move us to the desired state (assuming our analysis and definition of the *to be* is valid), training should be the major catalyst in developing the appropriate skill capability in the target population. However, just because they "can" do it, does not ensure they "will" do it. Impact is realized through performance not through capability. As a result, we must become partners with our clients. No matter how good our training might be, without field managers, coaching, reinforcement, and actual application to customer situations there will be no business impact.

The days of sending salespeople to class to be "fixed" are over, if they ever existed at all. When I work with sales management clients, the discussions focus not only on the skill gaps and how we will help in developing capabilities to overcome those gaps, but also on the reinforcement and coaching necessary to realize change on the job. The good news has always been that it is not a particularly difficult sale. Managers know this, but it is a lot easier to point to the fact that the training didn't fix the problem. Reality says training alone never will.

As trainers we have the responsibility to ensure we address the right skills and develop the capability of the target populations to overcome their skill gaps. Managers have the responsibility to turn that capability into performance on the job, where impact really happens. If you work with the sponsoring managers, identify their critical metrics and how they are captured, and get commitment about the roles and responsibilities related to capability and performance, they become part of the measurement process. Impact and results are validated by management, not just the training department. With shared responsibility there is also shared value, shared success, and shared impact.

RECOMMENDED RESOURCES

Robert O. Brinkerhoff, Ed.D.
Western Michigan University

Advantage Performance Group
http://www.advantageperformance.com

ADDITIONAL READING

- Robert O. Brinkerhoff and Anne M. Apking, *High Impact Learning*
- Robert O. Brinkerhoff, *The Success Case Method: Find Out Quickly What's Working and What's Not*
- Robert O. Brinkerhoff, *Telling Training's Story: Evaluation Made Simple, Credible, and Effective*

Notes

CHAPTER 1

1. Building Bridges, a sales and leadership training company based in Wisconsin, conducted an unscientific survey of 125 sales representatives throughout the United States in October of 2004.

2. AchieveGlobal is an international consulting and business training firm that has partnered with Delta College Corporate to deliver its programs.

3. Heather Johnson, "Field of Sales," *Training* (July 2004): 36.

4. Heather Johnson, "The Whole Picture?," *Training* (July 2004): 30.

5. Building Bridges conducted a phone interview with Susan Moll in October of 2004.

CHAPTER 2

1. Robert O. Brinkerhoff and Anne M. Apking, *High Impact Learning* (Cambridge, MA: Perseus Books Group, 2001).

2. Robert B. Miller, Stephen E. Heiman, and Tad Tuleja, *Strategic Selling* (Clayton, Vic., Australia: Warner Books, 1988).

3. Neil Rackham, *SPIN Selling* (New York, NY: McGraw-Hill, Inc., 1988).

4. Jerry Acuff and Wally Wood, *The Relationship Edge in Business* (Hoboken, NJ: John Wiley & Sons, 2004), *www.gottochange.com.*

CHAPTER 3

1. Neal Rackham, *SPIN Selling* (New York, NY: McGraw-Hill, Inc., 1988).

2. Charles A. Coonradt, *The Game of Work,* First Edition (Salt Lake City, UT: Shadow Mountain Press, Fourth Printing, 1989).

3. Ibid.

CHAPTER 4

1. Alan Greenspan, *The Importance of Financial and Economic Education and Literacy,* speech before the National Council on Economic Education, Chicago, IL, October of 2001.

CHAPTER 5

1. Jeff Thull, *Mastering the Complex Sale* (Hoboken, NJ: John Wiley & Sons, Inc., 2003): vi–x.

2. *Capabilities of the Future Sales Force Study* (Dechert-Hampe & Co., 2002) and *Great Selling Organizations Study* (Dechert-Hampe & Co., 2005).

CHAPTER 8

1. Professional Society for Sales and Marketing Training, *Trainer Talk, www.smt.org.*

2. Ibid.

3. Ibid.

CHAPTER 9

1. Malcolm Shepherd Knowles, *Andragogy in Action: Applying Modern Principles of Adult Education* (San Francisco: Jossey-Bass, Inc.,1984).

2. Sharan B. Merriam and Rosemary S. Caffarella, *Learning in Adulthood* (San Francisco: Jossey-Bass, Inc., 1991).

3. Ron and Susan Zemke, "30 Things We Know for Sure about Adult Learning," *Training* (1981).

4. "Some Characteristics of Learners, with Teaching Implications," retrieved 21 February 2006 from *www.rit.edu/~609www/ch/faculty/learner.htm*. Copyright 2000 by Online Learning, Rochester Institute of Technology. All rights reserved.

5. Allison Rossett and Jeannette Gautier-Downes, *A Handbook of Job Aids* (San Francisco: Pfeiffer, 1991).

6. Jim Richardson, "Training: Event or Process?," retrieved 24 February 2006 from *http://coe.sdsu.edu/eet/Admin/Biblio/index.htm*. Copyright 1994–2004, San Diego State University.

CHAPTER 12

1. Robert O. Brinkerhoff and Anne M. Apking, *High Impact Learning* (Cambridge, MA: Perseus, 2001).

2. Robert O. Brinkerhoff, *The Success Case Method: Find Out Quickly What's Working and What's Not* (San Francisco, CA: Berrett Koehler, 2003).

3. Robert O. Brinkerhoff, *Telling Training's Story: Evaluation Made Simple, Credible, and Effective* (San Francisco, CA: Berrett Koehler, 2006).

Contributors

BECKY STEWART-GROSS

Over the past 20 years, Dr. Becky Stewart-Gross has worked with thousands of leaders and emerging leaders, from small family-owned businesses to large multinational corporations. She is a sought-after trainer and member of the American Society of Training and Development. She is a member of the Professional Society for Sales and Marketing Training, coeditor of its newsletter, and recently elected to its board of directors. Becky was named a finalist in the Best Sales Trainer category in the 2004 American Business Awards. She is a professional speaker and member of the National Speakers Association.

Becky is an author and her recent book, *The Leader's Communication Toolkit* (HRD Press, Inc., 2004), focuses on how to select the right communication method in an electronic world. She recently completed the program on negotiation at Harvard University Law School. In 1996, she received the Michigan State University's Emerging Leaders Award. Becky earned her PhD from Michigan State University in 1991 and from 1987 to 1996 Becky served as an associate professor at Aquinas College.

Becky is president and founder of Building Bridges, which offers custom-designed communication training through seminars, consulting, and professional development coaching. She assists companies, teams, and individuals in building bridges to better communication.

Becky's business experiences combined with her interactive and energetic training style make her a trainer with a talent for showing others how to achieve their potential. She inspires, challenges, and motivates her audiences. You can contact her at *becky@buildingbridges.cc* or visit *www.buildingbridges.cc*.

JIM GRAHAM

Jim Graham is the VP of training and development at RR Donnelley. Jim is a longtime member and a past board member of SMT. He has presented best practice academies for the Professional Society for Sales and Marketing Training. His background is sales, sales management, channel management, sales performance improvement consulting, and training globally with an international firm, and a U.S. Fortune 250 company.

Jim started in sales in the pharmaceuticals industry with ICI Americas, now Astra Zeneca, as a sales rep and moved on to corporate sales trainer, district sales manager, and finally regional training manager with responsibility for the reps and managers in ten states.

Jim worked with Huthwaite, Inc., as a consultant, business development manager, and finally director of channel distribution. He worked with Neil Rackham (selling skills guru and originator of SPIN selling), and other thought leaders at Huthwaite.

At the Moore Corporation, Jim was the director of sales training, management development, customer service, and manufacturing training. When Moore acquired Wallace Computer Services, he was named a vice president and given all training responsibility in the newly combined Moore/Wallace organization.

Jim can be contacted at *jim.graham@rrd.com*.

DON STERKEL

Don Sterkel has over 30 years experience in the areas of retail consumer publishing and consumer product sales, recently retiring as senior director of learning and development for Time Warner Retail Sales and Marketing based in New York.

Don held field sales positions with Time as sales representative, district manager, and regional sales vice president. He was awarded District Manager of the Year honors for his key role in the early success of *People* magazine. Other major field successes included the internal sale of *Sports Illustrated* executive management to increase the number of copies distributed for local interest covers and stories and the promotion and increased distribution for the annual swimsuit issue, earning Don the first two *Sports Illustrated* Hall of Fame awards.

Over the past 20 years working within the New York office, Don developed and led strategic indicatives in the areas of sales, learning and development, marketing, organizational development, performance management, recognition, best practices, and human resources.

An 18-year member of the Professional Society for Sales and Marketing Training, Don has been a multiterm board member and served as president for the 2003 term. A presenter at many conferences, Don also was engaged with the Strategic Account Management Association (SAMA) as the SMT representative for the community of sales training practices.

Don is currently working on a business plan to begin the next stage of his career. He and his wife, Carol, now reside in Portland, Oregon.

ROBERT RICKERT

Bob Rickert is regional sales manager for Aarthun Performance Group Ltd. (APG), a full-service firm specializing in global sales and management training and consulting. He is responsible for sales and implementation of APG's financial and value selling programs in the Midwest and has over 20 years of experience in performance improvement consulting.

APG is the leading provider of customized, high-impact, financially oriented professional/managerial and value selling training programs that deliver bottom-line results. APG has delivered its solutions across 20 industries, including manufacturing, retail, banking, insurance, health care, foodservice, food and beverage, chemical, oil and gas, and many more. Bob is currently working closely with ITW, Deluxe Corporation, Siemens, Bandag, OfficeMax, Pella Corporation, HON Company, Pactiv Corporation, Ecolab, Grainger, and many others. In each case, he has been instrumental in building financial and value-selling competencies among senior sales leaders, sales managers, and account managers, resulting in significant profit improvement. You can contact Bob at 847-317-9711 or *brickert@aarthun.com*.

SUSANNE CONRAD

As director of organizational effectiveness and development at Dechert-Hampe since 1999, Susanne Conrad works with organizations to develop and implement business strategies to enhance their organizations' performance.

Susanne works in partnership with her clients to produce and sustain measurable results to support corporate goals by aligning the corporate structure and work processes with culture and employee motivation. Her practice focuses on structured change management, high-performance teams, and organizational learning and development.

For more than 20 years, Susanne has worked in consulting and management for manufacturing and service industries as well as industry associations, gaining an understanding of the issues and challenges faced daily by these organizations. She has worked with companies such as ConAgra, Masterfoods, Kraft, Gillette, Sprint, Bayer, Pfizer/Schick, and Time Distribution Services in areas such as training and development, customer development, customer relationship management, organizational restructures, process and workflow reengineering, and cultural realignments. She has also worked with associations such as the National Confectioners Association and the Grocery Manufacturers Association to develop strategic plans and implement industry initiatives.

Before joining Dechert-Hampe, Susanne was president of The Paragon Group, Inc., a management consulting firm focused on assisting midsize companies reach their business goals through organizational redesign and team management. Her work was directed at rethinking the fundamental system of work and organization by involving managers and employees. Her efforts typically resulted in highly motivated workforces focused on customer satisfaction.

Susanne is a keynote speaker; offers seminars and workshops on topics related to change management, team building, and skills development; and has been published in several industry publications. You can contact her at *sconrad@dechert-hampe.com* or visit *www.dechert-hampe.com*.

MICHAEL ROCKELMANN

For the past ten years Michael Rockelmann has worked in the HR, training, and organization development field. He has held full-time and project-focused positions within several Fortune 500 and 1,000 companies, including United Air Lines, Dade Behring, CDW, TAP Pharmaceuticals, Walgreens, and Quaker Oats. His training projects have included the areas of sales training, management development, employee development, and technical training. Other related experience includes competency mapping, organization development, process redesign, reward and recognition program design, performance management, and succession planning. Most recently, Michael was the training manager with 4Gen Consulting, a firm focused on consulting and training to help companies make and implement strategic sourcing decisions.

Michael has earned a BS in industrial psychology/organization development and an MEd in human resource education from the University of Illinois, Urbana-Champaign, and an MBA from Lake Forest Graduate School of Management. Michael is a member of the American Society of Training and Development and its Chicago Chapter.

Michael has his own practice, Driving Results, focusing on human resources, training, and business strategy consulting. More information can be found at *www.DrivingResults.com*. He can be reached at *info@drivingresults.com*.

RENIE MCCLAY

Renie McClay is an independent training consultant specializing in sales force development. After college, she began her sales career with Kraft Foods, eventually becoming Kraft's first female sales manager. Early on, Renie was bitten by the training bug and built a successful track record as a regional sales trainer. Her career includes several training management positions with Kraft and two other Fortune 500 companies – Novartis and Pactiv (makers of Hefty).

Renie is known for building solid sales force curriculum and creating training and selling resources for a variety of audiences, including direct sales forces, brokers, distributors and channel. She is also skilled in helping companies create exciting, productive national and regional sales meetings. One of Renie's training tools is using improvisation to help companies increase creativity, innovation, communication and to build productive teams (studied at Second City). She teaches people how to systematically build relationships with people they don't naturally connect with – both inside their organization and with customers.

Renie is the past president of the Professional Society for Sales and Marketing Training (*www.smt.org*). She also directs the

Sales Training Forum for the Chicago Chapter of the American Society for Training and Development (*www.ccastd.org*). Both organizations represent great resources for training professionals.

Renie has served as a judge for the American Business Awards. She is published regularly in the SMT Trainer Talk newsletter and various other magazines in the US and in India. She is a Certified Online Instructor through Walden Institute and conducts workshops in both traditional settings and on-line. She has used her corporate skills to participate in mission projects in Africa and India and has found those to help bring a better balance of spiritual and secular to her life. She can be contacted at *www.salestrainingutopia.com*.

DIANE M. BOEWE

Diane Boewe earned her BA in psychology and an MSEd in instructional technology from Northern Illinois University. She has 17 years of experience in the fields of instructional design, curriculum planning, and training.

Diane started her own consulting company, Performance Forum, in 1992. It was at this time that Diane had the opportunity to begin working with a number of Fortune 100 and 500 companies to help them develop their selling skills training curriculum. Over the next eight years, Diane provided selling skills curriculum consultation with Kraft, Gerber, Pactiv, and Ameritech, helping them design and develop creative, successful, participant-centered selling skills and new-hire curriculum, including product training programs.

In 1999, Diane joined the Drake Resource Group, Inc. DRG's primary business is the design of instructionally sound, custom learning products. Diane continues to provide selling skill curriculum consultation, as well as consultation in a number of other areas such as software, management, process, and leadership training. Diane is not only an instructional designer and project manager for client products, but is also a member of the company's leadership team. As the director of the consultant community, Diane manages a team of over 60 resources.

Diane is also a member of the national and Chicago chapters of the American Society of Training and Development. She has also written a number of articles for training industry newsletters on a variety of industry topics.

Using an instructional design systems approach and performance learning theories, Diane has conducted needs assessments and designed, developed, and evaluated a variety of computer-based, classroom-based, and on-the-job training programs. Diane has been the project manager and coordinator for many of these different projects. One of the projects Diane contributed to—DRG's new consultant orientation online course—was recognized with a Society for Technical Communication Merit award in 2003.

Diane has a unique ability to quickly grasp a client's individual performance and cultural needs and translate them into performance improvement solutions using state-of-the-art technology and tested learning and performance theories.

You can contact her at *dboewe@drakerg.com* or visit *www.drakerg.com.*

LUANN IRWIN

LuAnn Irwin, LAI Associates, has worked as manager/director of training for Eastman Kodak Company, Xerox Corporation, and HSBC (Hong Kong Shanghai Banking Company), all Fortune 500 (global) companies. As manager of learning and development at Kodak, LuAnn managed training professionals for sales training, leadership development, and other areas. The training was designed and developed for worldwide audiences and delivered virtually and in person for all Kodak employees and leaders. LuAnn submitted Kodak's performance and won the Training Top 100 Companies award from *Training* magazine. As manager of technical training design for Xerox, she managed a team of designers and developers and led eight worldwide training development teams. The training developed and conducted helped Xerox to win the Malcolm Baldrige National Quality Award for excellence. As director of training for HSBC, LuAnn designed and delivered customer service, sales, and leadership training for all employees in the region. She was the youngest and 13th woman promoted to officer of the company. All of this work involved interactions, budget, and support of the president, CEO, and VPs of Kodak, Xerox, and HSBC, as well as working with professionals, technical experts, and diverse populations of employees, to ensure performance improvements. She has also done consulting work for General Motors Delphi Division, the New York Governor's Office of Employee Relations, Blue Cross/Blue Shield, New York State Department of Education, county and city governments, Cornell University, Carnegie Mellon University, University of Rochester, Rochester Institute of Technology, and many other companies, educational institutions, and nonprofit agencies. LuAnn has a master's degree in adult learning from the University of Rochester. She is past president of the American Society of Training and Development (ASTD) local chapter and Literacy Volunteers of Wayne County. She has traveled to 23 countries and 49 states. Her husband, Lee, owns his own construction business. Her son, Michael, works in corporate strategy for Liberty Mutual; and her daughter, Alicia, works for Cornell University Graduate Studies (after just returning from Peace Corps service in Thailand). You can reach her at *luannirwin@hotmail.com*.

WILLIAM MAGAGNA

William Magagna earned a BS in secondary education and master's degree in instructional systems both from Penn State University. His continued studies included doctoral coursework in instructional systems at Penn State and an MBA that he is currently achieving at Millersville University.

William has over 12 years experience in teaching, training, education, and instructional design leadership as both a consultant/research associate and full-time corporate ISD/ training professional. He has produced several publications and conference presentations for both the academic and corporate practitioner audiences. During his time as a consultant, he worked with over a dozen Fortune 500 companies and numerous other small companies and governmental clients, providing leadership in a wide array of instructional design and training projects. William currently works for Dade Behring as a senior instructional designer. He can be reached at *William_Magagna@dadebehring.com.*

GARY SUMMY

Gary Summy has been involved with professional management, sales, and sales development throughout his career. Following graduation from DePauw University, he became supervisor for a road construction firm, managing over 40 laborers and teamsters. His sales career began in 1973, as sales engineer for Reliance Electric Company in the southern region. His association with sales training began in 1977 when he took a leadership role in the development of other Reliance sales engineers.

A series of progressive assignments and added responsibilities placed Gary as manager of training and development for sales and management, and manager of sales recruiting. During this period, Gary reduced costs over 30 percent, improved turnover, and put qualified people in the field 50 percent sooner. He also did sales consulting with other Reliance partners and area business concerns.

After nearly 15 years with Reliance, Gary moved outside of the industrial world as an internal consultant on sales development for a major regional bank, working with the bank, its affiliates, and its customers, delivering consulting services on sales development, sales training, sales compensation, motivation, and sales management. Sales frequently increased as much as 50 percent following Gary's intervention with particular business units.

Gary returned to line sales management in 1989, as regional sales manager for the newly created industrial division of Matco Tools, where he managed a sales force and other sales managers. Moving forward, Gary became senior sales engineer for Meier Transmission, a distributor of power transmission and motion control products. As a result of his experience and success, he joined Pioneer Standard Electronics, a global distributor of electronic components and computer systems, managing sales force development and implementing a strategic business partner program.

Using his wealth of experience, he created his own company, Outside the Cube. The company, dedicated to nontraditional thinking, sales growth, sales force development, and establishing strategic business partners throughout the supply chain, delivers innovative thinking and direction to customer-driven organizations. As a result of consulting work done for Motorola University, Gary became global director of performance development for sales and marketing for Motorola University. His work in sales leadership and strategic consulting with sales teams has generated several million dollars in revenue. *Sales and Marketing Management* magazine selected Gary as Sales Trainer of the Year for 2002 and the American Business Awards recognized Gary as a finalist for a STEVIE Award as Best Sales Manager in 2004. Gary is currently Director of Sales Development for Trane Commercial Systems. Gary is on the board of directors of the Strategic Account Management Association (SAMA, *www.strategicaccounts.org*) and the Professional Society for Sales and Marketing Training (SMT, *www.smt.org*).

Gary and his wife, Laurie, live in Mentor, Ohio, and are active in school, church, sports, and civic affairs in the community. They have two children, Kyle Stephanie and Gregory Ryan. Gary can be reached at 440-358-9661 or via e-mail at either *gsummy@trane.com* or *gasummy50@aol.com*.

Index